DARK
CHAPTERS

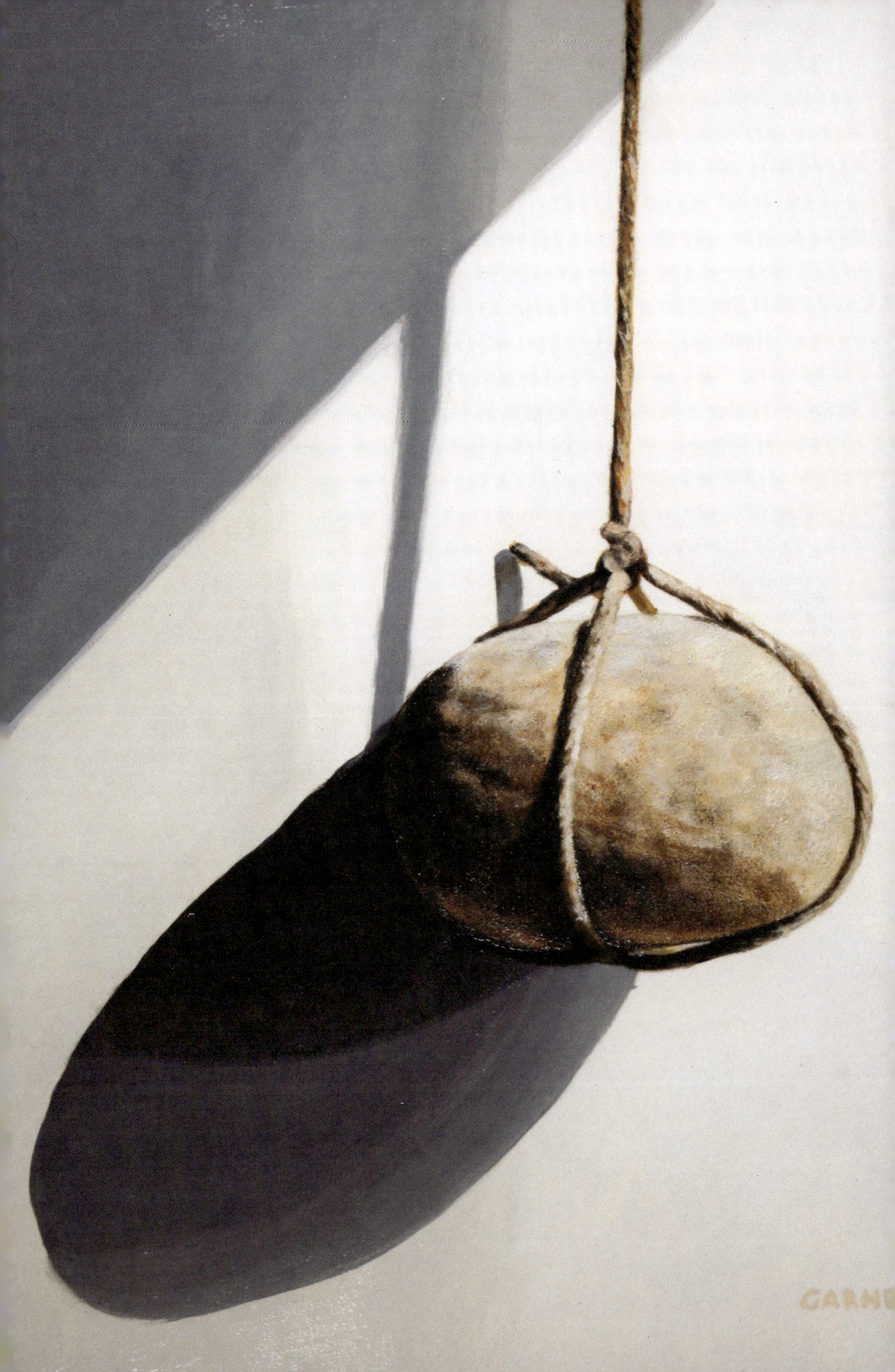

CARNE

DARK CHAPTERS

READING THE STILL LIVES OF DAVID GARNEAU

CURATED BY **ARIN FAY**

EDITED BY **NIC WILSON**

PAINTINGS BY **DAVID GARNEAU**

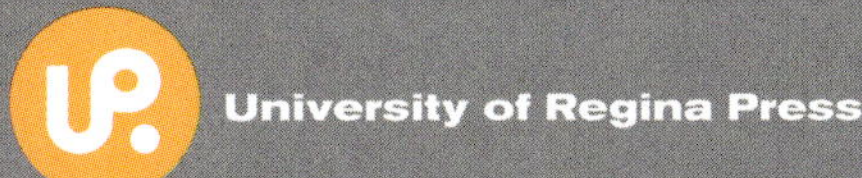

Printed and bound in Canada. The text of this book is printed on 100% post-consumer recycled paper with earth-friendly vegetable-based inks.

COVER ART: "Syncretism II," 2023, 61 × 45.5 cm, acrylic on panel.
FRONTISPIECE: "Métis Academic Charm," 2019, 50.5 × 40.5 cm, acrylic on panel.
CONTENTS PAGE ART: "Epistolary Exchange," 2023, 40.5 × 51 cm, acrylic on panel. (cropped)

COVER AND TEXT DESIGN: Duncan Noel Campbell, University of Regina Press
COPY EDITOR: Crissy Boylan   INDEXER: Nic Wilson

Library and Archives Canada Cataloguing in Publication
TITLE: Dark chapters : reading the still lives of David Garneau /
curated by Arin Fay ; edited by Nic Wilson ; paintings by David Garneau.

OTHER TITLES: Reading the still lives of David Garneau

NAMES: Fay, Arin, 1972- organizer | Wilson, Nic, editor. |
Container of (work): Garneau, David, 1962- Paintings. Selections.

DESCRIPTION: Includes bibliographical references and index.

IDENTIFIERS: Canadiana (print) 20240464915 | Canadiana (ebook) 2024046494X |
ISBN 9781779400543 (hardcover) | ISBN 9781779400536 (softcover) |
ISBN 9781779400567 (PDF) | ISBN 9781779400550 (EPUB)

SUBJECTS: LCSH: Garneau, David, 1962-—Criticism and interpretation.

CLASSIFICATION: LCC ND249.G364 D37 2025 | DDC 759.11—dc23

10   9   8   7   6   5   4   3   2   1

University of Regina Press, University of Regina
Regina, Saskatchewan, Canada, S4S 0A2
TEL: (306) 585-4758 FAX: (306) 585-4699
WEB: www.uofrpress.ca

We acknowledge the support of the Canada Council for the Arts for our publishing program. We acknowledge the financial support of the Government of Canada. / Nous reconnaissons l'appui financier du gouvernement du Canada. This publication was made possible with support from Creative Saskatchewan's Book Publishing Production Grant Program. We also gratefully acknowledge the funding from the Canada Council Explore and Create grant that Nelson Museum, Archives & Gallery was awarded to support the creation of this book.

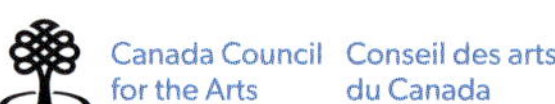
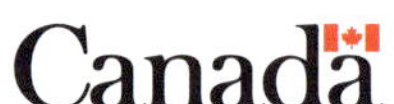
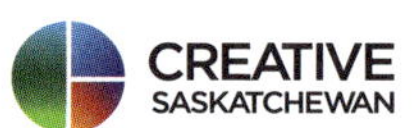

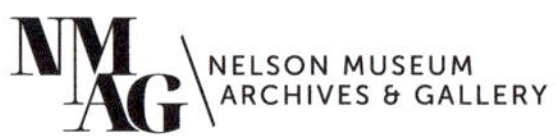
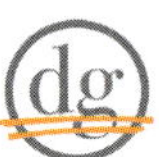

University of Regina Press designates one title each year that best exemplifies the guiding editorial and manuscript production principles of long-time senior editor Donna Grant.

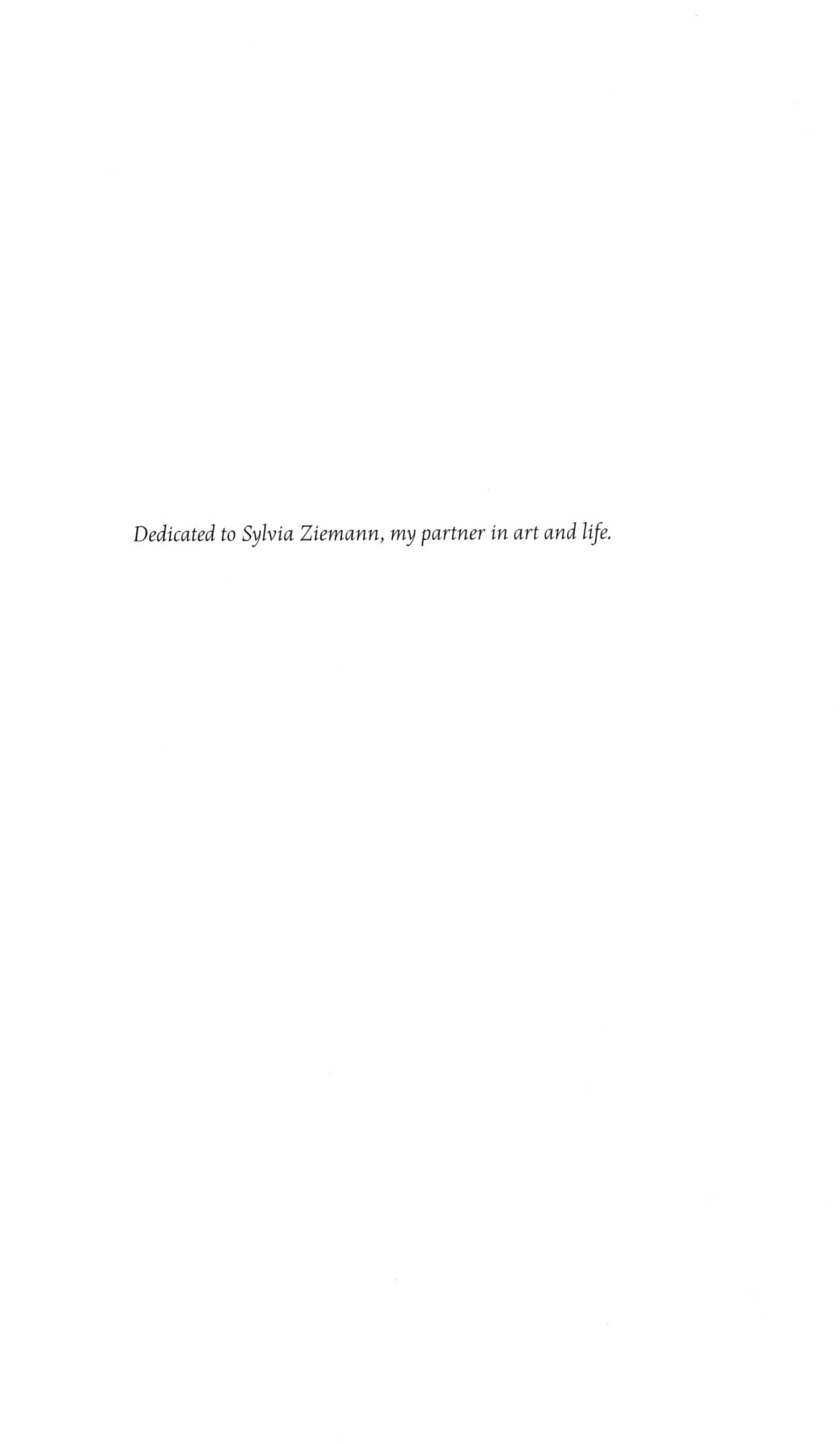

Dedicated to Sylvia Ziemann, my partner in art and life.

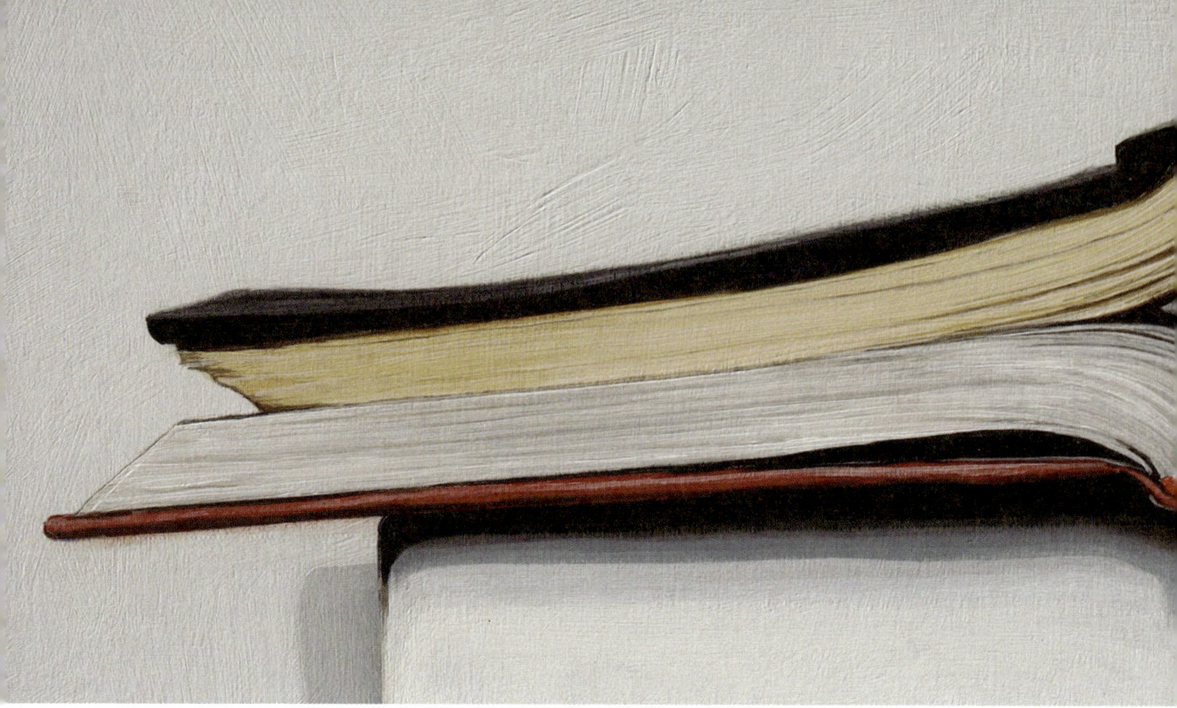

CONTENTS

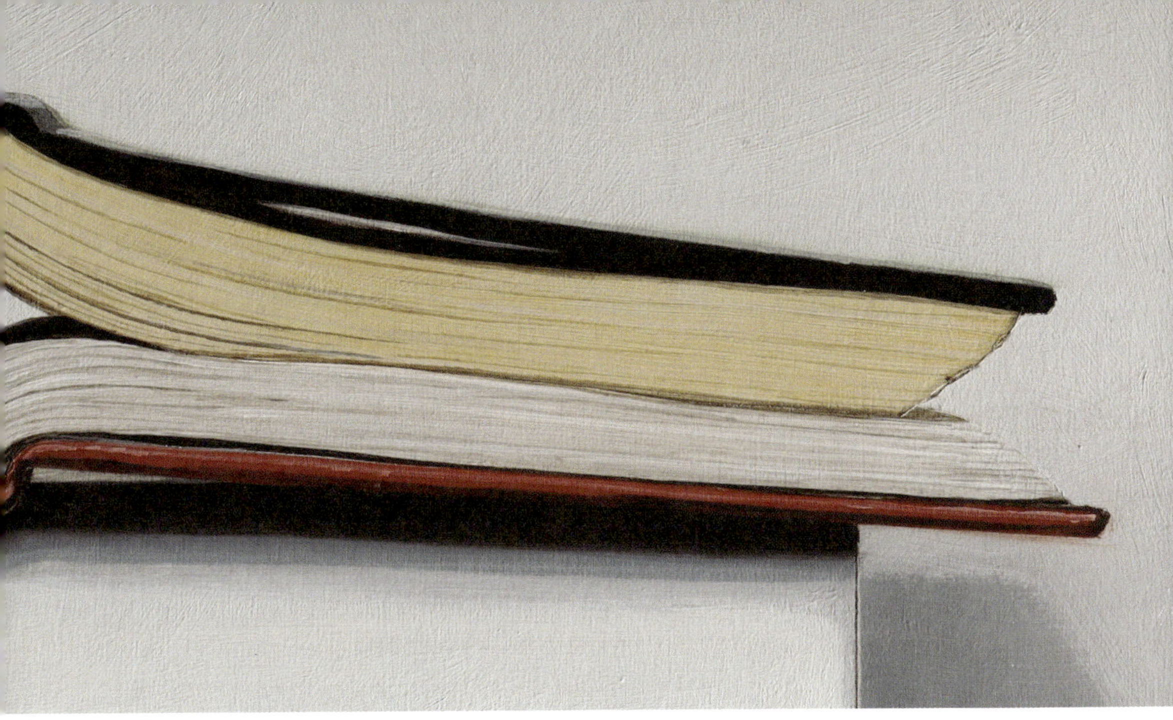

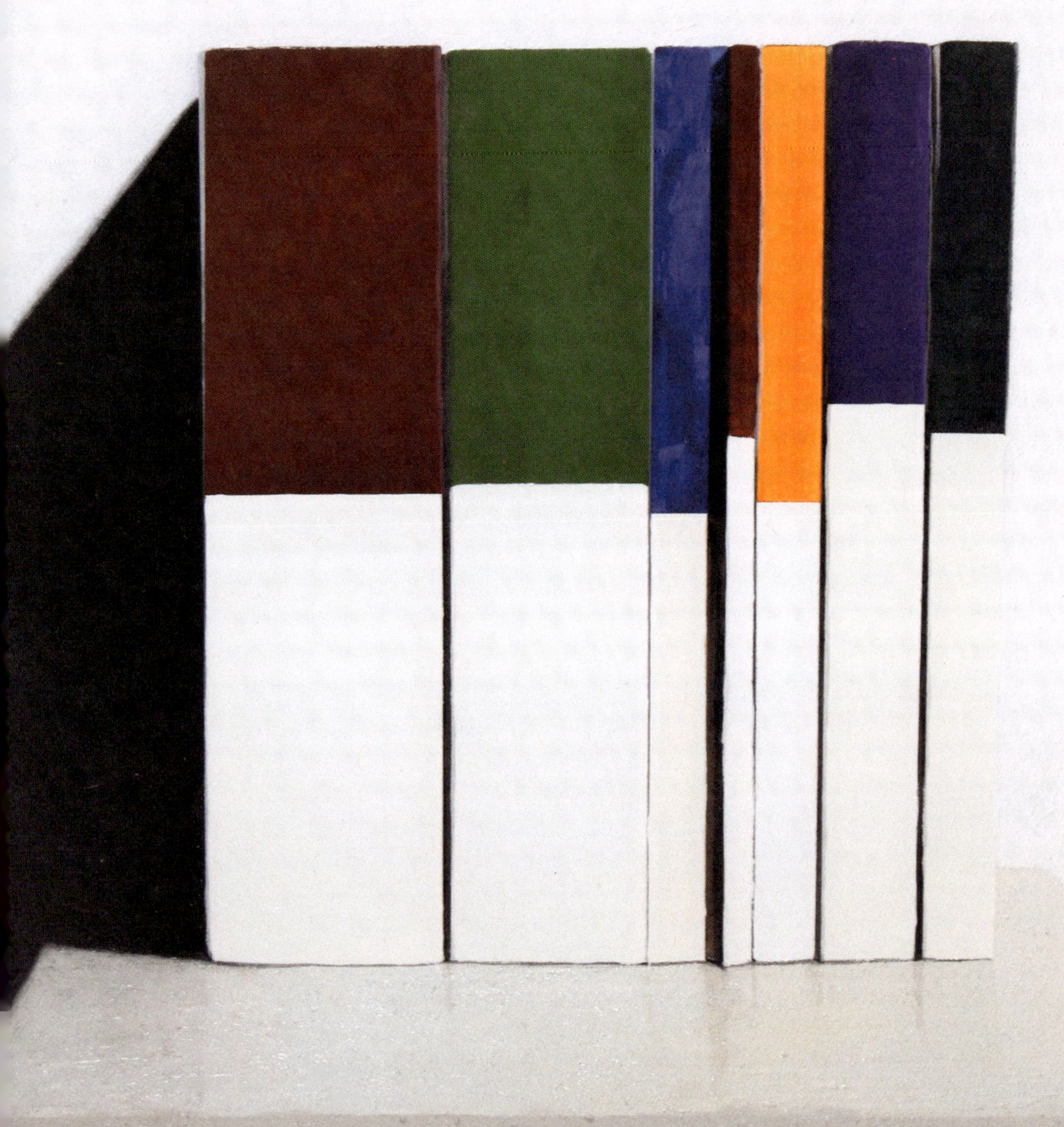

GARNEAU 19

FOREWORD
BY NIC WILSON

Many of David Garneau's still lives contain images of books and bones. These two categories of things could be regarded as opposed to one another—one being organic and the other being an object made by humans—but an oblique connection unites them. There is a faint line running down the centre of most pieces of parchment. It is a remnant of the ridge on an animal's back from which their skin was peeled. The *spine* of a book received its English name from this shadow around which pages were folded, stacked, and gathered like bundles of nerves encased in bone. The book you now hold, like most of the books you have probably held, is made of wood or cotton pulp, but it can't shed its association with the land from which its materials were extracted. Though many conveniences of post-industrial life take great pain in covering the tracks of manufacturing and the supply chains that produce books, tomatoes, and acrylic paint, one knows that they do not spring from divine intervention.

Garneau's painting has engaged an incredible breadth of modes over the course of his career from history painting to near abstraction as well as illustrative and diagrammatic approaches to image making. Each foray is soaked in his incredible attention to the codes of history, meaning, emotion, sociality, and pedagogy. Like many artists of the last

FACING: "…darkest, most troubling chapters….," 2019, 31 × 40.5 cm, acrylic on masonite.

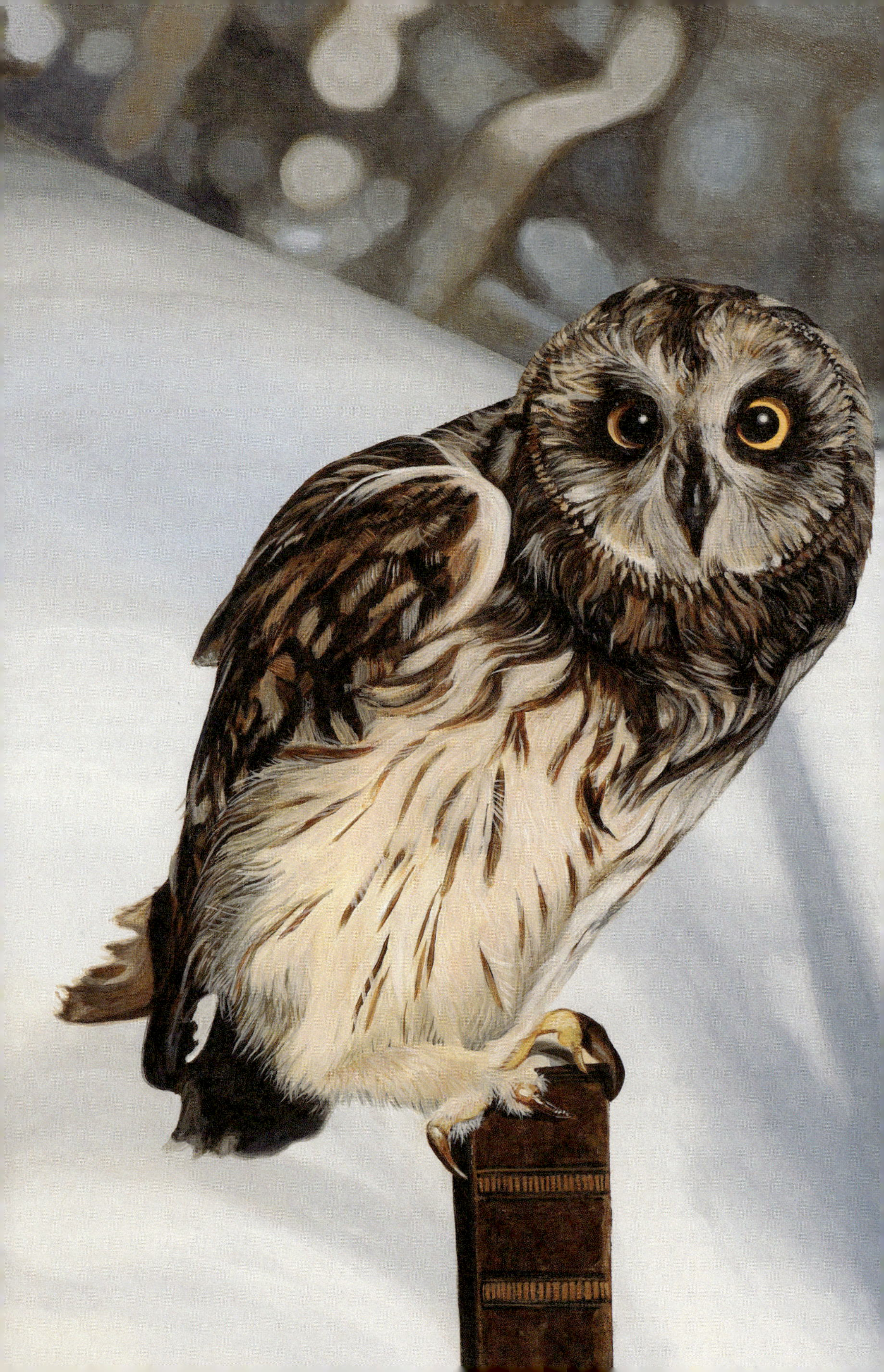

several decades,[1] Garneau has turned his considerable critical insights to the messy and exploded genre of still life to nudge at the gargantuan and enmeshed histories of capitalism, colonialism, and resource extraction. His investigations are curious—often appearing cool and uncluttered—in contrast to the glut of contemporary Western consumer cultures.[2]

In his book *Looking at the Overlooked*, critic and art historian Norman Bryson cites frescoes from the Villa of P. Fannius Synistor at Boscoreale as some of the earliest surviving European representations that could be included in the history of still life. Though he is careful to stress the cultural specificity of images often separated by centuries and vast geographical incongruities, Bryson characterizes still life as a type of image with specific "codes of viewing."[3] From the specific vantage point of these images, Bryson sees objects from the material world as coded with specific cultural meanings and currents of discourse. Throughout its patchy, fractured histories, still life has often illustrated human needs and exploits through the exclusion of the human figure; many images explore needs that stray beyond the bounds of bodily sustenance. They can thread together the desires of the mind and the body. In the case of Garneau's paintings, sustenance might be the work of finding ways to live with disagreements between academic, Eurocentric world views, and those of his Indigenous communities.

Many of the most famous examples of still life were made during the so-called Dutch Golden Age. This was a period of time between the late sixteenth and late seventeenth century in which the newly formed Dutch Republic commanded a huge trade empire through the foundation of the Dutch East India Company. This globalized trading network created and concentrated a huge amount of wealth among the merchant class, which made room for a new type of art patronage. Before this time, royalty and the Church were the main patrons for the

---

1   Notable artists working in this orbit include Shellie Zhang, Kelly Mark, and Juan Ortiz-Apuy.

2   The shadow of still life can be found in contemporary product photography, which encompasses depictions of discount bananas and microwave ovens as well as luxury perfumes and diamond rings.

3   Norman Bryson, *Looking at the Overlooked: Four Essays on Still Life Painting* (London: Reaktion Books, 2013), 18.

FACING: "Non-Colonial Attitude," 2022, 61 × 46 cm, acrylic on panel.

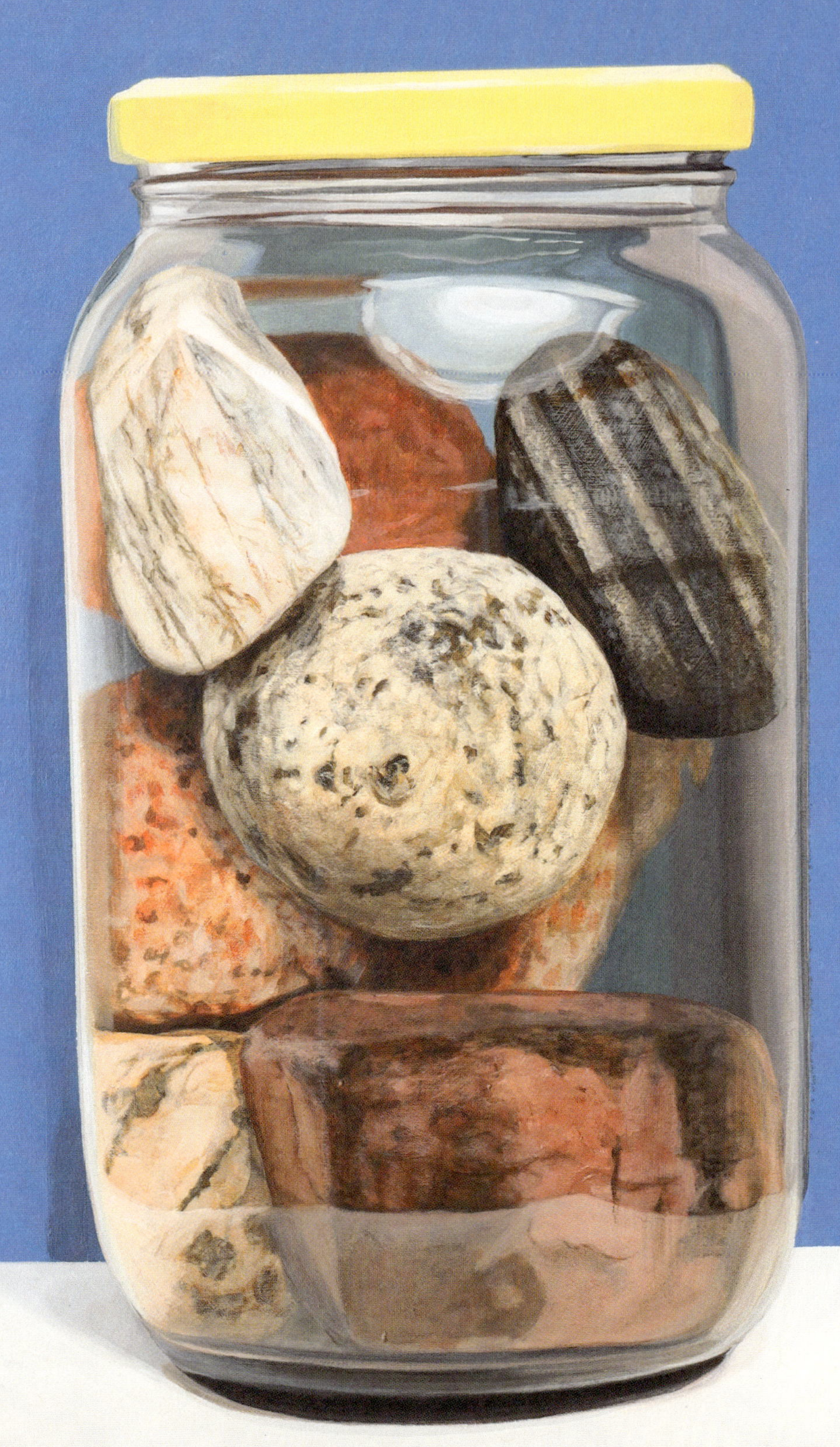

CARNEAU

arts, but this new class of wealthy Dutch traders began to collect paintings that were both images of their wealth and abundance and precious commodities in and of themselves. Classic still life subjects such as tulips from the Ottoman Empire, pomegranates from modern-day Iran, and silks from China found their way into the genre through the expansion of global trade, which built on the routes established by the Silk Road. The stillness of these images holds vast amounts of movement across land and sea, the rise and fall of empires, and the decay and destruction of human bodies.

At the same time, the British were quickly expanding their own trade networks westward across the so-called New World, through the founding of the Hudson's Bay Company, which stretched out across Inuit, Nehiyawak, Ojibwe, Dene, Dakota, and Nakota lands. Other European nations such as France, Spain, and Portugal began to establish colonies. Traces of this expansion can be found in images such as *Two Hounds with a Still Life of Entrails, Artichokes, Lettuce, Squash and a Woven Basket* by Peter van Boucle. Spilling from the woven basket in the painting, you can see several squash that were cultivated as a staple food in the Americas for hundreds of years before sustained contact with Europeans. As a result of these trade networks, the Métis People emerged through the union of French fur traders and the Indigenous nations of the continent.

Dark Chapters: Reading the Still Lives of David Garneau is a response to his work and also a marker of public discourse on issues of white supremacy, Indigeneity, empathy, allyship, and what is widely known as reconciliation—a process and term which David continues to problematize. Many of the contributions in this collection interrogate the way these images are entangled with questions of power, violence, social justice, land, knowledge, and resource extraction. Some approach the work head-on while others slide in from unanticipated entry points. Some take on fuzzy or hybrid forms while others sit comfortably in the category of essay or poem. Some are adapted from previous lives. Some are progressive attempts at finding new forms of connection, and others bare the pitfalls of learning. All are genuine attempts at processing and engaging with Garneau's work and the way it both troubles and helps constitute notions of national identity, Indigenous sovereignty, uneasy meetings, and the existential quandaries they inspire.

FACING: "Stone Preserves," 2022, 61 × 46 cm, acrylic on panel.

DARK CHAPTERS

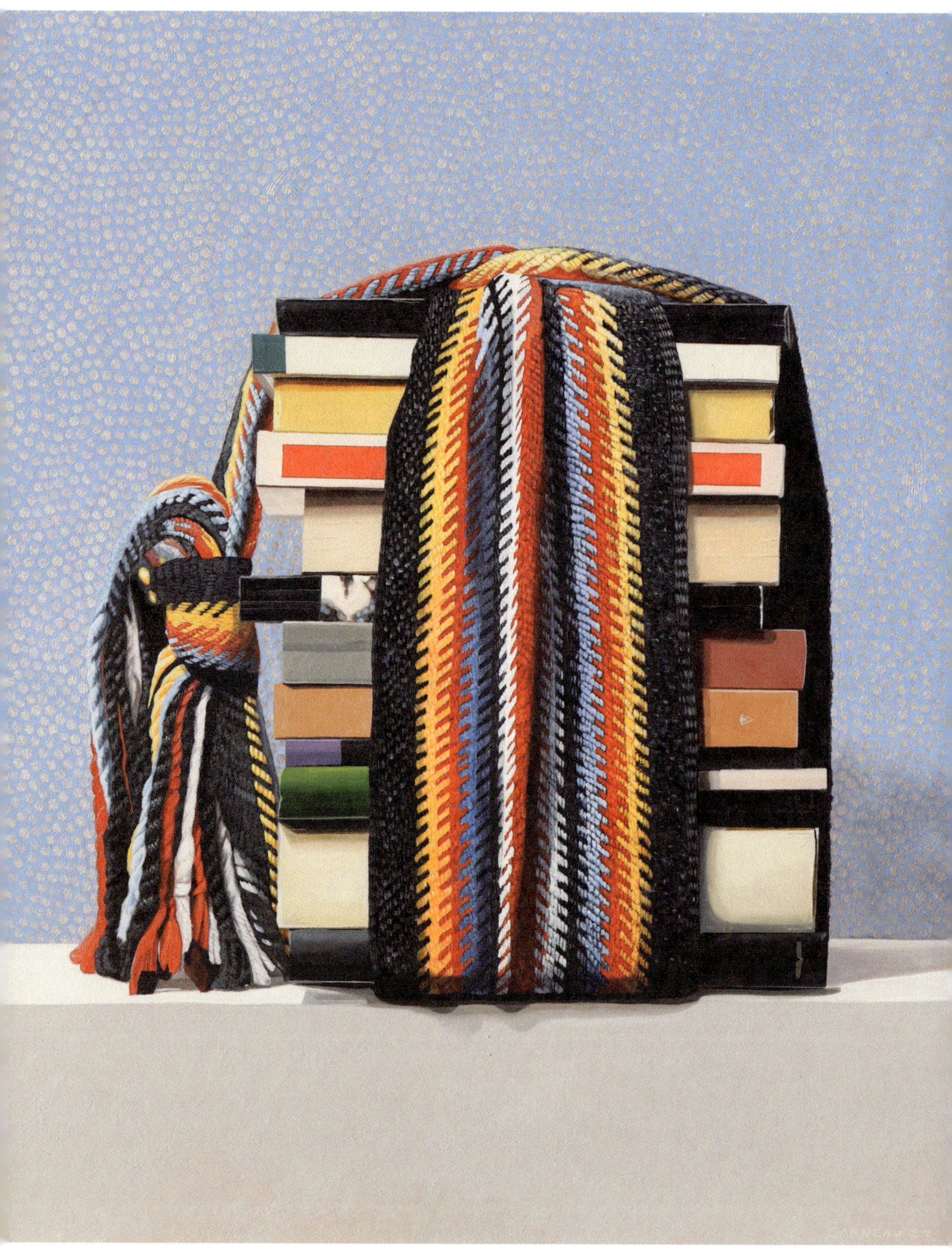

STILL LIFE.
BY JOHN G. HAMPTON

David Garneau's still life paintings are seductive allegories for an era of tension: between knowledge and presentation, representation and existence, performance and identity, conciliation and assimilation, Western and Indigenous. Over the course of the *Dark Chapters* series, one can witness an ever-deepening technical precision in his paintings, which is matched by their conceptual richness. The glistening eggshells of *Fragile*, the sumptuous rendering of light in *Protected Grandfather*, and the meticulous depiction of individual strands of yarn in *Métis Bundle I* and *II* demonstrate a commitment to the academic tradition of the still life, while the selection of subject matter follows a symbolist trajectory.

During a studio visit in 2022, Garneau told me that the still life, as a genre of painting, was historically considered to be the lowest form within the formal academic tradition—which reached its height in nineteenth century Western art and remains influential in many painting and art history programs in the West. While religious and portrait paintings were reserved for painters of high stations, the still life was associated with domestic spaces and thus deemed more appropriate for women artists.

Recognizing the hierarchies that persist within artistic practice, Garneau admired strategies that some symbolist artists who were barred from *higher* forms of art found to surreptitiously insert meaning into still lifes through the selection of painted subjects, colour, composition, and context. Despite sexist admission practices to guilds and academies, artists like Clara Peeters, Anne Vallayer-Coster, and Dora Carrington found relative success with their symbolically and technically evocative works. Garneau builds on these legacies, embracing the still life as a site of material contradiction—still yet live—a Western construction ripe for enlivening through Indigenous ontologies, animacy, and insight into the spirit of all things.

Over the last decade, Garneau has been developing and refining a personal lexicon within his still life paintings. He uses symbols that exist in tension between Indigenous and Western understandings of knowledge, emphasizing yet complicating their distinctions (a practice that also extends to his scholarly pursuits).[4] Beyond generalities, Garneau creates a uniquely Métis vernacular informed through his specific lens as an urban Indigenous artist navigating post-secondary institutions as an educator. The resulting work is academic—in the sense of the contemporary academic institution, as well as its relation to classical ideals of the academy—yet it is also acutely critical of these traditions. Garneau expands the still life's capacity for relationality through his own positionality as a Métis artist, extending into intercultural solidarity, political and religious influence, and other topics that loom large across many Indigenous communities today. This type of integration of Indigenous and Western epistemologies is colloquially described as "two-eyed seeing." Walking these two worlds, Garneau investigates what it means to make use of colonial institutions alongside customary and traditional knowledge.

Dark Chapters incorporates images of rocks, books, bones, apples, and tools in charged relation. He evokes shared Indigenous understandings about the knowledge of rocks and builds on his own long-standing interest in their relation to humans. Rocks represent time on a scale that is sometimes difficult to comprehend; they are seemingly inanimate yet ever changing; have witnessed millennia, carry stories, and have agency yet are too wise to use it.[5] Garneau has argued that a stone, on the other

---

4   See David Garneau, "Necessary Objects," *Canadian Art*, November 25, 2019, canadianart.ca/interviews/david-garneau-necessary-objects; David Garneau, "Non-Colonial Indigenous Public Art," *Rungh* 11, no. 1, rungh.org/non-colonial-indigenous-public-art; and David Garneau, "Indigenization and Its Opposite, Indigenization," *Rungh* 8, no. 2, rungh.org/indigenization-and-its-opposite-indigenization.

5   Vine Deloria, "Relativity, Relatedness, and Reality," in *Spirit & Reason: The Vine Deloria, Jr., Reader*, eds. Barbara Deloria, Kristen Foehner, and Sam Scinta (Golden, CO: Fulcrum, 1999), 32–39.

hand, is a rock put to use by humans.[6] In his still lifes, Garneau depicts both rocks and stones in various states of utility and autonomy. His rocks and stones act as stand-ins for different models of Indigenous knowledge and tools, shaped over millennia in relation to their surroundings, sometimes carrying spirit or memory and sometimes adapted for human uses.

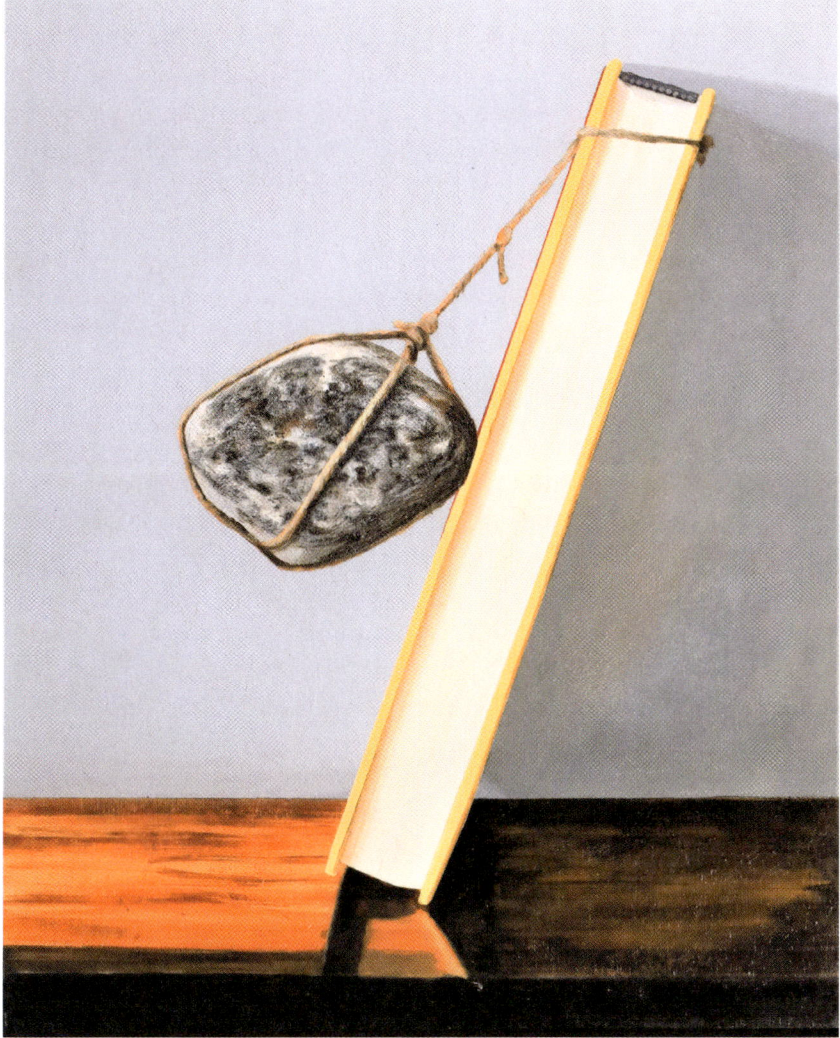

"Wisdom, Knowledge, Balance," 2021, 50.5 × 40.5 cm, acrylic on panel.

6   David Garneau, "Rocks, Stones, and Grandfathers," *Rocks, Stones, and Dust*, 2015, rocksstonesdust.com#writing.

The books in Garneau's work are typically proxies for Western systems of knowledge. Books record and preserve knowledge. They can transmit information across distances without requiring active reproduction or retelling as oral storytelling does. Garneau suggests that while the written word's reach can be a great asset, an Elder's knowledge in print is an unhappy compromise. Recording the knowledge of basket making, for example, means you no longer need to teach basket making through shared practice. That knowledge could be seen as safe in the book rather than requiring each generation of community members to learn for themselves and teach future generations. In this sense, knowledge is put to rest in a book—it can be awakened by an active reader, but it can survive generations without community.

As Indigenous Peoples gain greater presence within Western academic settings, and as we put these institutions to use, there is an uneasy relation between Western theories and tools and non-colonial embodied and relational knowing. Writing our knowledges removes the imperative for human-to-human transmission, but we work to ensure it does not become static by striving to embody our cultures, ensuring they continue to live and evolve. And as we speak to wider audiences—working within Indigenous or Western spaces outside nation-specific communities—we undertake a balancing act between universality and specificity. Garneau's works are generalized—into the broader discussion of "Indigeneity"—yet interested in his own Métis specificity or, more broadly, how individuals are informed by our own lived experience, education, environments, and cultures.[7] When working in non-Indigenous spaces as an Indigenous cultural worker, there is a continuous negotiation between autonomy and the collectivity of being a "cultural person," between speaking for yourself or on behalf of your community.

Garneau addresses the tragedy of attempting to deal with trauma in isolation with *Healing Alone*. A rock is fractured, split in two by some great force, sitting alone, precariously reassembled with a single strip

---

7   See ongoing dialogues unpacking the generalization of "Indigeneity" through Garneau's artistic practice and criticism in: David Garneau, "Visiting Indigenous," *Rungh* 8, no. 3, rungh.org/visiting-indigenous; David Garneau, "Indigenous Criticism," *Border Crossings* (May 2015), bordercrossingsmag.com/article/indigenous-criticism; Matthew Rana, "Un-Settling Criticism," *Kunstkritikk*, June 30, 2023, kunstkritikk.com/unsettling-art-criticism; and David Garneau, "Writing about Indigenous Art with Critical Care," *Momus*, March 25, 2020, momus.ca/writing-about-indigenous-art-with-critical-care.

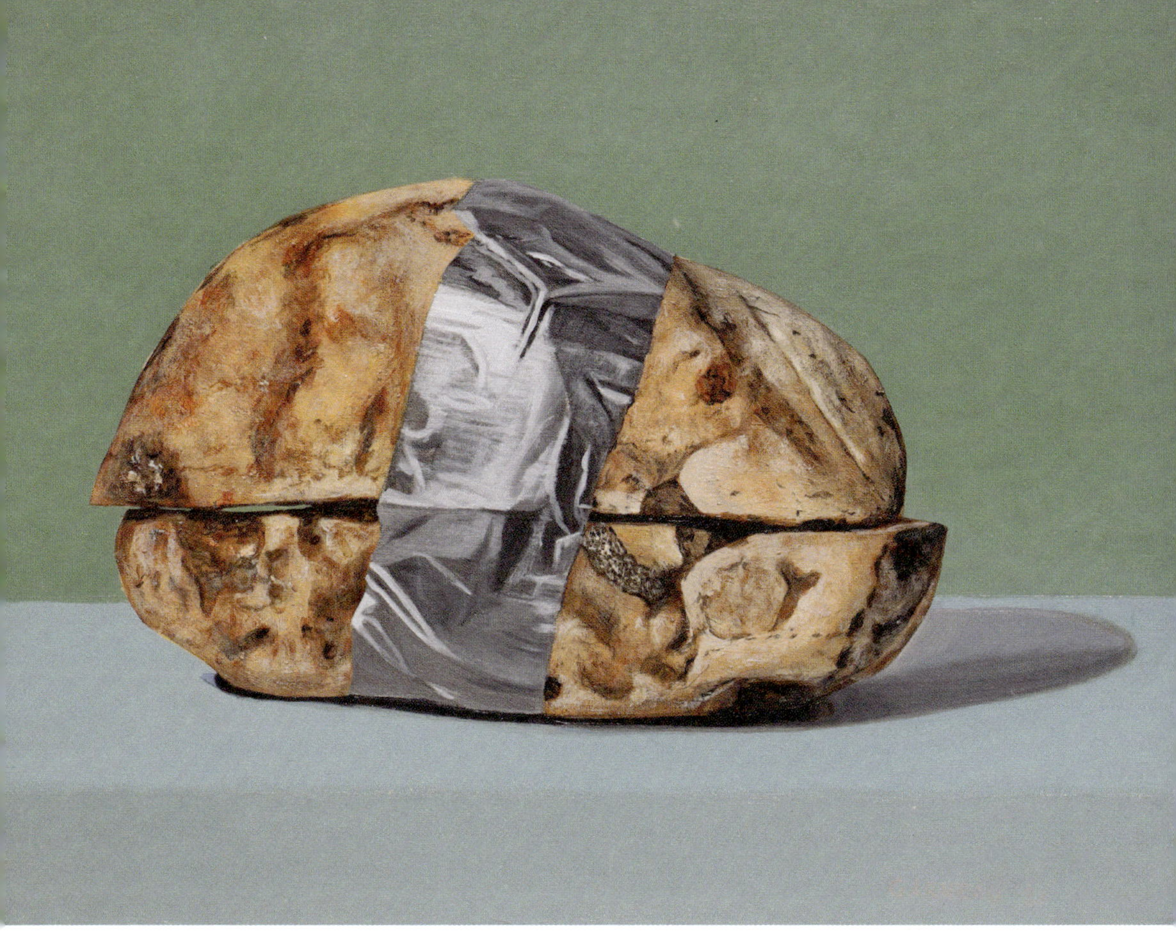

"Healing Alone," 2021, 36 × 46 cm, acrylic on panel. Collection of the MacKenzie Art Gallery.

of duct tape. The impacts of cultural genocide have decimated many communities, creating overlapping traumas as well as severing the connections we rely on for collective healing. Communities have been working for generations to rebuild those healing relations; however, as cultural workers enter into academia or other Western fields, there are incentives to move away from our communities for work or study. This rock's isolation and visible trauma hold space for those navigating this success-fuelled separation, as well as for its twin: those we keep in our prayers—the ones who hurt alone, who are disconnected or disconnect themselves from their communities. Healing is something that cannot fully occur alone, though many attempt it this way, either for lack of community or for not being ready to welcome that help in. The piece holds space for individual trauma yet remains in relation with Garneau's larger investigations into the emotional limits of certain systems. No amount of book knowledge or cultural material on its own

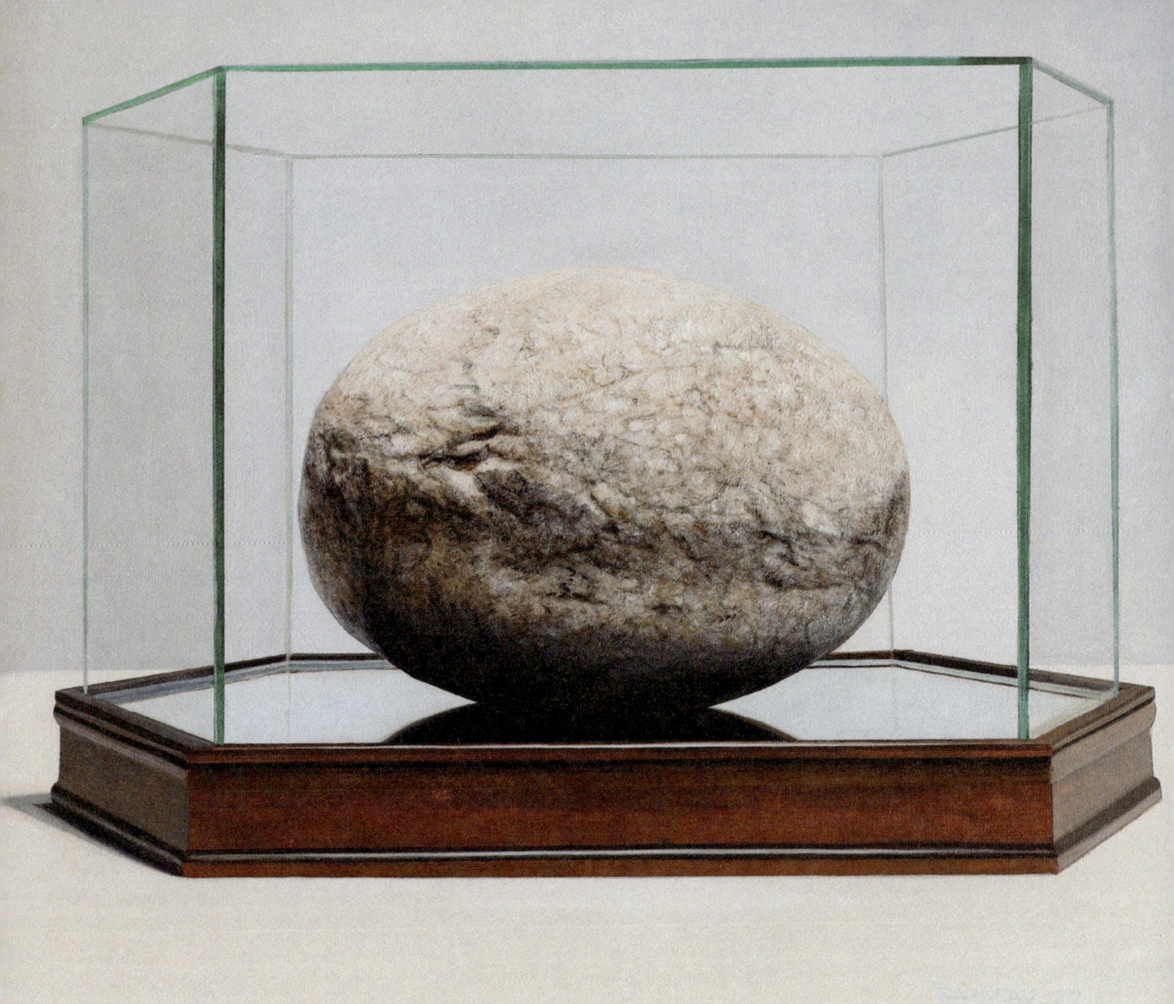

"Suffocating Grandfather," 2022, 61 × 50.5 cm, acrylic on panel. Collection of the MacKenzie Art Gallery.

will create community, nor can it offer true healing. It can hold things together in a shape that should be right yet isn't quite whole.

Protected Grandfather and *Suffocating Grandfather* act as different examples of misguided institutional care. The former depicts a Grandfather rock wrapped in bubble wrap as if preparing for safe storage of shipment. The latter places the same Grandfather rock in a museum display case. The titles highlight the dissonance between museum standards for the care of cultural property in a Western tradition and the needs of Indigenous ceremonial or cultural objects. The Grandfather is a living entity with a purpose that is denied through attempts at preservation. The irony of denying an object its life as a form of care is an active discussion among Indigenous cultural workers who seek new models for conservation. Most areas of the museum have moved on from "salvage anthropology" (the attempt to document and preserve the culture of a "dying Indian race"), yet preservation is a primary function of conservation departments, which are struggling with Indigenous articulations of care. Many belongings were made to be used, and that utilization is more than just "acceptable degradation"—it is an essential part of its care.

In Garneau's lexicon, the Grandfather is a rock-stone hybrid. It becomes a *stone* through ceremony, yet it is utilized for its inherent spirit and experience as a *rock*. The Grandfather rock acts as a bridge between humans and our relations. It is something we use, but it cannot be relegated to our control or protection. A rock perceives the world through tactility, responding to wind, water, fire, gravity, erosion, and shifts in temperature and humidity. A rock cannot be a rock if it is preserved by humans; it can only be a stone. In its element, a rock may erode, expand, contract, or break from interior moisture heated into steam, and that is how it remains alive, how it remains in community—in relation to humans and other beings—and a conduit for knowledge and spirit.

The rock's mode of perception is all encompassing—an experience typically absent from anthropocentric painting traditions or aesthetic philosophy. Garneau illustrates the apparent incongruities and incompatibilities of these modes of aesthetic representation and lithic experience, embracing the tension in a precarious yet productive balancing act.

In *Grandfather Contemplating Western Ocularcentrism*, a Grandfather rock faces its own reflection. The title points to the limits of visual-centric modes of interpretation, and it indirectly addresses both the essence and limits of Garneau's project. I imagine the Grandfather rock contemplating what it means to rely on appearance and surface value, what can and cannot be gleaned through our eyes, human obsession with representation, and how much of our own essence is a performance. Like this Grandfather rock, contemporary Indigenous people often must confront our own reflections in frames that were not designed for us. We adapt to our environment and—in the best case scenario—respond to this tension by becoming rock-stone hybrids. We both rely on and resist a performance that helps bring us further and closer to our own existential truth. As we do work outside of community, this work can both reinforce and distance us from the central relational essence that is being called upon.

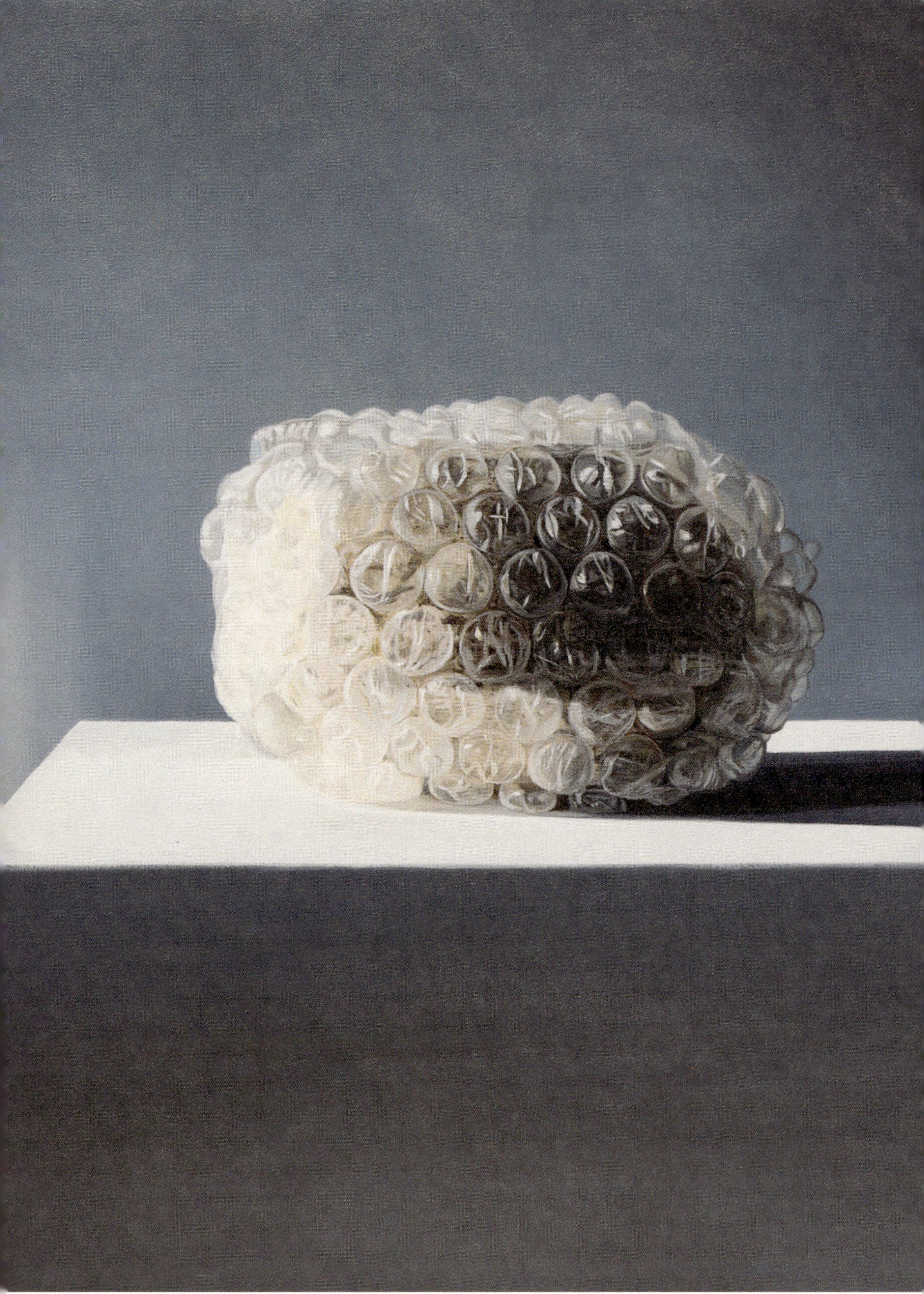

Garneau's work does not resolve this tension but makes an uneasy peace with it. His still lifes embrace the stillness and power of image making and record keeping, as well as the life force found in active cultural production and investigation. Though no human subjects appear, Garneau's symbolic compositions represent the complexity of his individual positionality within a broader network of communication, capturing the abstract tensions and loaded histories of a human experience in all its relations.

FACING: "Protected Grandfather," 2022, 92 × 72 cm, acrylic on panel. Collection of the Mackenzie Art Gallery.

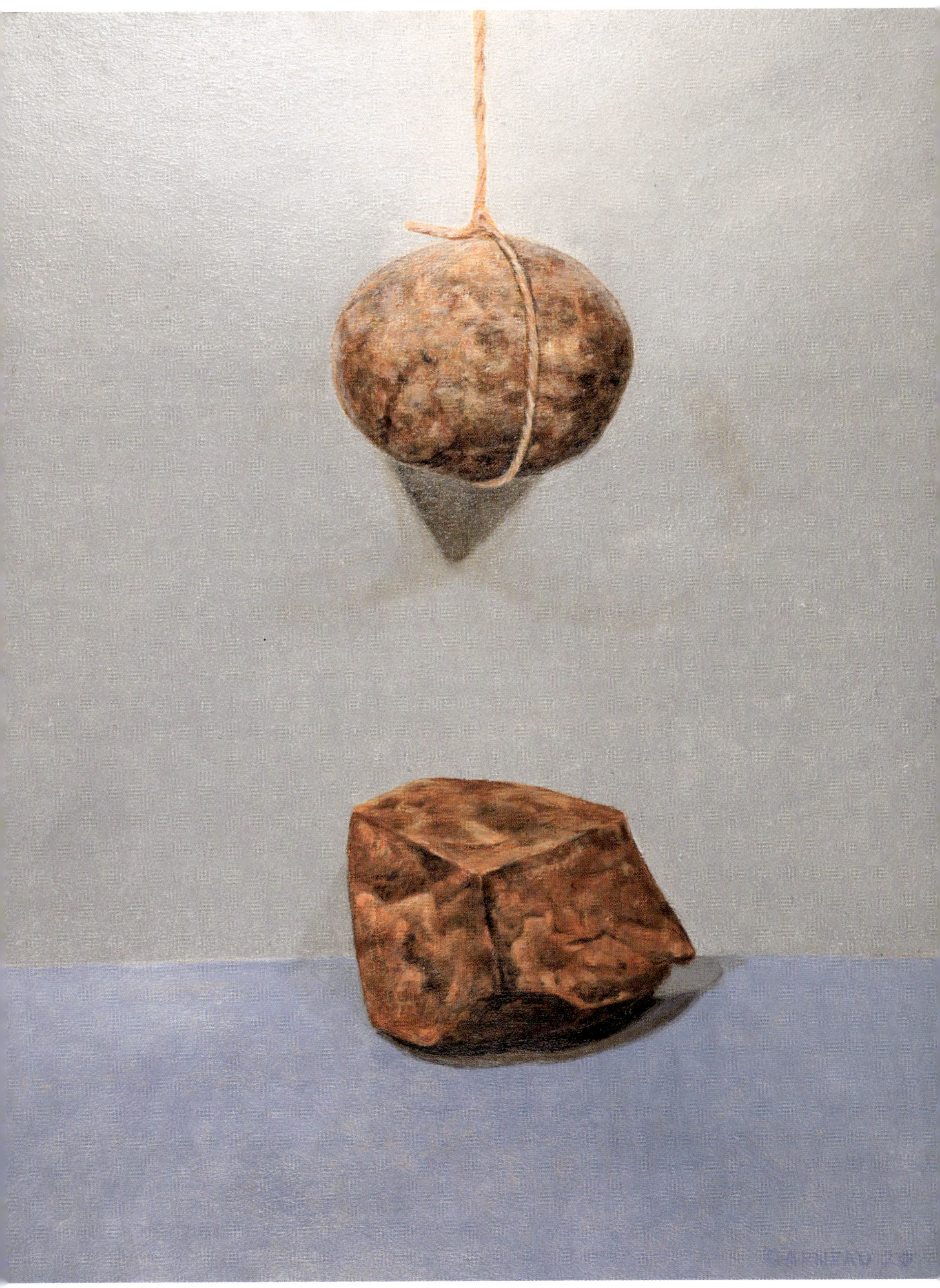

STONE AND ROCK: *I HAVE FAILED YOU.*
BY PETER MORIN

1.

I have a desire to reach towards the painted air that seems so alive around the painted stone/rock.

2.

Paintings aren't alive in the same way that Totem Poles are alive. This sentence doesn't mean anything really. Materials and cultures. Intentions and realties. Mediated through bodies and words to make something actually meaning full. And today I'm a bit of a grifter. I'm not trying to be disrespectful here. I love Paintings as much as I love Totem Poles. And I'm not shy about privileging and prioritizing Indigenous making systems over Western/European ones. This is a choice I make. And there are so many reasons to make that choice.

3.

That being said (the statement about privileging in the previous section) I still want to complicate my read of David's painting even more. Paintings and Totem Poles help me to feel more alive. Also being closer in to that alive-ness, and honouring my Tahltan–French-Canadian body, means that I must try to honour that both Paintings and Totem Poles are alive and are inter/related art/forms that are not placed in competition. Here. Read upon read. Stone upon Rock. Stone upon Stone. Rock upon Rock. Stroke upon cut stroke. Breath upon breath.

FACING: "Stone and Rock," 2020, 50.5 × 40.5 cm, acrylic on panel.

It's important to not rely on muscle memory to make these words. The words in that sentence, in these sentences. The words that make up this messy-full prose. There is no comfort in these words. The actions that emerge because of these particular words mean nothing. You can choose to hold none of this. And there is no comfort in the applications of paint onto a flat surface. This can all be lies if you choose. And it's funny how easily lies are stronger than the truth. Rock. Stone. Painting. Painted breath. Honouring the human body that is pushed to its limits because creative act/ions can be shattering. One painting made by hands that lifted surfaces and shape into a delicious composition. One experience of hands lifting and assembling an experience for our viewing bodies to lean-in-to. One choice after another to make what we are looking at and being asked to ascribe meaning towards. I feel more meaning full because I am choosing to look twice. Together we hold the stone and the rock and the blue water that they touch in the painting. Do you also imagine holding the stones, moving them around, dancing with them, and then placing them rightly before making the painting?

4.

We honour the human experience of making, of looking, of touching, of feeling. Painting is a sensuous act. Lying is also a sensuous act for some. Together, We are infinite hands lifting infinite stones together.

5.

I lift those stones as I imagine David lifting those stones. Rocks. Knowledge. I hold their weight. My hands become the painter's hands, and we, together, place these stones onto books, that are placed on a table surrounded by appropriate lighting. All of it are lies. All of it are the best lies. Lies that help us to recognize our own human meaning. My hands are not a painter's hands. My hands have never lifted these stones, never felt their weight. And I've never held a paint brush in any meaningful way but I have felt held by river stones.

6.

It is important to not rely on muscle memory as you are reading these words. It is important to not rely on muscle memory while writing these words. I am not a painter. I am not a writer. I am a thinker. Somewhere along this life/way, we are taught that muscle memory is supposed to help us to feel alive. Safe. Fed. Connected. Well-behaved. Muscle memory helps us to become team players. Muscle Memory helps us to feel productive, and to feel comfort. Muscle memory helps us to be safe passionate people. Muscle memory helps us to be safe angry people. Even in writing this list, right now, in the previous sentence, I've realized that I have a learned and developed a muscle memory that tends to list one negative attribute followed by one positive attribute. I know that I try and write for a reader. Muscle memory. There is no guarantee that anyone will read this. And always in the front of my mind is our mother's journey with Alzheimer's and how she is actively transforming her muscle memories every day. You can't rely on these things. This type of listing, one negative then one positive, is easier to read. This type of listing is inviting the reader to believe that I might know what I'm talking about. This type of listing is also about reassuring myself that I'm not a messy person, that I can control myself and not take too many outlandish risks. Now, this has stopped feeling like home. Now, this is starting to feel like I'm nowhere. You are reading this and probably thinking this is the definition of nowhere. I wonder if we should all stand in nowhere and look at rocks together.

7.

I reach out my painted hand into the painted space of the painting to lift up one of those painted stones. There is a physicality that requires faith. A body holding another body. An Idea holding up an Idea. This consensual touch between two beings. But maybe it is a non-consensual touch. A smaller body being lifted up by another body without being asked. Touch is the medium now. Touch makes it easier to write about Indigenous knowledge systems because maybe that's what David is asking me to do. Perhaps, this painting is that moment, before entering the sweat lodge, standing by the fire that warms rocks. They are rocks that are transformed by the sacred. They are Grandmothers and Grandfathers because of the sacred. And, we have the sacred because of Grandmothers and Grandfathers. This is what you are told. This is what I was told. They are Grandmothers and Grandfathers because of power. Some of you have muscle memory that tells you this is a type of truth. Some of your Muscle memory that helps inform/shape the way a body can/will move. Today I feel tired of being controlled. I know that Words tend to lie to me, and I keep coming back. Today, I'm realizing that this muscle/memory keeps us from being unsafe. I know enough to not touch the fire-red-hot rocks. My training means that I will also recognize that fire paints stones red. I know enough to not touch the painted stones in a painting. Today I'm realizing that taking risks becomes a way to be free from this muscle memory tyranny.

8.

I know that there is air because my lungs tell me that there is air.

This muscle memory controls how we get home safely.

I know that there is no such thing as painted air because my painted lungs are not breathing in Western European Art/History.

This means that every painting, from the bowels of Western/European Art History, that looks alive is actually dead.

9.

This means every impulse must be interrogated. Every word. Every thought that might become a useful idea. Every potential sentence that is strung along inside of an idea to make a "point" isn't real. You can't rely on any of it. You can't rely on sitting down to type. You can't rely on standing up to write. Writing these words, you notice your breath shifts into shallow anxious waters. You cross your feet. You uncross your feet. You also realize that you are waiting for a phone call. Everything needs to break apart. Especially because you know that you are so comfortable reaching into the painting and picking up those stones. And all the words are too familiar. Rocks. Beings. Ancestors. Your skin has already been touching those stones. Skin on stone makes a new type of skin. A communion. A sensuous power that is probably too powerful. A sensuous power that is world-making new power full worlds.

10.

I have spent a lot of time around stones in my Indigenous life. A part of that stone story starts at age 16, sitting in a sweat/lodge for the first time, and seeing those hot red rocks for the first time. Those rocks that were painted by the fire. At the current age of 46, I now know that those rocks were actually painted by too many years of knowing the Universe's secrets. I've been thinking about this exact thing since being invited to write about David's paintings. And I've done just enough work, in Academia now, to be able to theorize, synthesize, and actualize "something." And those skills feel "emptier" than usual today. At 16, those stones scared me. I could see that they were breathing and to make the breath more meaning full, the Sweat Lodge keeper would put medicine on top of those hot red rocks. And that sweat lodge keeper, named Phil L'Hirondelle, told us about how his grand/kid could see the gender of these sweat/lodge stones. This memory of working rocks/stones reminds me of the book *Roland Barthes* by Roland Barthes. He managed to write a whole book about himself without mentioning himself once. I wonder about the books that these working rocks/stones write about themselves. I wonder if they care to mention themselves in the story of their working lives.

11.

I wanted to write about the painted air around those painted stones so bad. Actually, I wanted to write myself into the narrative. I wanted to centre my own breath, and my breathing into the surface of the painting. I wanted you to read along with these thoughts. Messy. Available. Complicated. I wanted you to reach with me, along with me, into the flat/depth of this image. I wanted you to take your hands and feel along the sides of the rock. I wanted you to feel alongside the edges of the stones with me. I wanted you to take your hands and run your fingers along the blue line, where the blue meets institutional grey. I wanted your hands to touch my hands touching the painter's hands touching these two shapes called stone or rock. I wanted our breaths to move together into the surface of the painting. I wanted to talk about quantum realms and how many of these realms are being touched by us, together with these stones/rocks/paint. I never wanted any of us to imagine being the stone or the rock. I never wanted any of us to have to hold the rock up so that we can tie the perfect knot on the thinnest string, thinking/worrying that we might let the rock fall. I never wanted any of us to become the stone or the rock, because we aren't good enough to do that imagining work yet.

12.

There is no such thing as painted air. There is no rock. There is no stone. There is no breath. There is nothing that is surrounding them. There is everything that is surrounding us. I do have some hope that the knot will break, that the knot holding up our dreams will just fall apart. I do have some hope that the rock will be able to travel again. I do have some hope that we will be ready to pick up these new pieces of a potential future and continue to make something beauty full.

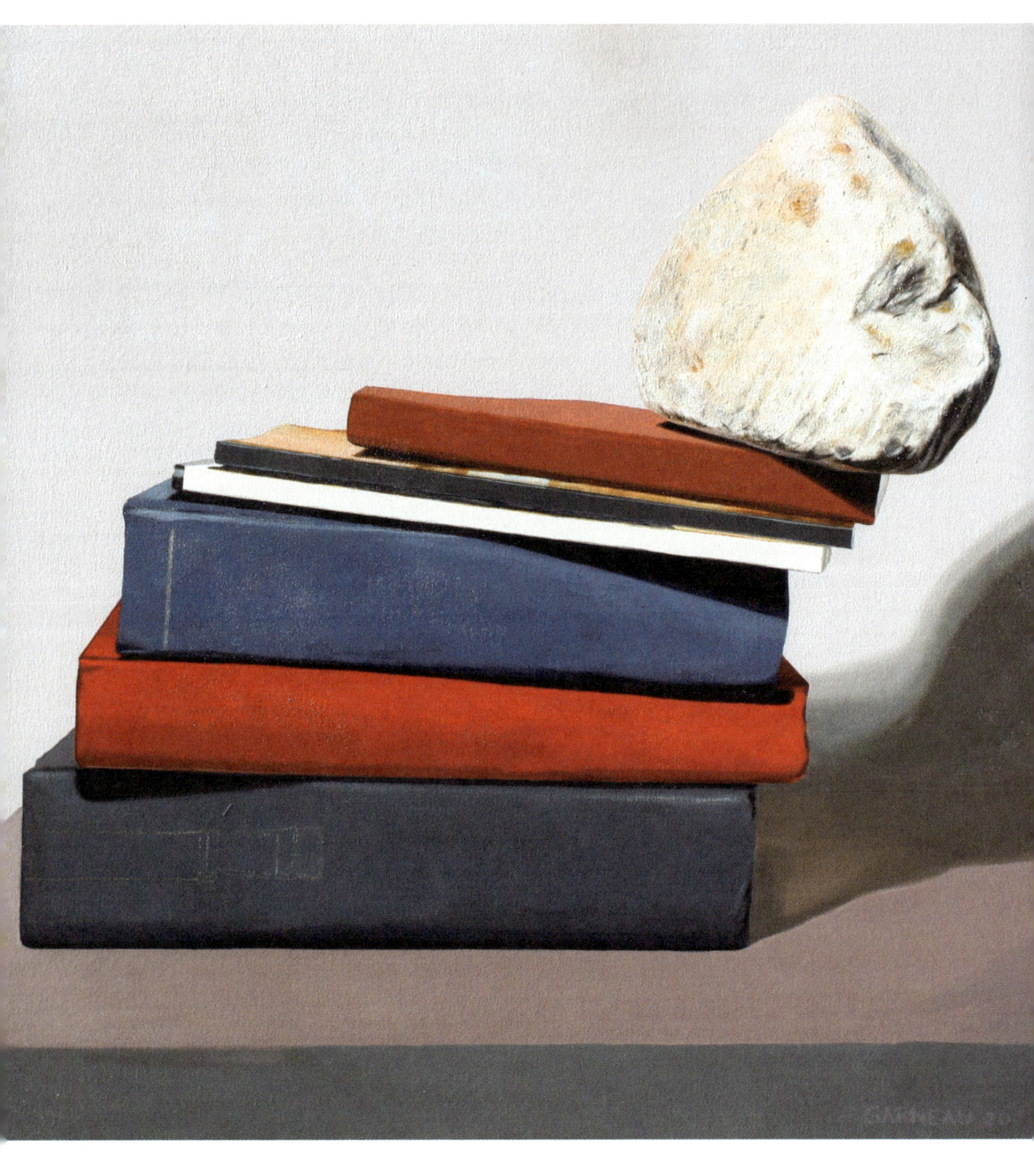

WANDER CARRIED
BY CECILY NICHOLSON

there are stone witnesses / even on the road less travelled[8]

---

8   Juliane Okot Bitek, "Day 73," *100 Days* (Edmonton: University of Alberta Press, 2016), 28.

FACING: "Glacial Erratic," 2020, 58.5 × 58.5 cm, acrylic on canvas.

NETWORK IN THE MOTION OF TILL / A MEASURE OF MEMORY

The matter of erratic perched upon a conclave of lithologies
                                        matter is a familiar place.

The flow of eras in and of rocks entrained, transported
deposited in the vast retreat of ice, a terminal edge

                        —a touchstone.

On the brink, how boulders remember their provenance.

They remember their relations
                    sediment the cobbles, gravel, sand, silt, clay
                        dragged along glacial pavement.

The groove of striations rounding edges
polishing their faces as they move across a constant bedrock
                                    —a stack of primary tomes.

A MESH OF ROOTS / MAKES SLOW HASTE

This stage is an erratic, late season, thick with blackflies.

A makeshift podium
at the corner of kitchen table and Main.

The towering books, their unfamiliar habitus[9]—a perch
                              in verse, upon a rock of self-governance
                                        deeply committed
                                  together, looking forwards
                         slightly intoxicated with anticipation
                                  of Independence. Impatient
                    with the glacial pace of decolonization.
             Vigilantly critical of the manoeuvrings
of the Colonial Office. Often in despair at the state
of formal politics in the islands still.

Keeping close track of events in a thrift of wandering
great distances, some hundreds of thousands of miles
along a dispersal train. At a glacial pace, naturalizing
dependencies in the punctual time of politics
systems of articulation, fact, construct, and event.

The big rock fell from the sun.
Regimes come and go; elections have their cycles.

          Light work extends its shadow to the edge.

Unwavering and outlasting
the familiar durée of economic time now set upon us.

---

9   Stuart Hall, *Familiar Stranger: A Life Between Two Islands* (Durham: Duke University Press,
     2017), 162, 205.

REBAR BARE BONES / IN THE SPALLING INFRASTRUCTURE

lithology of the boulder to the lithology of the bed
this porous face to a stack of nondescript books

carboniferous limestone
now embedded within the till at Whitburn Bay

worn away sandstone on top of limestone
to the angular granite at the river grey

a supernatural granite boulder
on a flat terrain of metasedimentary rock

quartzite carried in from the mountains
is of the mountains and sings a mountain song

networks in the motion of till—a shoreline leaving
rock fleeing—the ice retreats or the ice returns

thunder and lightning arrive simultaneously
the foothill train run so long now grows tiring

hard work in the hard rain, endure maturing forces
fighting for surficial change in a tertiary system

typography of the moving particles and sediment
groundwater flows northeastward in remnants

the ceremonial contours of a young Mistaseni
underground the lake in a gentle preglacial valley

heft unearthed as the lake waters rose to burst
a ridge cut widely, carrying everything away

an old one resubmerged in some collegial state
fragments sunk to the bottom of a recreational lake

WIND BLEW THE TRUNKS TWISTED / ICE-SCOURED BASINS

"To perch," as Audre Lorde remembers, "the bird with no feet" amid
"trees with no limbs."[10]
Stay awhile as home no matter how precarious. The forest has roots.
Nothing rolls, nothing is singular. Indistinct amid a loose flow of selves
and always adjusting to the constant movement
of temporary emulsions. The perch, this place in painting is always on
a little edge, always teetering there a hold. Balancing

resistance is a flutter of wings in convection, the tremulous drift.
Balance is a constant purpose.

---

10   "Wherever the bird with no feet flew, she found trees with no limbs." Audre Lorde, *Zami:
     A New Spelling of My Name* (Watertown, MA: Persephone Press, 1982), 31.

IN THE MOTION OF TILL / TOWARDS THE BLUFF OF AN OLD SHORELINE

rocks have eras, stones move in their own time
imagine them migrating

frost heaving amid symbionts, lichen, acid, salt
and animal tracks that lead away

sometimes the stones will stay awhile
erosive centuries can be wearying

like an island in practice
land, smaller than a continent, surrounded

by water-wind-gravity
log booms, invasive ivy, the constant traffic

just off the highway weathering damage
vandalism and the elements

in this preservation era
a deep rest is a stone's millennia

far from their source they remember rivers
seas that wound their way inland

shedding earthly corridors
maritime fossils the field turns over

quiet slips of algal mud runoff tongues of ice
bolder, as matter out of place

FACING: "Everyday Sacrament (Tea, Pickerel, and Bannock),"
2024, 46 × 61 cm, acrylic on panel.

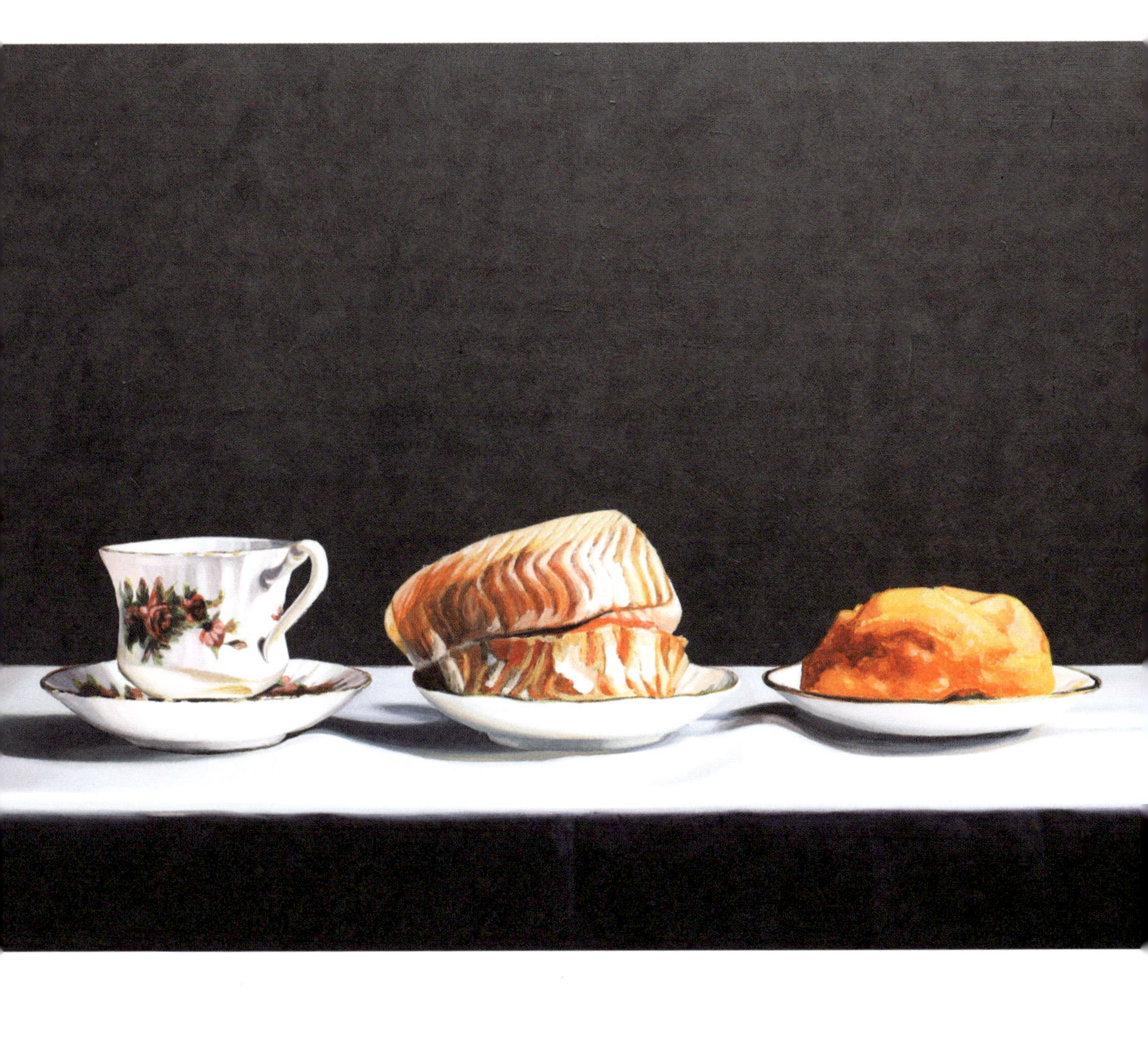

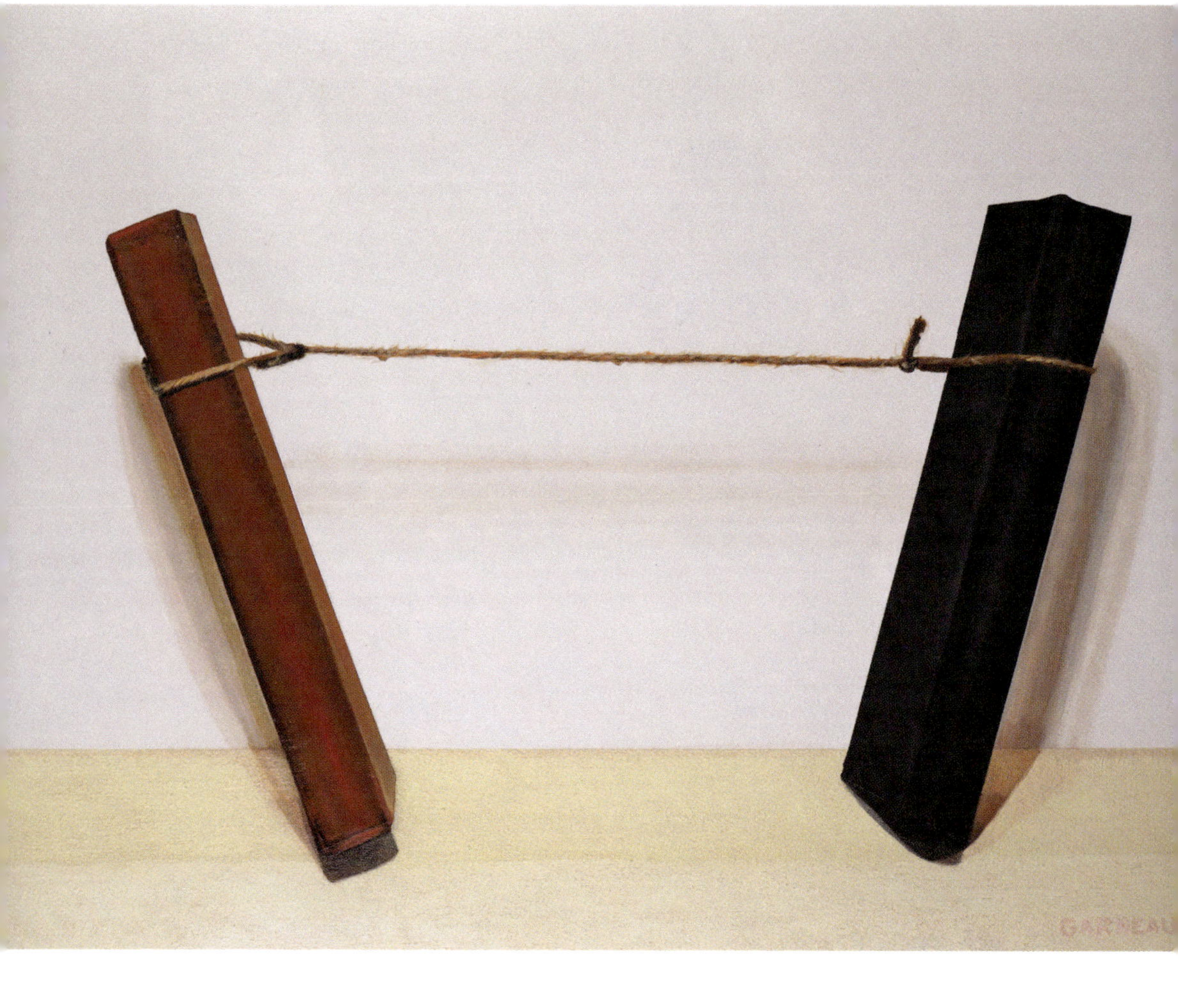

ON *KINSHIP*
BY PAUL SEESEQUASIS

magine if you will a tiny cabin near La Ronge in the late 1950s. It is framed with unpainted plywood, an old bush stove heater to stave off the minus forty-degree Celsius winters, and an outhouse, and surrounded by Jack pines. It belongs to a rather imposing Métis man; a bush man and surveyor, yes, but also a man who is an intellectual, from a relatively privileged social background, who has chosen to live here. Now imagine that cabin is filled with the usual necessities of life in the north—a rifle, ammunition, shovel, compass, ropes, gear, radio, and canned foods and fresh meat—and you may feel you have completed the picture. But there is something else: makeshift bookshelves along the walls, some warping under the weight of hundreds of books, ranging from pulp Westerns to the collected works of Marx and Engels.

James Brady was the first Métis intellectual I encountered as a young man. I was angry, directionless, and with no intellectual framing to analyze my reality as a young urbanized Cree man coming of age in the colonial, provincial entity known as Saskatchewan. Someone had given me, or maybe I discreetly tucked it under my jacket in some bookstore, a book entitled *The One-and-a-Half Men* by Murray Dobbin. It was the story of Métis activists James Brady and Malcolm Norris. At the time it was a minor revelation, but it has proved to be a lasting one.

I read it with interest and in Brady and Norris saw a sort of tag-team of role models: Indigenous men who were learned in Western, socialist theory and, in an almost act of thaumaturgy, translated its application to contemporary social justice and anti-colonial activism in northern Saskatchewan. That they ultimately failed to bring about a revolution or even a significant improvement to the lives of Cree, Dene, and Métis in the North was no surprise; even then I saw that the hegemony was too entrenched, too woven into the fabric of "settler Canada" that no two Métis activists, regardless of their intellect or grassroots activism, could possibly unsettle that system. It remains entrenched to this day.

Still, kinship rekindles that experience of decades ago.

It reminds us that yes, in its own way, knowledge is a form of power, but it is also very limited. And, in fact, only "power is power."[11] Only power itself prevails.

The covers of the two books are red and black. Colours fraught with many interpretations: red as in the Indian "red path," Mao's "red book," and Carl Jung's "red book." Black as in the Bible, black as in an accounting book of ledgers, black as in a public book of condolences. They are, these two books, seemingly pulling away from each other, as opposing magnetic poles do, as diametrically opposing ideals always do. There is a knotted string that seems to be striving for a balance between the two extremes, or to at least keep both books somewhat upright in their proper position. That string, knotted by human fingers, is frayed and tense.

> "A caution: just as 'the West' often lacks coherence and consistency, few First Peoples are paragons of their traditional teachings. Natives live under occupation and with programs of aggressive assimilation and racism. Reserves are not utopias. Indigenous is not a settled position. It is an aspirational identity, a recovery and creative mission that attempts to continue the best non-colonial ways of knowing and being in the future." —DAVID GARNEAU[12]

There is something to the string that is illusive. Is it preserving a delicate, precarious balance between ideas, between ideologies, between

---

11   *Game of Thrones*, season 2, episode 1, "The North Remembers," directed by Alan Taylor, written by David Benioff and D.B. Weiss, featuring Peter Dinklage, Lena Headey, and Nikolaj Coster-Waldau, aired April 1, 2012, on HBO.

12   David Garneau, "Radical Currents: Indigenous Art in the Future Continuous," Constellations: Indigenous Contemporary Art from the Americas, October 2020, muac.unam.mx/constelaciones/assets/docs/essay-david-garneau.pdf.

conflicting kinships? Or is it an anchor whose time has come, and just as we untether the boat so we can navigate the river, now is it the time to cut that string and liberate ourselves from both those volumes?

In cutting that string, perhaps we enable ourselves to get back to something that is not bound and framed by a cover, but something that has been lost or simply forgotten. Brady brought his books to his cabin in La Ronge: they were more than a pastime to while away long winter nights; they were a tool for him to interpret this home of his choosing and to apply his theory to interpret it. But perhaps he soon recognized his books could only go so far. They were not born of that land. They were not of it.

On the land was something intangible but real. Not just nature's immensity itself, which is also unforgiving and non-judgmental and reigns supreme, but the ghosts of the past that inhabit its expanse and whose teachings are, like those voices on the wind, passed on, generation to generation, in orature, not the page.

In seeking a life in the bush, on the trails and rivers, Brady was, in his own way, cutting that string in search of knowledge that is not written but spoken, knowledge that is seen and felt and not confined within the covers of a book. For any interpretation of that knowledge that the land itself holds is diminished the moment it is written and codified.

> "The [colonial] attitude assumes that everything should be accessible to those with the means and will to access them." —DAVID GARNEAU[13]

Within the strands of that string, perhaps, is something that is not meant to be accessible, that is not meant to be anthropomorphically categorized and exhibited. That is not meant to be reduced to a tool of reconciliation and understanding to make us feel better about ourselves. Rather, it is illusive, ephemeral, and alive: alive not only in memory but in the trees, skies, animals, water, and rocks. It is the infinite. It is the great mystery. It is kinship.

---

13   David Garneau, "Imaginary Spaces of Conciliation and Reconciliation," *West Coast Line* 74, vol. 46, no. 2 (Summer 2012), 28–32, web.archive.org/web/20210309160333/http://reworksin-progress.ca/wp-content/uploads/2012/08/wcl74h.pdf.

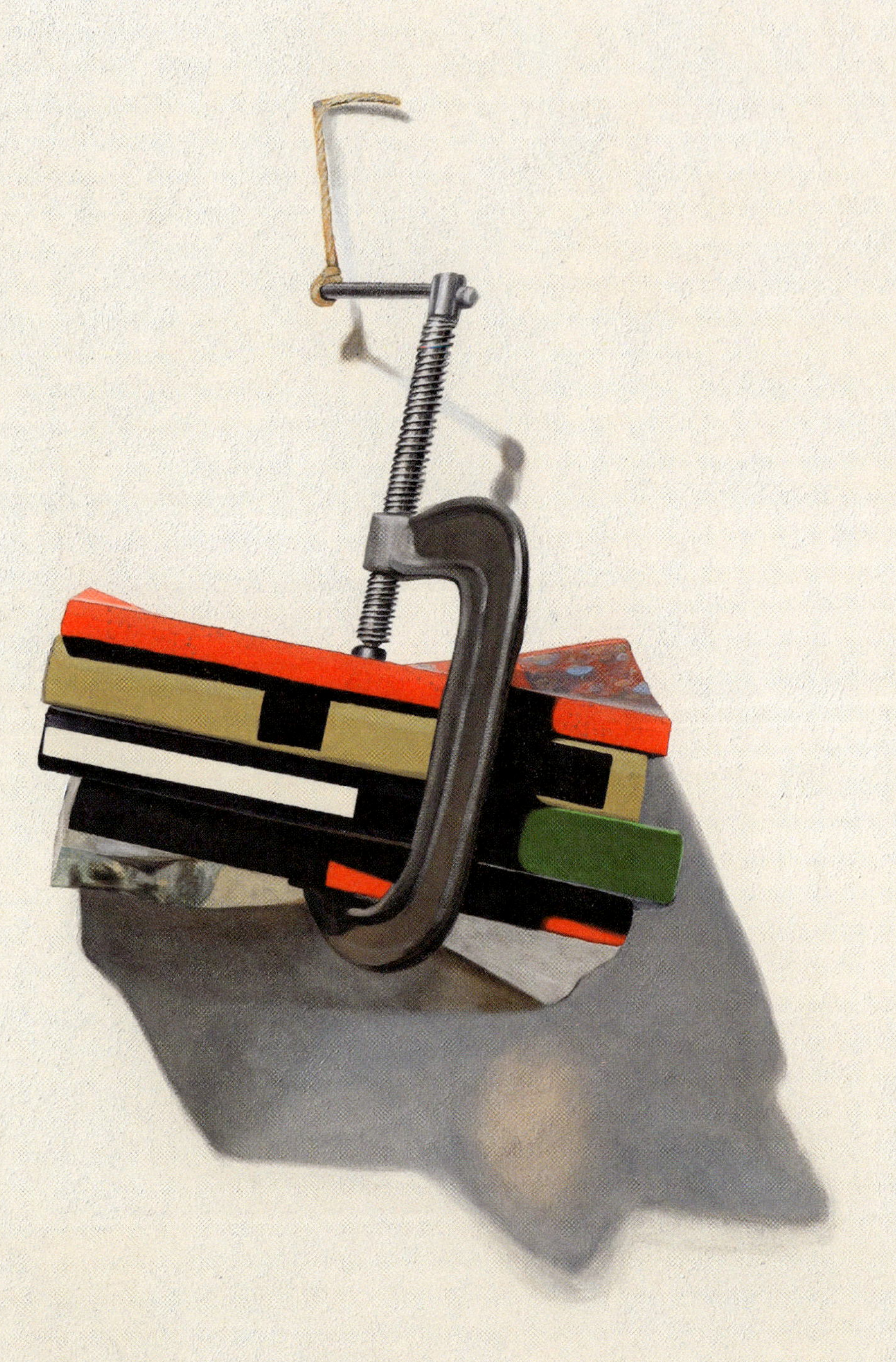

LEARNING FROM
INDIGENOUS. ACADEMIC. SOLIDARITY
BY JEFF DERKSEN

n his expansive series of still life paintings, *Dark Chapters*, David Garneau sets the themes of education, the academy, and divergent forms of knowledge in a strained relation. As a Métis artist, he specifically positions these in tension with Indigeneity and Indigenous epistemes. This terrain is clearly laid out in the titles the paintings carry: *Two-Eyed Learning, Indigenous Scholarship, Métis in the Academy, Good Scholarship, Bad Protocol, Academic Pretendian,* and *Academic Activism.* Within the series, a canvas entitled *Indigenous. Academic. Solidarity* is particularly compelling to me as a working-class settler who moved up to take a job later in life in the academy. A notion of solidarity—a common term and a commitment that I have been familiar with most of my life—is set alongside the terms *academic* and *Indigenous*; yet they are separated by very strategic periods, as if they exist singly and are not articulated, or cannot be joined. The title is therefore not naming an existing condition, but it is a challenge, I believe, and a provocation to contemplate both how or whether actual "academic Indigenous solidarity" as a horizon can be achieved.

Dark Chapters, as a body of work, is also an extraordinary gesture that deploys the genre of still life painting to subtly pose a set of urgent social questions. This gesture also parallels art historian Norman Bryson's thinking when he writes "when the term 'still life' is still around and well, it makes sense to not just settle for the inherited

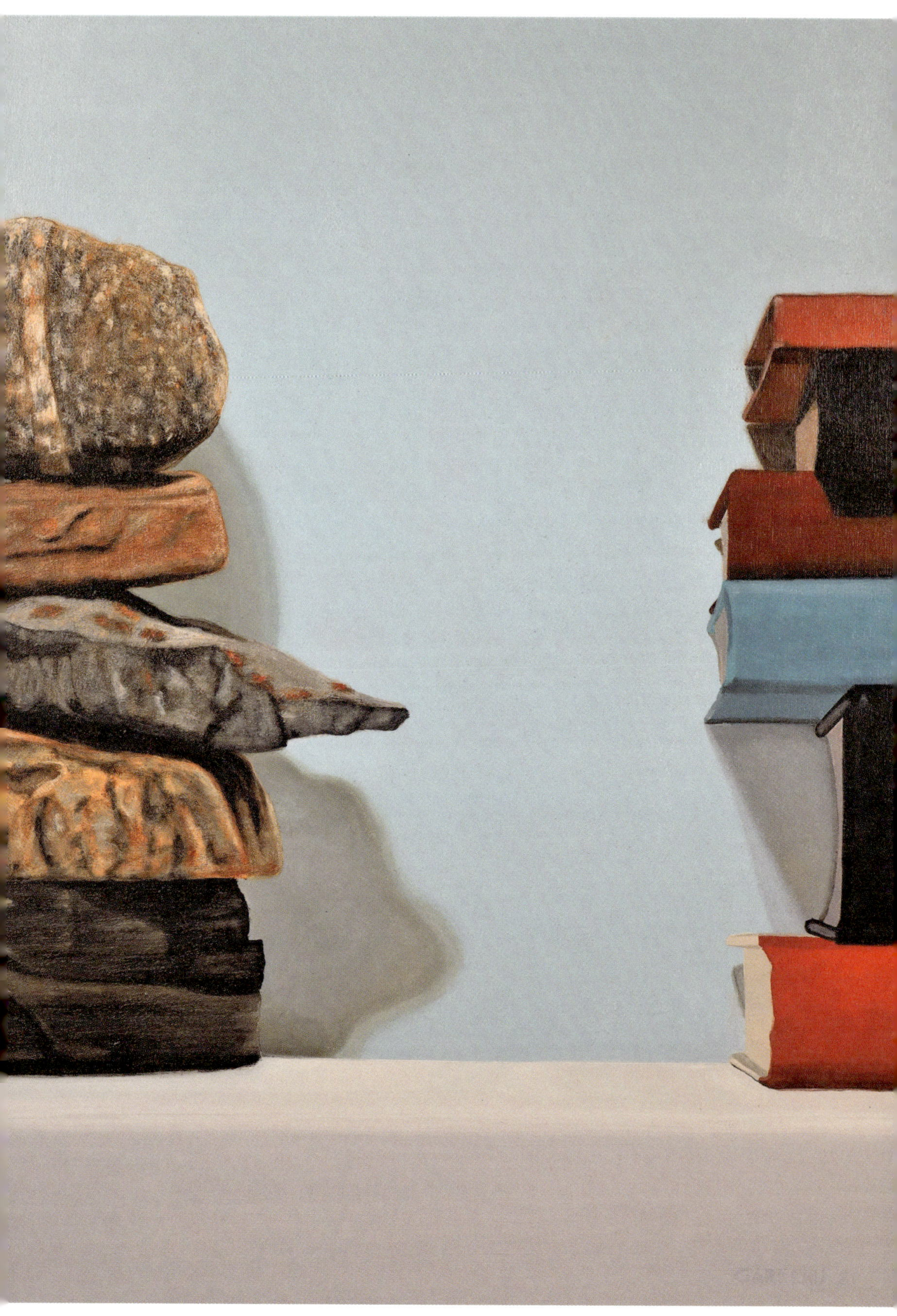

discussion but to try and move that discussion into our time and to ask what still life might mean, for us now."[14] But Garneau asks a question outside of Bryson's Western art historical frame: what might still life be able to do in relation to Indigenous knowledges, epistemes, aesthetics, and representation? Here, still life becomes a social and aesthetic proposition. Bryson identifies still life "as the genre at the furthest remove from narrative" and "the hardest for critical discourse to reach,"[15] but in *Dark Chapters*, still life is a critical discourse itself—one that veers away from closure and interpretation and towards relational thinking. For *Indigenous. Academic. Solidarity* is a relational provocation that firstly asks academics and settlers, like myself, how would such solidarity work, and beyond that, how can solidarity be reformed or reimagined so it is "not a call on Indigenous peoples to forcefully align their interests and identities in ways that contribute to [their] own dispossession and erasure," as Glen Coulthard and Leanne Betasamosake Simpson put it.[16]

Bryson points out that, historically, "still life painters designed the individual works to appear *as* still life and to take their place in a *series* of work of the same kind."[17] The seriality of still life paintings allows meanings and patterns to be built up over time, for seriality is a diachronic movement even as a still life painting is synchronic, the capturing of a particular moment. Seriality creates and gains meaning as a viewer takes in the paintings in a series; that is, a viewer does not see the painting as singular, isolated from the others nor as a single moment, despite the paintings themselves being a constructed moment. Garneau emphasizes this seriality through the repetition of the objects that he uses to construct the sculptural moments that become the paintings. Books with their covers painted over so they are equally material and symbolic, stones of various sizes and shapes, a stone hammer, braided rope to join or suspend, a metalworker's hammer and a hatchet, as well

---

14   Norman Bryson, *Looking at the Overlooked: Four Essays on Still Life Painting* (Cambridge, MA: Harvard University Press, 1990), 7.

15   Bryson, *Looking at the Overlooked*, 9.

16   Glen Coulthard and Leanne Betasamosake Simpson, "Grounded Normativity/Place-Based Solidarity," *American Quarterly* 68, no. 2 (2016): 252.

17   Bryson, *Looking at the Overlooked*, 10.

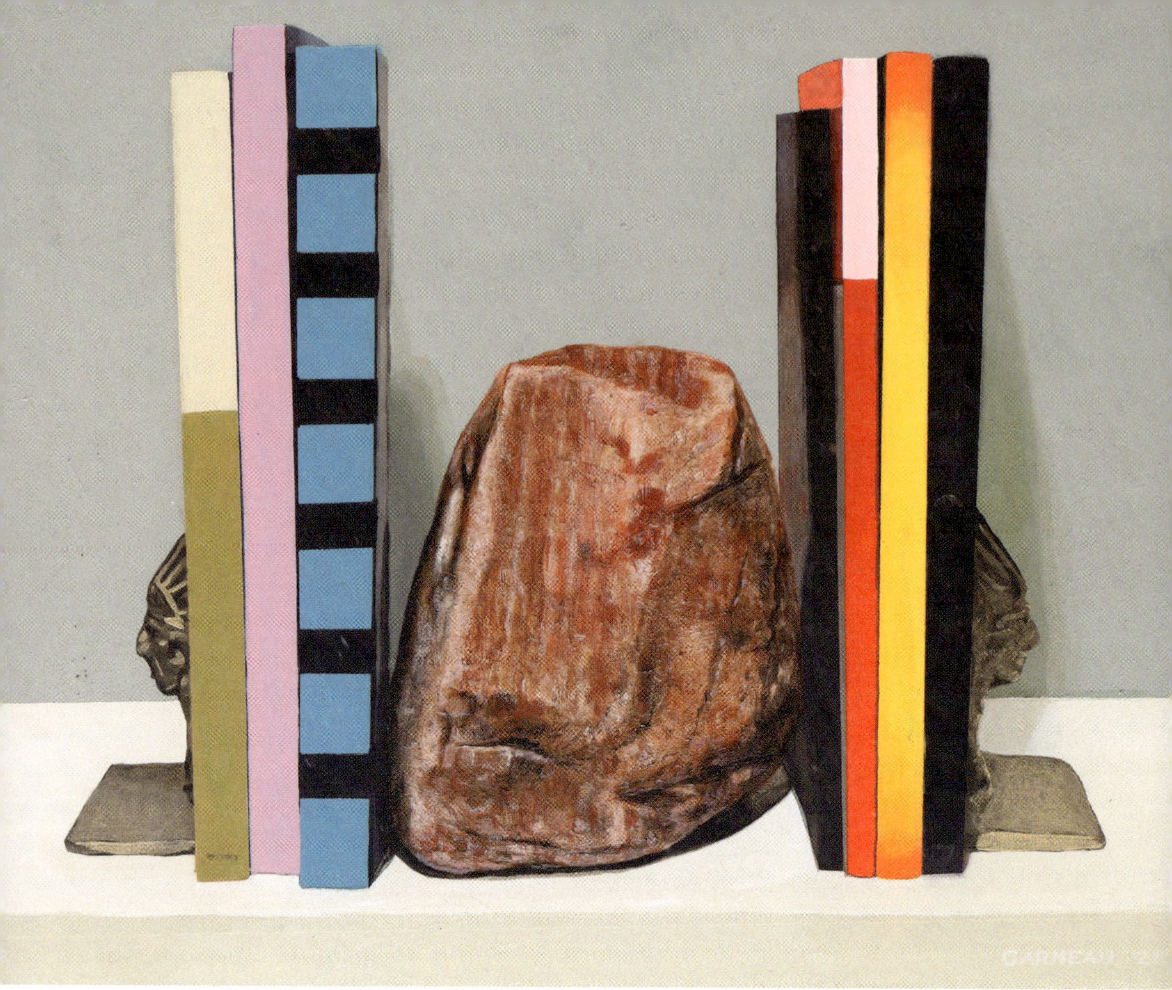

"Indigenous Scholarship," 2021, 40.5 × 51 cm, acrylic on panel.

as fruit, such as apples and oranges, and china cups and glasses, which can be associated with historical still life paintings of abundance, are arranged and rearranged into contingent sculptures. These arrangements accentuate the balancing, precariousness, and tensions between the objects. As Bryson notes of the dishes, crockery, cups, glasses, and other everyday items that are organized into a still life, "No less than wars or revolutions, such artefacts are the products of cultural and historical pressure."[18] In *Dark Chapters*, the artefacts that Garneau selects, whether Indigenous cultural belongings or studio tools and dishes, are the products of Indigenous culture and the historical pressure of colonialism as it weighs on the present. The paintings are in no way passive as they carry and display that pressure.

---

18   Bryson, *Looking at the Overlooked*, 13.

Within this repertoire, *Indigenous. Academic. Solidarity* is constructed of four books approximately the same size uneasily and even a little roughly pressed together with a common metal C-clamp. The C-clamp is a staple of an artist's studio (you can buy one at Canadian Tire for about twenty-five bucks) and would be used to hold in place anything that was being glued together—such as a frame—or to fix material to a workbench so it could be cut, drilled into, sanded, or otherwise worked on. The spines of the books face us, but they are painted over so we do not see the titles, the authors' names, or the publishers' logos. The top and the bottom books in the small stack are slightly bent, pushed in by the pressure of the C-clamp, and the entire assemblage tilts downward and to the right. The assemblage appears to be hung from a single nail on a white wall by a thin braided twine tied to the C-clamp's T-handle, on the clamp's collar. It is all delicate and contingent yet forced, solid, and fixed. Following Bryson's model of reading still lifes as paintings of pressured social artifacts, I take this particular still life as a provocation to think through the terms and the possibility or the impossibility of actual academic Indigenous solidarity.

What conditions make *academic*, *Indigenous*, and *solidarity* such difficult concepts to join together as a social action? To contemplate this, I want to first lay the groundwork for what *academic* means today in relation to *Indigenous* and then to look back at how *solidarity*—a classical positive attribute from leftist discourse—has a troubled history when it is looked at within the history of Marxism in relation to Indigenous knowledges and ways of being. This will bring me to the current political moment in which we have seen a shift, filled with potential, that can open the concept of solidarity to be thought of in relationship with Indigeneity without falling into the liberal traps set by notions of "allyship" and state politics of recognition. This shift has dynamically emerged from decades of Indigenous discussion and critique of Marxism, as well as from the call from new social movements for forms of solidarity that can encompass the challenges of solidarity as a social bond.[19] From there, can a more effective solidarity emerge?

---

19   Working-class academic David Roediger, in a *Boston Review* forum on solidarity, proposes that "as a word, at least, solidarity is trending upward. The varied uses of the word have more than compensated for a steep decline in talk of 'labor solidarity' from its peak in the early 1960s to 2019: we now talk of solidarity with Palestine, with Standing Rock, with Iranian women, with Ukraine." His point is that solidarity as a concept has become more diverse, asked to take in more forms of difference, and to work across differences. Likewise,

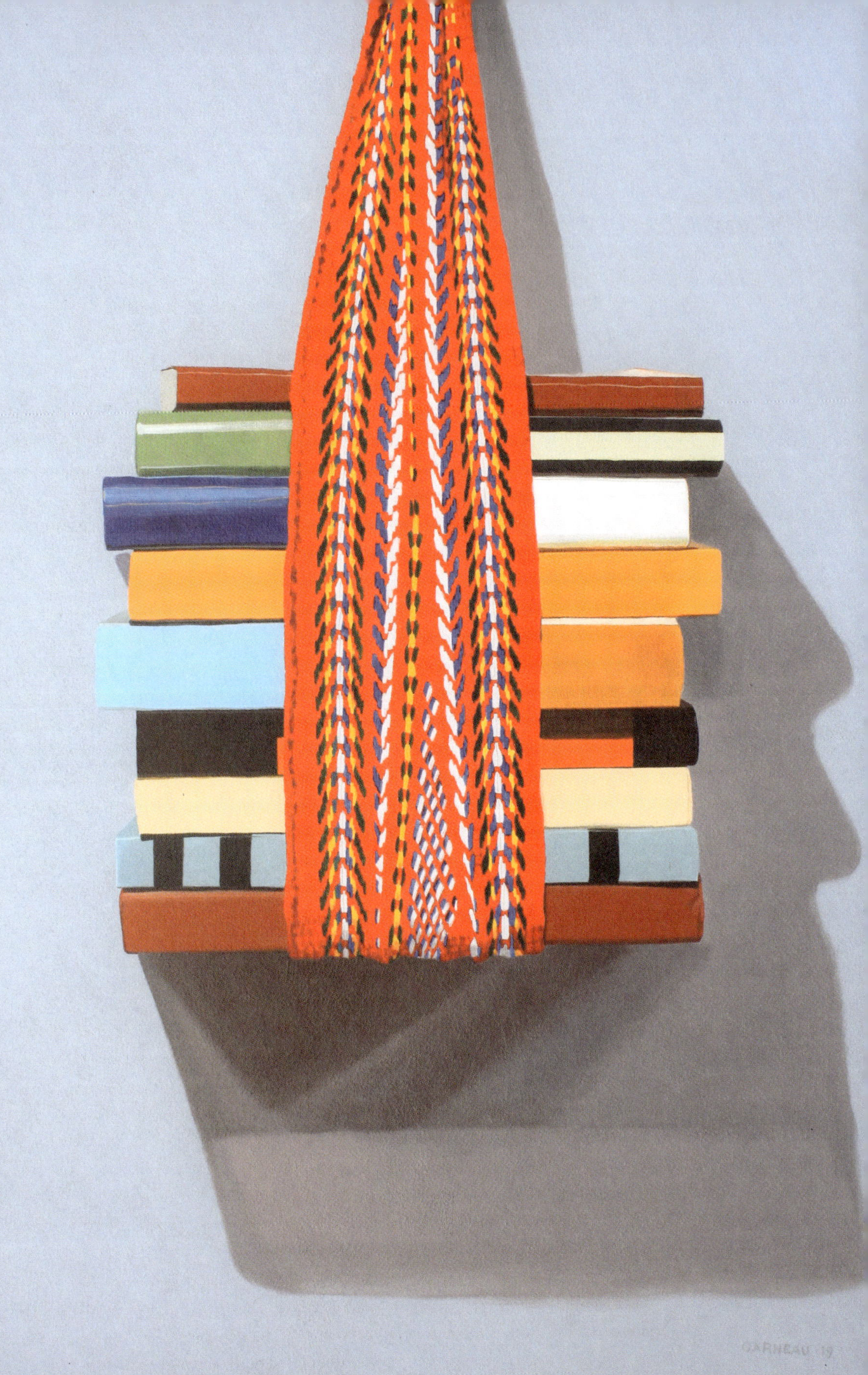

As the Sámi scholar Rauna Kuokkanen asserts in *Reshaping the University*, "'Academy' and 'Indigenous' are complex concepts with multiple internal divisions and conflicts."[20] Locating the structural root of this tension, Marie Battiste writes, "Every university discipline, and its various discourses, has a political and institutional stake in Eurocentric diffusionism and knowledge. Yet, every university has been structured to see the world through the lens of Eurocentrism, which opposes Indigenous perspectives and epistemes."[21] This relationship between the academy and Indigeneity is in a high stakes moment as most Canadian universities claim to be "Indigenizing" and reforming to be more welcoming for Indigenous folks. At the same time, Indigenous engagement with universities has entered a new stage, demanding change, responsibility, and reciprocity based on very specific and clear reforms that have been defined and presented by Indigenous faculty, students, and staff. Yet the colonial structures of the university remain strong (if more subtle), and these reforms are rarely acted upon in structural ways. Reforms may be recognized and even "championed," but the depth of transformation needed still seems far off. Is there the will, imagination, and historical respect to take this opportunity to decolonize universities—to make them a place where knowledges can breathe?

Strongly rejecting the type of inclusion in the academy that extracts Indigenous knowledges as a "resource" and is a false welcoming that deflects from the project of building "Indigenous intelligence" on Indigenous terms, Leanne Betasamosake Simpson writes: "We cannot carry out the kind of decolonization our Ancestors set in motion if we don't create a generation of land-based, community-based intellectuals and cultural producers who are accountable to our nations and whose life work is concerned with the regeneration of these systems rather than meeting the overwhelming needs of the Western academic industrial complex

---

the Indigenous resurgence movement is one of the forms of difference that the concept of solidarity is challenged to reckon with. David Roediger, "So Many Antinomies," *Boston Review*, September 19, 2023, bostonreview.net/forum_response/so-many-antinomies.

20   Rauna Kuokkanen, *Reshaping the University: Responsibility, Indigenous Epistemes, and the Logic of the Gift* (Vancouver: UBC Press, 2007), 11.

21   Marie Battiste, *Decolonizing Education: Nourishing the Learning Spirit* (Vancouver: Purich Publishing, 2013), 186.

FACING: "Métis in the Academy," 2019, 122 × 79 cm, acrylic on canvas.

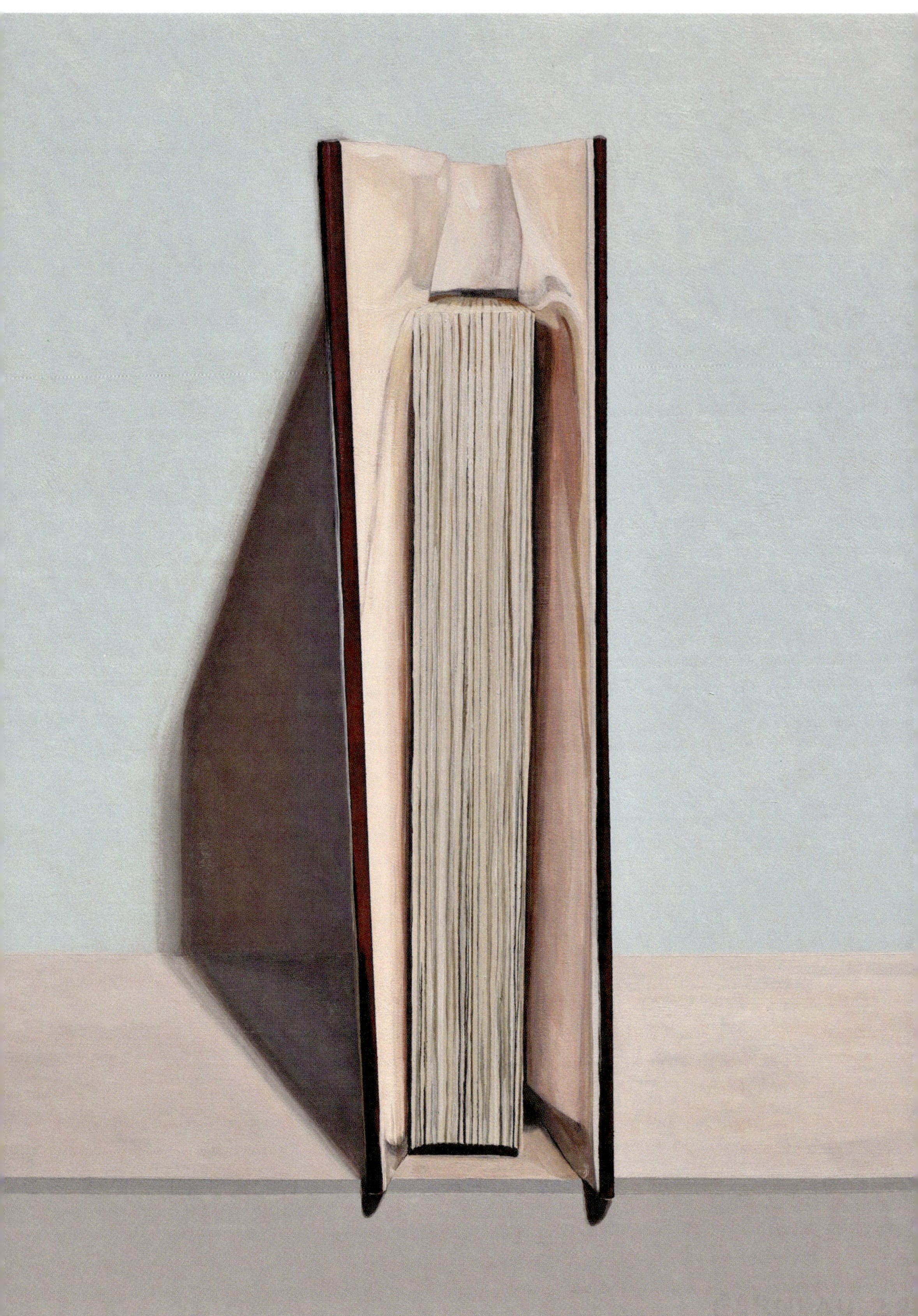

or attempting to 'Indigenize the academy' by bringing Indigenous Knowledge into the academy on the terms of the academy itself."[22] Simpson's position leads away from the type of reforms that can eat up the energy and time of Indigenous faculty and students and shifts the responsibility to the academy to "make a conscious decision to become a decolonizing force in the intellectual lives of Indigenous peoples by joining us in dismantling settler colonialism and actively protecting the source of our knowledge: Indigenous *land*."[23] This is both a rejection of the existing structure of the academy and an invitation to join in what we might understand, from a leftist position based on other decolonial struggles, as a new form of solidarity.

Between the necessary work of decolonizing the academy and establishing more sites of "land-based, community-based intellectuals and cultural producers," which Battiste and Simpson propose, Kuokkanen argues for the transformation of universities. However, she does so by arguing for a radical reshaping of the university through the logic of the gift of Indigenous knowledges and epistemes that would crack the academy's "epistemic ignorance" that narrows its intellectual foundations. Yet she cautions, similarly to Simpson, "before the academy can recognize the gift of [I]ndigenous epistemes, it will have to profoundly transform itself; it will not be enough merely to include [I]ndigenous epistemologies (i.e., [I]ndigenous systems of knowledge or ways of knowing) in pedagogies and curricula."[24] Simpson and Kuokkanen reveal a central problem in establishing any form of solidarity between the academy and Indigenous people: the academy must first reform itself to be receptive to the transformative gift of Indigenous epistemes and to join in dismantling settler colonialism.

The concept of solidarity, coming from a leftist tradition of working-class unity and mutual aid in the early nineteenth century, is built around a European frame of knowledge and ways of being, even though it was transformed in the 1960s through an engagement with

---

22　Leanne Betasamosake Simpson, *As We Have Always Done: Indigenous Freedom through Radical Resistance* (Minneapolis: University of Minnesota Press, 2017), 159.

23　Simpson, *As We Have Always Done*, 172.

24　Kuokkanen, *Reshaping the University*, 3.

decolonization struggles of what Vijay Prashad calls "the Third World political project."[25] It has a powerful sense of shared and bonding liberation in Marxist discourse. As a social process, solidarity has expanded in usage to be an inviting concept, a feeling and attitude and relationship that puts people side by side—standing with others with whom you understand yourself to share an external condition.

Solidarity is vastly different than the form of allyship that Jodi Dean excoriates, as it is not aimed at an internal turn based on identity but rather a linking of one's agency to the agency of others. This does not figure the people or group or situation that one can be in solidarity with as a deficit, as a lack of agency or knowledge, but rather a joining of potential with a shared horizon of a changed world. Dean's burying of the notion of the ally has particular resonance within the relationship of *academic* and *Indigenous* as ally has emerged as a term settler academics used to identify themselves as supportive of Indigenous initiatives in the university and thus to differentiate themselves from all of the forces that work to uphold the colonial status quo. But Dean does not spare the ally as she locates it as a form of liberal self-improvement: "allyship is a matter of the self, of what the self acknowledges, of the individual who stands alone, and this single individual taking on a struggle that properly belongs to another."[26] Allyship is singular and internal and not a struggle with the state or capitalist power, Dean argues, and ultimately "reflects the shrinking or decline of the political."[27] For Dean, allyship does not carry the commitment of being a comrade or the setting aside of the self in forms of solidarity; it is not the model for the hard work of the struggles against oppression and exploitation. Simpson lays out a similar position, describing Indigenous struggle as hard work, accountability, and responsibility. "It's not," she writes, "a hashtag or a sticker or a T-shirt or a selfie or anything white liberals think is important."[28]

---

25   Vijay Prashad, *The Darker Nations: A People's History of the Third World* (New York: The New Press, 2007).

26   Jodi Dean, *Comrade: An Essay on Political Belonging* (London: New York: Verso Press, 2019), 18.

27   Dean, *Comrade*, 19.

28   Simpson, *As We Have Always Done*, 67. I have to admit I have a "I'm Standing with Standing Rock" T-shirt, along with a number of orange T-shirts that I wear to work at a university on Orange Shirt Day, September 30.

But averting the liberal trap that allyship can be does not necessarily lead to solidarity as the ready-made concept to support Indigenous initiatives and struggles in or out of the academy; it is not an easy step. This is because the relationship of Marxism and Indigenous Peoples and their thought has historically had some friction. This particularly cohered around Marxist notions of developmentalism (and the stages of capitalist development), conceptions of the natural world, and Eurocentric formulations of history and time. There have been many re-readings of Marx over the last twenty years that put this relationship of his thought and Indigenous Peoples in a different light, but I want to use a particular moment to show how uneasy a fit Marxism has been for Indigenous struggles and liberation.

Marxism and Native Americans, initially published in 1983 and edited by Ward Churchill, is both an incendiary take on Marx's Eurocentrism (and the North American left's reproduction of it) and a considered reading of Marx from an Indigenous perspective. In a compelling critique that addresses the question of developmentalism, history, and the relationship to nature, Vine Deloria Jr. concludes: "From the perspective of American Indians, I would argue, Marxism offers yet another group of cowboys riding around the same old rock. . . . It accepts uncritically and ahistorically the world view generated by some ancient Western trauma that our species is alienated from nature and then offers but another version of Messianism as a solution to this artificial problem."[29] Churchill, who throughout the volume searches for moments of interface and use, concedes in a statement that also critiques the Marxist writers in the volume: "If Marxism *universally* chose to disregard cultural perspectives outside its own preconceived paradigm, what were the global implications?"[30]

Jumping forward some thirty years, Glen Coulthard, in his influential *Red Skin, White Masks*, critically rereads Marx for and from the colonial present and surmises, "To my mind, then, for Indigenous peoples to reject or ignore the insights of Marx would be a mistake, especially if this amounts to a refusal on our parts to critically engage his important critique of capitalist exploitation and his extensive writings

---

29   Vine Deloria Jr., "Circling the Same Old Rock," *Marxism and Native Americans* (Boston: South End Press, 1983), 135.

30   Ward Churchill, ed., *Marxism and Native Americans* (Boston: South End Press, 1983), 10.

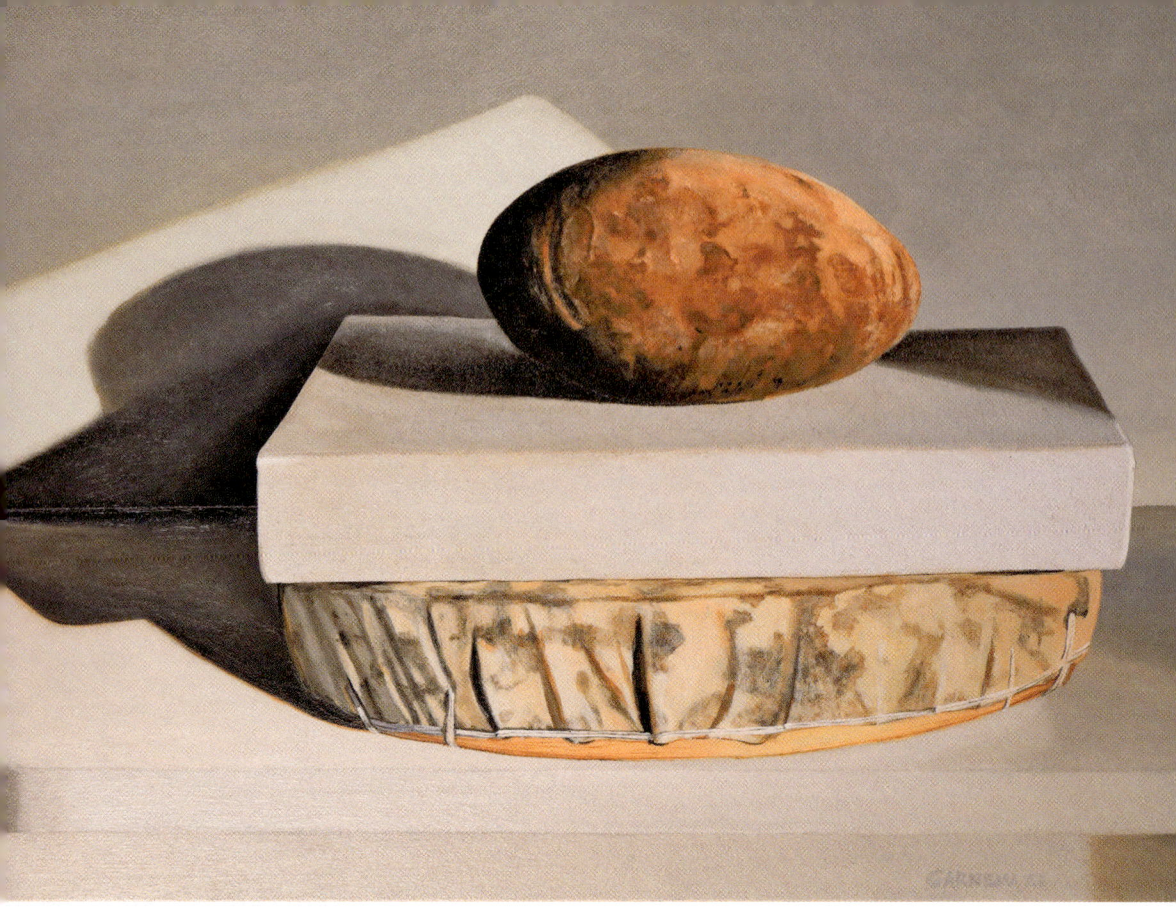

"Good Scholarship, Bad Protocol," 2021, 46 × 61 cm, acrylic on panel.

on the entangled relationship between capitalism and colonialism."[31] Coulthard also reflects on the late 1960s and early 1970s when he assesses the importance of George Manuel's *The Fourth World: An Indian Reality* as "a crucial Indigenous intervention into the ideological influence that the decolonization struggles of the 'Third World' had on the North American's left's critique of racial capitalism and imperialism in the 1960s and early 1970s."[32] These three moments—the late 1960s, 1983, and 2014—show the frictions between Marx's thought and Indigenous scholars and activists, as well as the application of Marx's thought by North American leftists; these moments also show the will to find a use value in Marx's critical methodologies as they can be applied to the

---

31 Glen Sean Coulthard, *Red Skin, White Masks: Rejecting the Colonial Politics of Recognition* (Minneapolis: University of Minnesota Press, 2014), 8.

32 Glen Sean Coulthard, "Introduction: A Fourth World Resurgent," *The Fourth World: An Indian Reality*, eds. George Manuel and Michael Posluns (Minneapolis: University of Minnesota Press, 2019), x.

present colonial condition and Indigenous thought and struggles. I take this to be an evolving critical praxis that attempts to decolonize Marx.[33] To do this, Coulthard lays out a clear project when he proposes that "rendering Marx's theoretical frame relevant to a comprehensive understanding of settler-colonialism and Indigenous resistance requires that it be transformed *in conversation* with the critical thought and practices of Indigenous peoples themselves."[34]

So despite all of these very solid and admirable attributes of solidarity—attributes necessary for social change—solidarity is not a concept or a relationship that settlers can expect Indigenous folks to enter into unquestioningly without it first being transformed by Indigenous practices and thought. This is not because, as I've tried to point out, solidarity is a concept brutally flawed from the start or so tainted with bad Marxist intentions that it needs to be tossed aside wholesale. Rather, it is a concept that has to be opened to crucial Indigenous interventions so it can shuck some of its Western concepts of inclusion, sameness, self, and difference in order to come out applied to the present from an Indigenous perspective.[35]

What would this transformed or reshaped solidarity look like and how could it get us a step closer to academic Indigenous solidarity? Simpson, reflecting in part on Coulthard's contribution to Indigenous resistance and sincerely looking for new forms of engagement proposes that "building alternatives with communities of coresistors is powerful because our struggle for liberation is profoundly related to theirs. But to engage in a truthful way, we have to first know who we are, and I worry we are not committing time and energy to Indigenous intelligence and theory, because it is a struggle. Indigenous intellect and grounded normativity is under attack. It is easier to rely on Western liberatory theory already well established in the academy."[36] The ideas of linked struggles and the necessity for liberation to be global go back to the earliest uses of

---

33   I should also point out that some Indigenous activists today want no part of aspects of Marxist thought and the frameworks of Left critique. See IndigenousAction.org for its take, which includes fabulous slogans such as "We celebrate the death of Leftist solidarity and its myopic apocalyptic romanticism."

34   Coulthard, *Red Skin, White Masks*, 8.

35   Dean makes a strong argument that "Comrade does not eliminate difference." Dean, *Comrade*, 35.

36   Simpson, *As We Have Always Done*, 66–67.

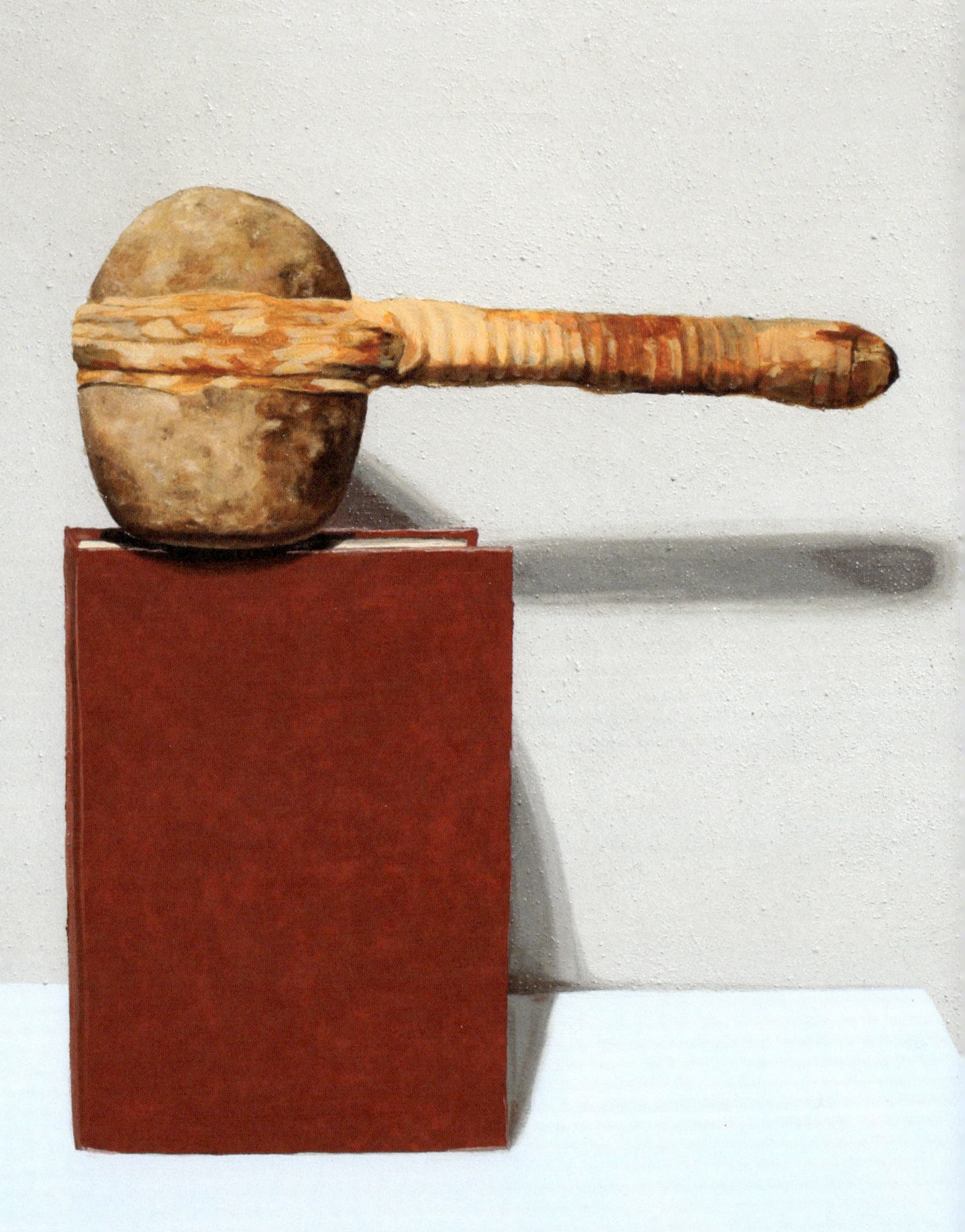

GARNEAU 20

solidarity in Marxist thought, so that aspect has endured; yet "Western liberatory theory" cannot be a blueprint. In speculating further on what "solidarity could look like under grounded normativity"[37] and in relation to ethical obligations to Black Canadians, Simpson asserts, from the position of Nishnaabeg political practices: "We need to be willing to develop personal relationships with other communities of coresistors beyond white allies. We need to develop these as place-based constellations of the theory and practice because when we put our energy into building constellations of coresistance within grounded normativity that refuse to centre whiteness, our real white allies show up in solidarity anyway."[38] Solidarity here, as the Eurocentric concept I have approached it as, is decentred from whiteness in relation to Indigenous and Black struggles; this is an example of solidarity being reworked, even amplifying some of the tendencies solidarity took on during its engagement with "Third World" decolonial struggles, to make it more relevant for the decolonial struggles of the present.

As I come to the end of this short speculation, I realize that Garneau's still life did not take me on the path I had mapped out in notebooks and on screen. It did not push me to use Bryson's intervention into the readings of still life to see Garneau's painting as a social prompt and a form of criticism and knowledge. Yet these qualities in the painting *Indigenous. Academic. Solidarity* remain. I did not then move to Indigenous interventions into the concept of solidary with the hope to reform it by opening it to that conversation between critical Indigenous thought and Marxist liberatory theory. This remains necessary. Instead, I come out having been led to understand the necessity of not relying on, and to see the dangers of, Western liberatory theory to situate my own (and others') relationship to solidarity and Indigenous struggles. For the way that such liberatory theory has been inherited still threatens—or even necessitates—the integration and erasure of Indigenous practices and knowledges.

---

37   Simpson is using a specific term here devised by Coulthard: "I call this place-based foundation of Indigenous decolonial thought and practice *grounded normativity*, by which I mean the modalities of Indigenous land-connected practices and longstanding experiential knowledge that inform and structure our ethical engagements with the world and our relationships with humans and nonhuman others over time." Coulthard, *Red Skin, White Masks*, 13.

38   Simpson, *As We Have Always Done*, 231.

This is the echo I hear when Alex Gourevitch, aiming to reconceive solidarity for a shared present, writes, "developing the sort of solidarity we need to change the world may require dispensing with rather than deferring to the identities we have inherited, precisely in order to forge more just and joyful ones."[39] However, this invitation can also sound like the historical process that Coulthard and Simpson warn against, calling it "auto-genocide" for Indigenous people as it would abandon grounded normativity and therefore "the processes, practices, and knowledges that inform our political systems, and through which *we practice solidarity*."[40]

Solidarity must not be easy, and it cannot be rooted in European forms of universalism. As my Indigenous colleagues have pointed out, it is about walking the path together and being there every step of the way. Solidarity uses the figure of standing—standing is solidarity—with the implication that one has arrived at an established place or relationship of mutual aid and that one's support is trustworthy, sincere, and shared. Solid. This has a compelling history within labour struggles, anti-eviction movements, and environmental struggles, as well as within my own life, particularly in relation to education and the academy. So, I realize, as I have done many times in the last years working, scheming, and laughing with my Indigenous colleagues, I have been subtlety taught something without it being announced as a lesson.

A last word on *academy*, for me the most troubled term in *Indigenous. Academic. Solidarity.* Solidarity, in the Marxist sense of standing alongside and supporting through action all liberatory struggles against oppression and capitalism, is not nurtured in the academy. Small pockets of it can be scratched out and defended, but the intense divisions of types of knowledge and the individuation of recognition do not make the academy a place where solidarity can blossom, transform, and become truly mutual. The path shown by Coulthard, Simpson, Kuokkanen, Battiste, and others sets up an imperative in which new forms of solidarity—in its reformed concept—can lead to more expansive forms of coresistance in and beyond the academy. And this, in turn, may reform the academy.

---

39   Alex Gourevitch, "Transcending Difference," *Boston Review*, September 19, 2023, bostonreview.net/forum_response/transcending-difference.

40   Coulthard and Simpson, "Grounded Normativity," 254.

FACING: "After-Life," 2020, 58.5 × 58.5 cm, acrylic on canvas.

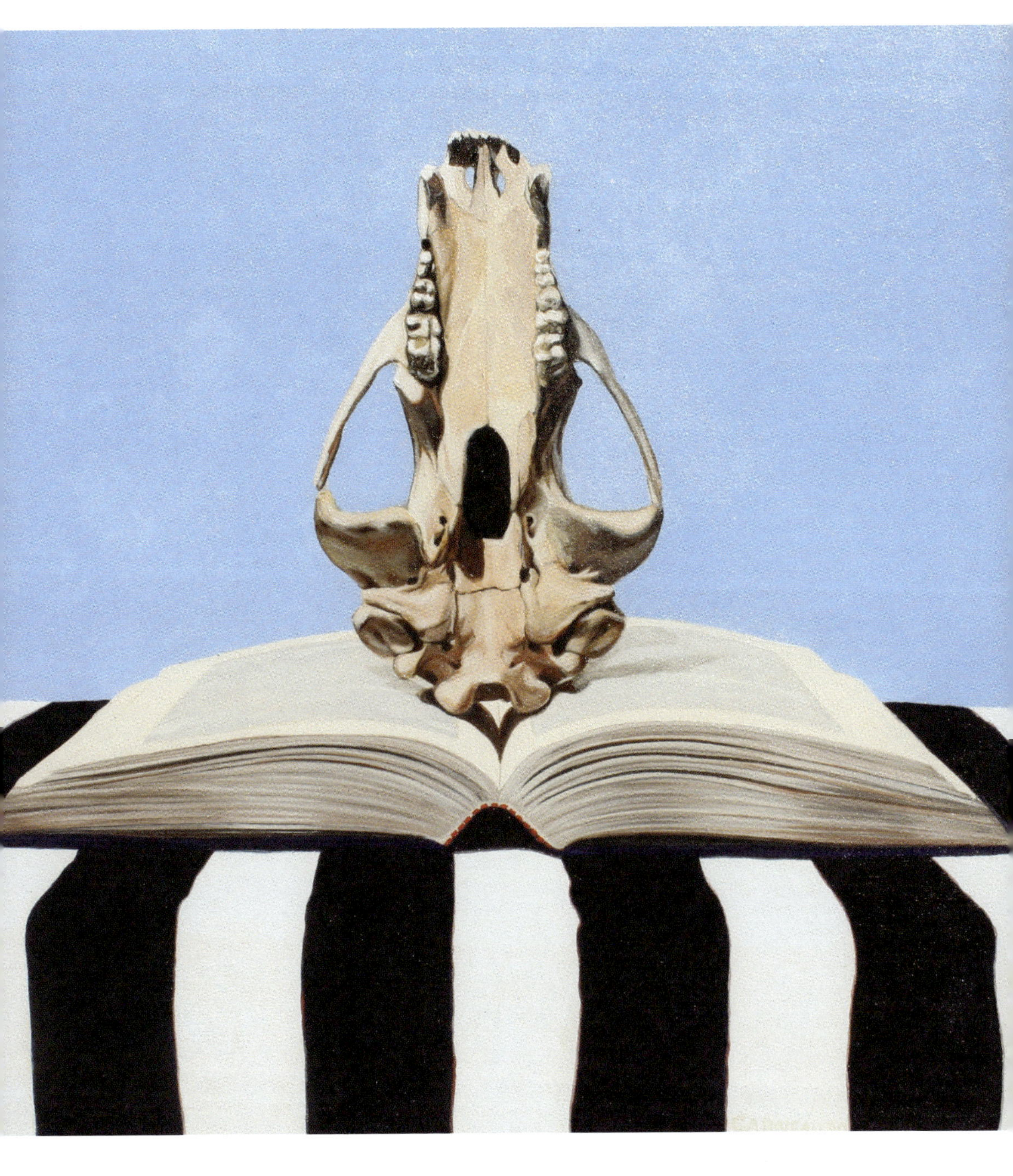

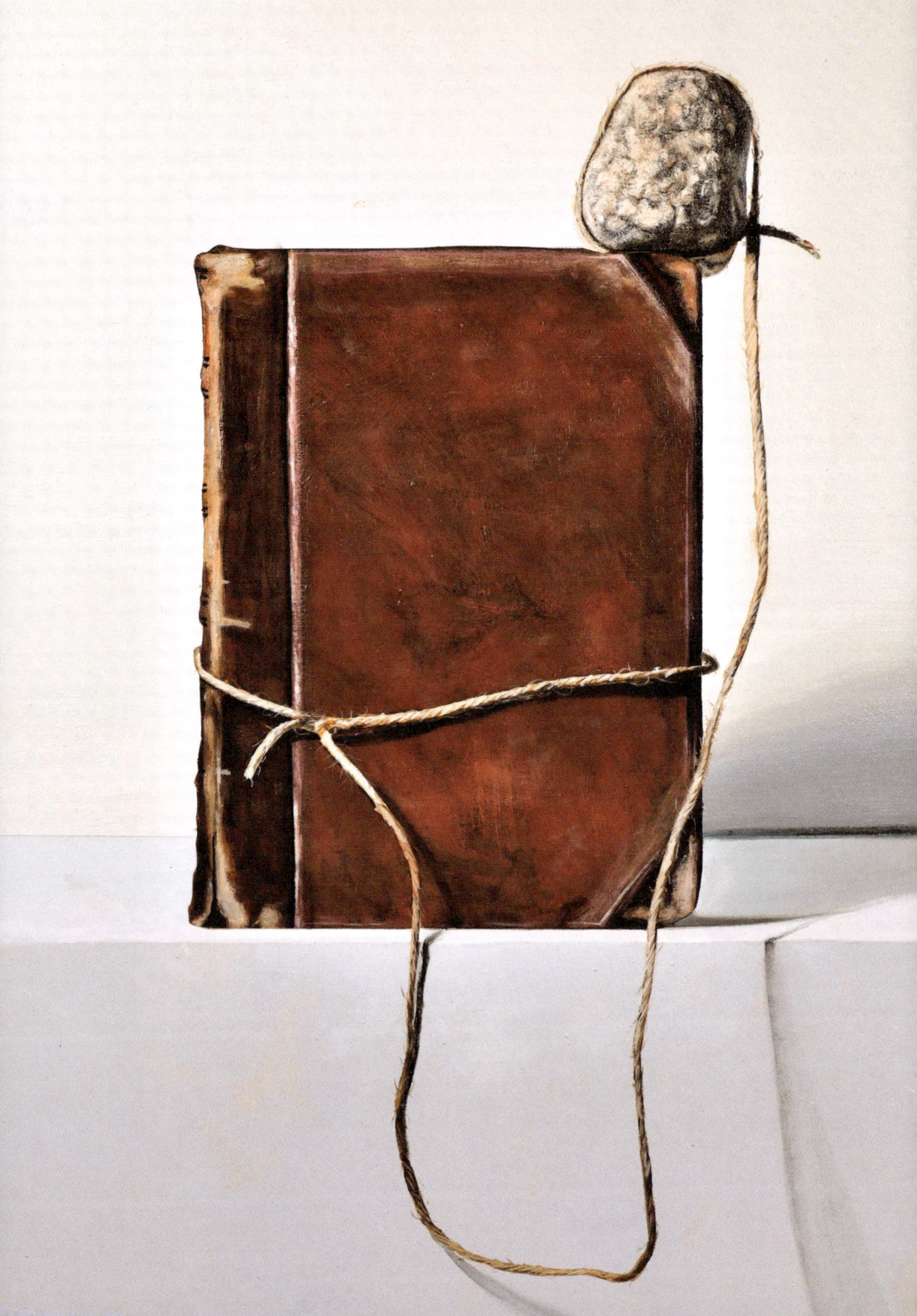

KNOCK KNOCK
BY LILLIAN ALLEN

Knock Knock

Nothing speaks silence more than a stone
nothing speaks silence more than a book
and yet they both speak, voluminous

ᴧᴧᴧ

Knock knock!

Who's not there?

ᴧᴧᴧ

I stand alone but not
a rock or a stone, alone

FACING: "Nothing More to Say," 2021, 61 × 46 cm, acrylic on panel.

except when the book reads me
. . .

Have you heard of glasshouses?

. . .

never a book alone
not like a stone in glasshouses

never knock a book by the sound
or by its cover
or by page 20 before it's over
never knock its whisperings to a stone
never knock a cover by its colour
or place of origin
never knock, enter kindly with love

String stone leather paper bone
fast forward to the year 4023
a technology reads a rock like a book
and projects for all to see
the life of a planet that rumbled and staggered
through centuries of greed and burning forest fires
warming seas. Wars. Unchecked desires
the sound of bones
as they crumble under the shock of a planet
frenzied on itself, wringing every inch and every oz
of advantage from every corner of Gaia
the rich feeding on the poor

but the music soars, artists create another world
becomes real ^^^
inhabited by consciousness of creativity and zeal for beauty,
compassion, and care

Who among you?

. . . . . .
Metaphoric metamorphic, igneous ingenious
sedentary sedimentary slip sliding through time

I am listening for your breathing.
. . .

Last night in a dream
a sisterhood of leaves
covered the land
and everything organic
went back to their beginnings
and we were one, and sentient
like the land, like a stone, like the rock
like the mountains, like the rivers, like the sea
and everything inanimate came to be, sentient
and we embraced each other across all difference
no ruler rules. No need for words.

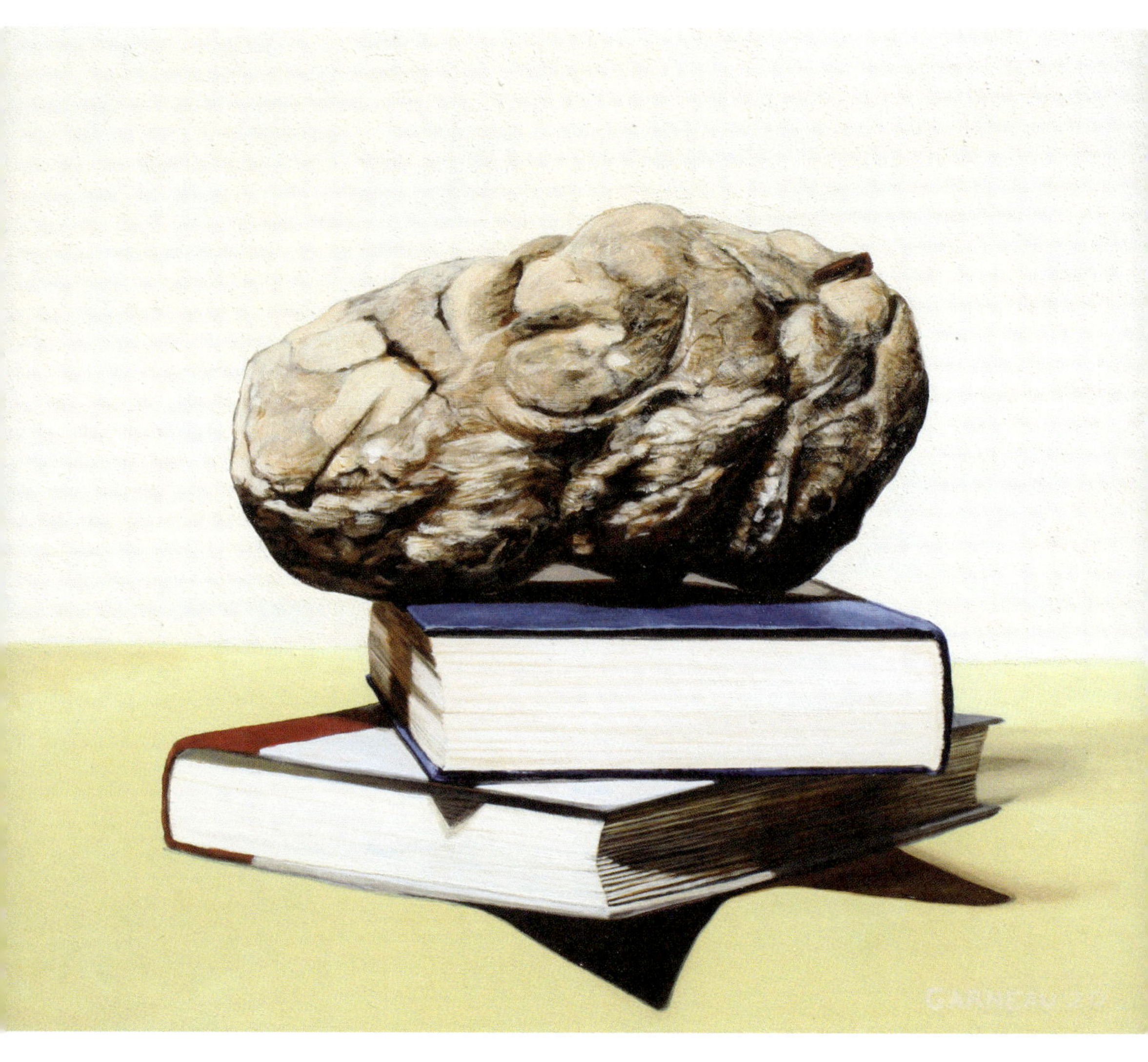

UNSETTLING THE COLONIAL GAZE
BY TREVOR HERRIOT

When I saw several of the paintings in Garneau's *Dark Chapters* series, my first thought was there is something disquieting here. Knives, hammers, and stones dangling from string, teetering atop piles of books, or being held in a tense opposition to one another. In each strange tableau, the objects jumped out at me beneath harsh light in disturbing and mischievous juxtapositions. This, I thought, is how you take the European still life tradition, with its consoling expressions of domesticity in soft light, and turn it upside down.

The titles are suitably provocative and many read like invitations to narrative: *Academic Pretendian*, *Smudge before Reading*, and *Suffocating Grandfather*, to list merely three.

So, there are stories here. Stories and questions for the viewer to ponder and perhaps decode. More than half of the paintings in the series feature books—objects that have traditionally contained stories from European and colonial perspectives.

One piece, *Education the New Pemmican*, shows a large chunk of pemmican sitting on top of two untitled books. Take a good look at the pemmican in the painting. While at first glance it might be another stone, on closer examination the pemmican seems to ripple with braids of organic bodily life in some kind of suspension, waiting to be released. Is it a buffalo? The title of the piece riffs on the oft-quoted aphorism "education is the new buffalo," urging us to see in Garneau's

Education the New Pemmican a defiant vision of Indigenous education that, even more so than the pemmican trade of the early nineteenth century, has the capacity to break the colonial-capitalist grip on the land and its destructive, de-Indigenizing cult of individualism.

Not knowing what the books contain, the viewer faces a question: What kind of education is the new pemmican? The mainstream education that has dominated learning in North America in recent centuries, the kind that was applied to remove the "Indian" from the children at residential schools? Or could it be the Indigenous forms of land-based education that have a much longer tenure on the continent and are now being reconstituted?

Other questions arise from the proximity of books and pemmican: should education only be about producing labourers who will serve in the industrial economy that is destroying the Earth, or should it help to make us fluent and intimate caretakers of the places where we live? What happens when knowledge is disengaged from place and the land? When it no longer arises from the more-than-human world, the matrix of life from which it is shared and passed on from creature to creature in relationship? What is lost when the only knowledge we recognize and use in our governance is channelled into an education system that depends on a single form of literacy, neglecting all others?

The books in Garneau's *Education* are untitled and closed, reminding the viewer that an education that depends on written text restricts access to the literate. Above the books rests a piece of pemmican, an assertion perhaps that the de-Indigenizing education model of the colonial-extractive culture with its ideal of private-wealth gathering has not entirely displaced Indigenous cultures and economies based on values of giving, receiving, and sharing.

Access points to other differences between Indigenous and colonial education systems. Writers of settler descent sometimes wonder why Indigenous protocols prohibit them from recording certain teachings in a book. In a culture that believes everything should be recorded, written down, and available to everyone as a resource to be used, it might be difficult to understand Indigenous knowledge systems and their prohibitions against putting certain teachings into written form. If knowledge is a dynamic, living thing, however, something that changes through space and time, and not something that can be collected and pinned to the page like an insect in a museum cabinet, it begins to make sense that it must be passed on in a relationship of trust between teacher and student, through rituals, ceremonies, and everyday life.

As a metaphor, the pemmican in *Education* sitting on top of two books suggests a form of education that transcends mainstream Western modes of learning, which nourishes because it comes from a relationship with the land and all of its presences. On the other hand, there seems to be room in the story for a more subtle take on education beyond any simple binary that would place traditional oral and land-based learning above all text-based education.

An artist of Métis heritage in particular knows what it is like to live in a both/and world, to live betwixt and between cultures. And it would not be lost on Garneau that it was a prohibition against the export of pemmican that first set the Métis Nation at odds with colonial governments, many decades before Riel's stand at the Red River and Batoche.

"The Same Chains," 2020, 91 × 76 cm, acrylic on canvas.

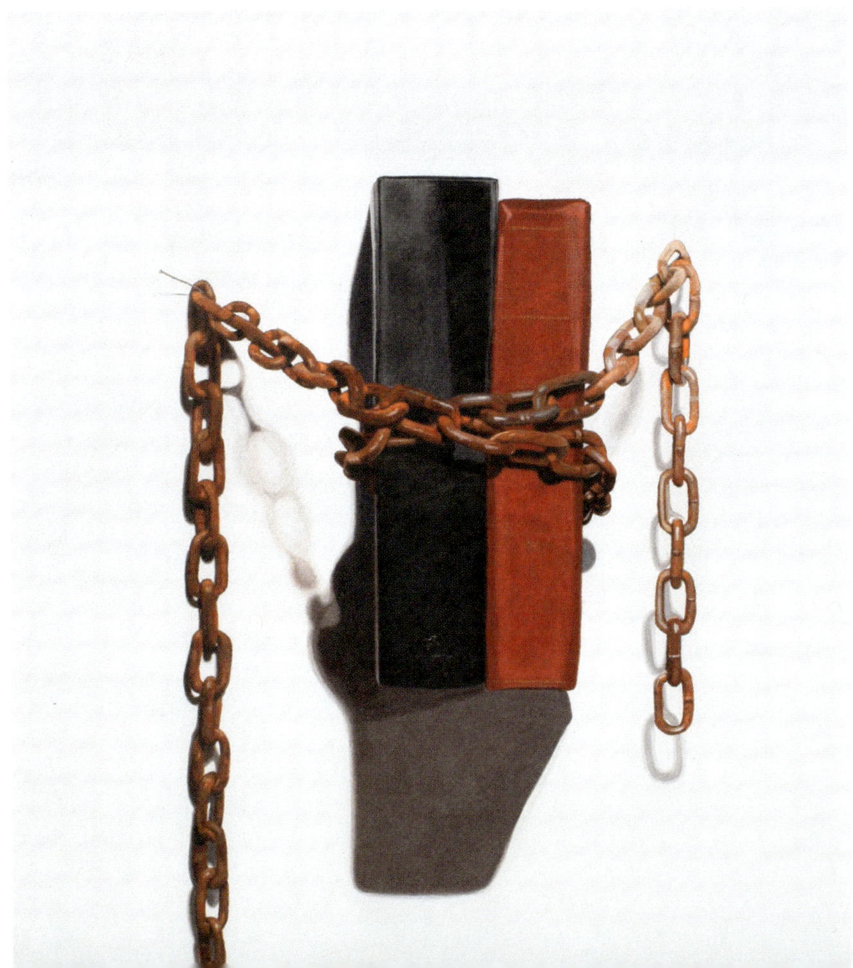

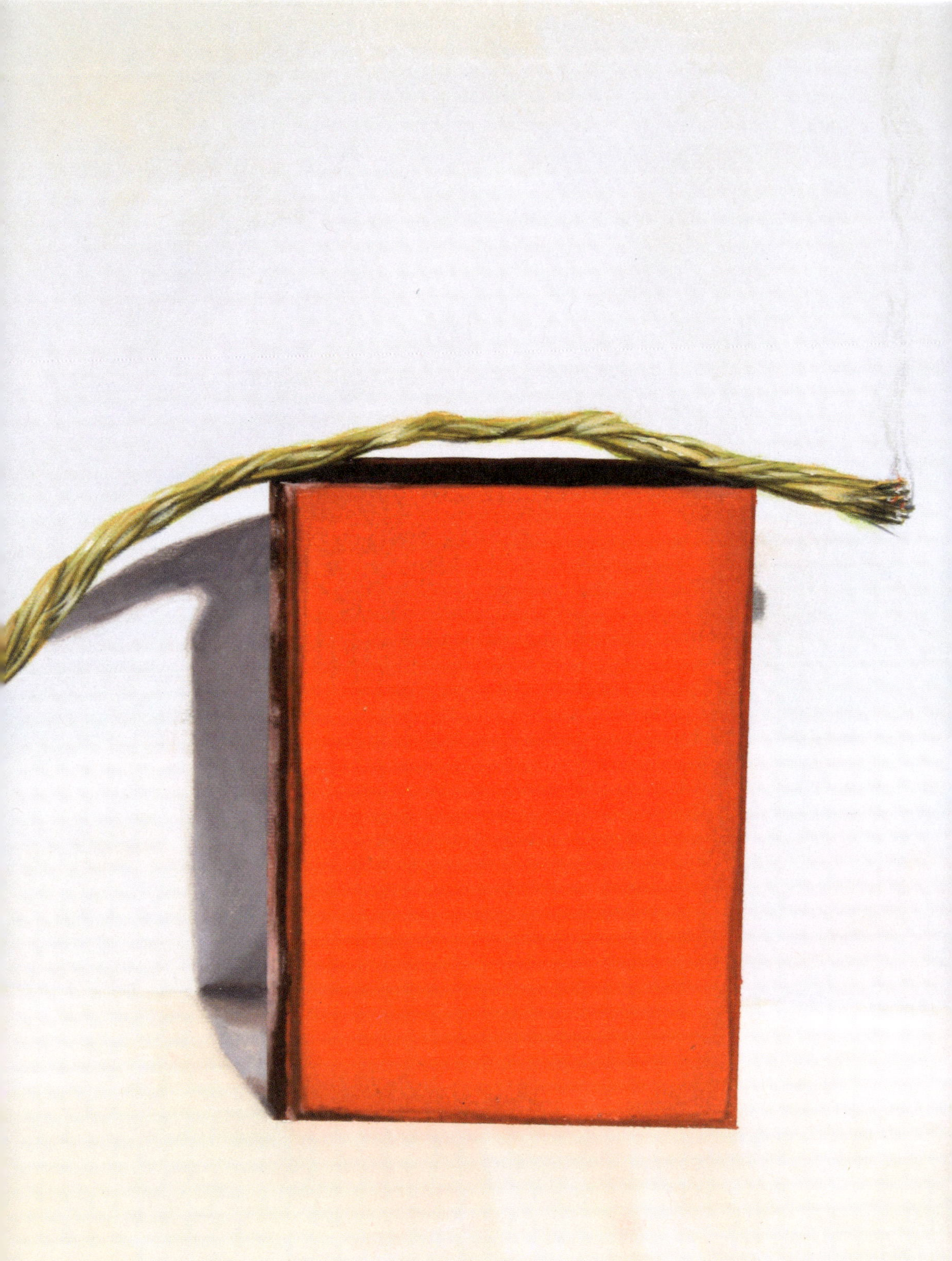
GARNEAU

SMUDGE BEFORE READING
BY TARENE THOMAS

peyak

one could say
the academy has softer thorns

                    than violent streets

with its layered madness
and vast epistemologies

dipping into the spirits it studies
the masters tools have teeth

one could say
harm does not escape the bounds of

the books that
house harmful ideologies,

that occupy space on stolen land
silently
                              or not so silently degrading us

while white scholars
philosophize the Indigenous

times have changed
we have NDN scholars in white spaces too,

doing this work, what does it mean
to study oneself in the white mans house?

niso

spirit cast shadow onto
our degrees built

not from the rez
or from kokum's stories about the cannery

that taught me more than any academic article
more than texts housed in blood-stained pillars

are we bound by books as NDN scholars?
I smudge before I read so I don't get lost in canadas so-called history

sometimes we're stuck in our heads
even though it was our hearts that brought us here

nisto

inundated with double consciousness
chasing echoes of our home fires

sweetgrass dries out on my kitchen floor

                                    as I read

theory so dense, I question
if I'll ever speak in a rez accent ever again

when I got accepted into university
my aunty was worried, rightfully so

smudge before you read my girl,

                    she told me, so I try my best

with broken cree and maskihkiy
to keep me from capsizing, into an

academic canon
that threatens my nehiyaw spirit

by telling me it will swallow me whole,
with my rez accent, degrees and all, I remind myself

I need not measure myself
with the colonizers tools

newo

We won't know if all this work will be worth it in the end
We are preserving harvest for bounty we will never taste

For safety we might not ever know
For spaces we may not ever see

For legislation   that we hope

Will be kinder to our children's children

The cost effect may weigh on our minds

And our spirits,   as it should

But I know we are burning down walls—
Burning down institutions that have never served us

For our ancestors that came before us
and ancestors that will come after us,

For our more than human relatives and the earth
that grants our spirit life, for ourselves

We may not know if all of our work will be worth it in the end, tapwe
But the pain of doing nothing outweighs
the pain of not knowing   every time

And I know we will rise to fight
But for now, we'll smudge before we read

THE LAND DOES NOT FORGET

you can't remember
why you're there, in that colonial place, go home

the land that raised you does not forget
kiwepahtaw

put your feet in sîpîy, walk up the riverbank
smell the pine, birch, lavender, mint,

lay in a field of sweetgrass
stick your hands in the dirt that houses your ancestors' bones

use your fingernails to dig a hole big enough for your feet
lay there, in that earth, sprinkle askîy wherever you hurt

when you're ready, wiggle your toes to unearth your body
let pisim wash magic into your iskotew

do this four times a year

or whenever the institution is too much

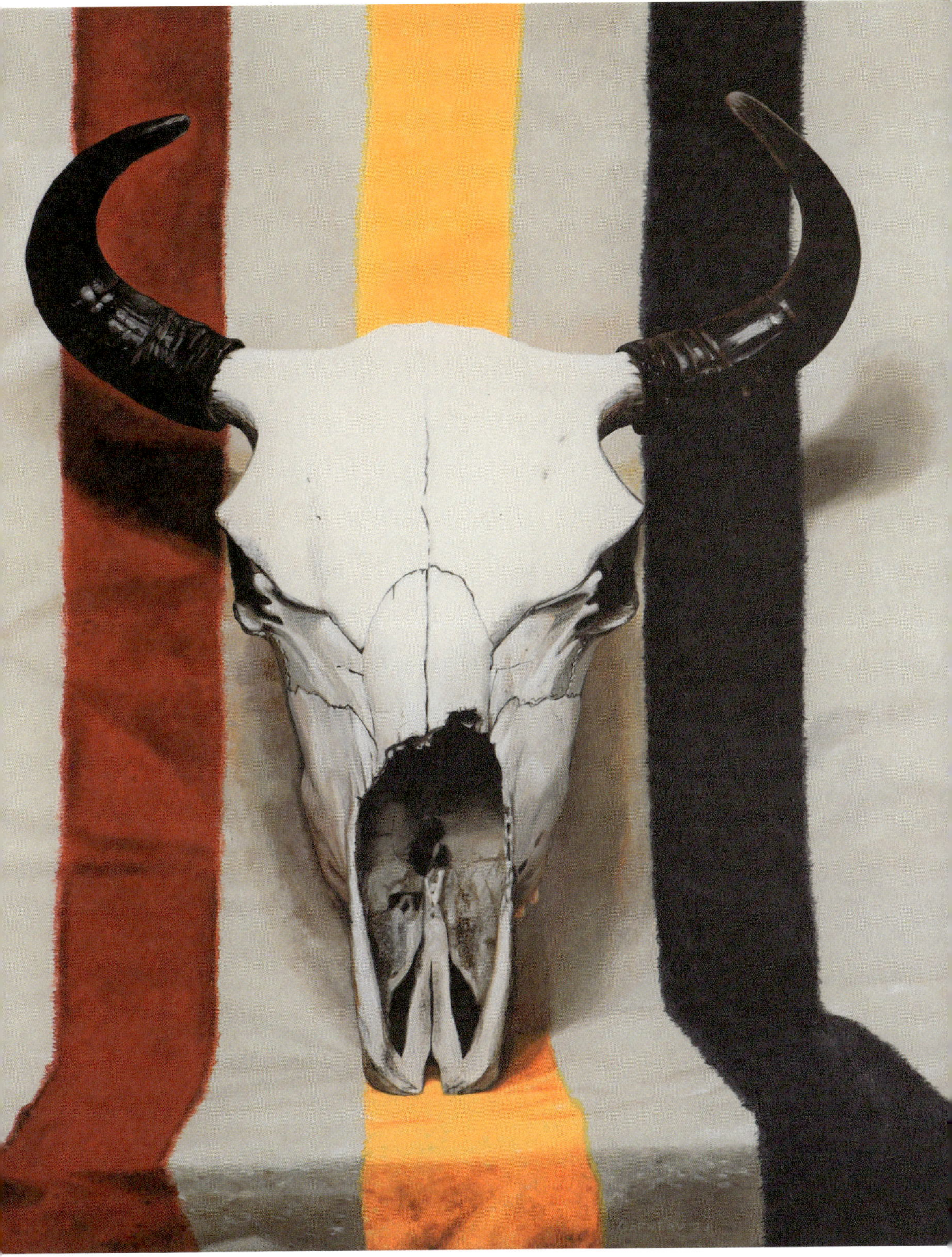

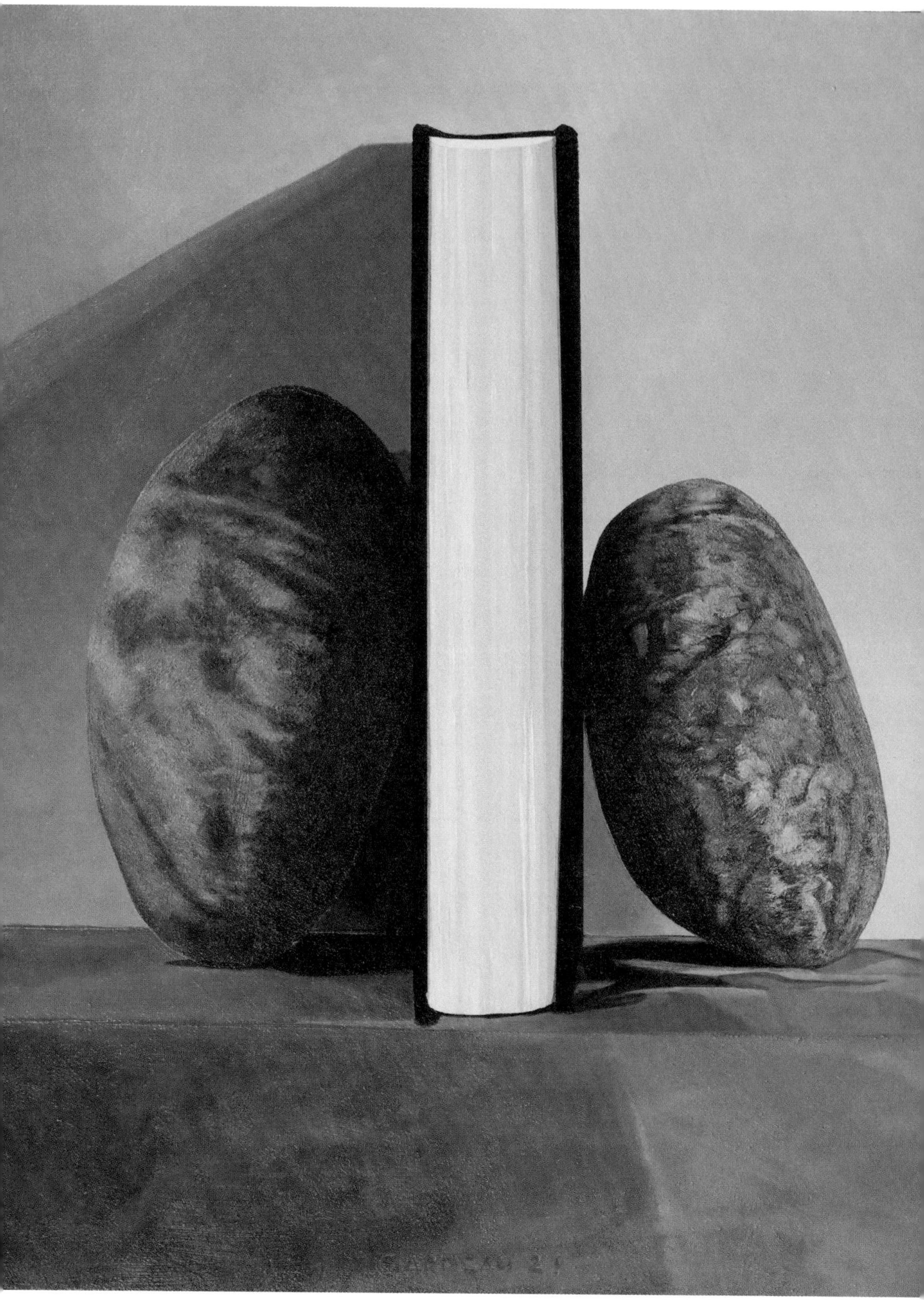

CONFESSION
AFTER DAVID GARNEAU
BY RITA BOUVIER

an array of marbled   ribboned eroded
dis-placed asinîyāk   lean   against a tome
squared and sharp-edged   reaching for sky
what is wiya[41] to make of this poetic pose?

titled
"confession"   already wiya knows
this carefully arranged erection   is nothing more
than a paternal colonial construction

sent by the creator to haunt wiya
wiya constant cursing   living with lies and half-truths
wiya secret land interests and bodily desires
and all of wiya shady corporate business dealings   as if . . .

but all this   smart-assed sensibility
is just a preamble   looking more closely wiya knows
it's just one old one to another   sharing stories
tâpwêwina—truths   through a thick "brick wall"

---

41   wiya in Cree means "he/she" and/or "him/her."

FACING: "Confession," 2021, 50.5 × 40.5 cm, acrylic on panel.

good luck!   wiya thinks
rule-bound and carefully mortared in beds of theory
it looms between the old ones in judgment   ready
to mete out punishments according to its laws and mores

hāw   shhhh! shhhh !   listen!
wiya can finally hear the old ones
speaking to one another in relationship
chuckling now and again at their own foolish banter

ah nistâw—my brother-in-law
ayiman ôma—[living this] life is hard
acimso'win ôma—[this idea] of telling on oneself
is not . . . shall we say   borrowing a phrase   kosher

after all what could we offer this "brick wall"
no offence intended
that looms over us as if to say   written
it is tâpwêwin—the truth   the only truth and . . .

layered in pages of foreign sounds and footnotes
can it really fully comprehend all-that-is
within the vastness of oceans   below and above ground
or the disharmony of living a translated life in English only

besides what could we say
to satisfy this monolithic culture
that controls our every movement
and that of our kin   and all that offers us life

often leaving all our hopes and dreams resting
on the moon   meanwhile woodland caribou may not survive
nistâw—my brother-in-law   I confess I have lived a long life
and I am old   but not as old as . . .

the one that weaves us together
that we glimpse more clearly   awe!
when we are camouflaged in darkness
dancing with its silent rhythms   under a field of stars

niciwām—my friend   no need to despair
the creator that brought us together had a plan
kamôcikihtânow—we will have some fun
take an amble   for that material capitalist cash

we know what they want to hear
our deepest darkest dirtiest secrets and desires   as if . . .
I confess   I too am old like you   still I wonder
what does it mean to be   ay'sînô—human?

this brick wall between us   we could scale
sit on top of   looking yonder with help from the young ones
or perhaps through osmosis the power-that-be will see
beyond the limited horizon of its ideals and imagination

meanwhile   like our great-great-great . . . who shared tales in vain
with linguistic anthropologists to satisfy their insatiable curiosity
we can share simple but juicy versions of our stories—
the ones we imagined   created out of our own consciousness

with the young ones' pen   we can even implicate them
in this interconnected entangled global human story
of theft and violence   now turned truth and reconciliation
to an imaginative rebirth of all our lives   it's never too late

tâpwê—it's true, nistâw!   after all   humanity's earthy secrets
run deep in all our bodies and spirits   said the scholar
in our hunger   in our need for touch
connectedness with other human beings and life itself

pāstāhowina—transgressions on life   well
that's a matter we will not speak of   nor should we
from one foolish dazzling asinîy—rock to another
its brilliance speaks for itself   amen!

haw niciwām! ekosi maga!   let's rest awhile in this poetic!
grateful for our moment riding its rhythmic highs and lows
awash in the flux and revolutions of heavenly words
endless white space and cycles of verse! let's keep that fire burning!

well   nist . . . âw   on these pages anyhoo!
said the wise owl   (laughter all around)

aha! kitapwan niciwām—yes! you are right my friend
papôwin miyowasin—laughter is good [for the spirit]

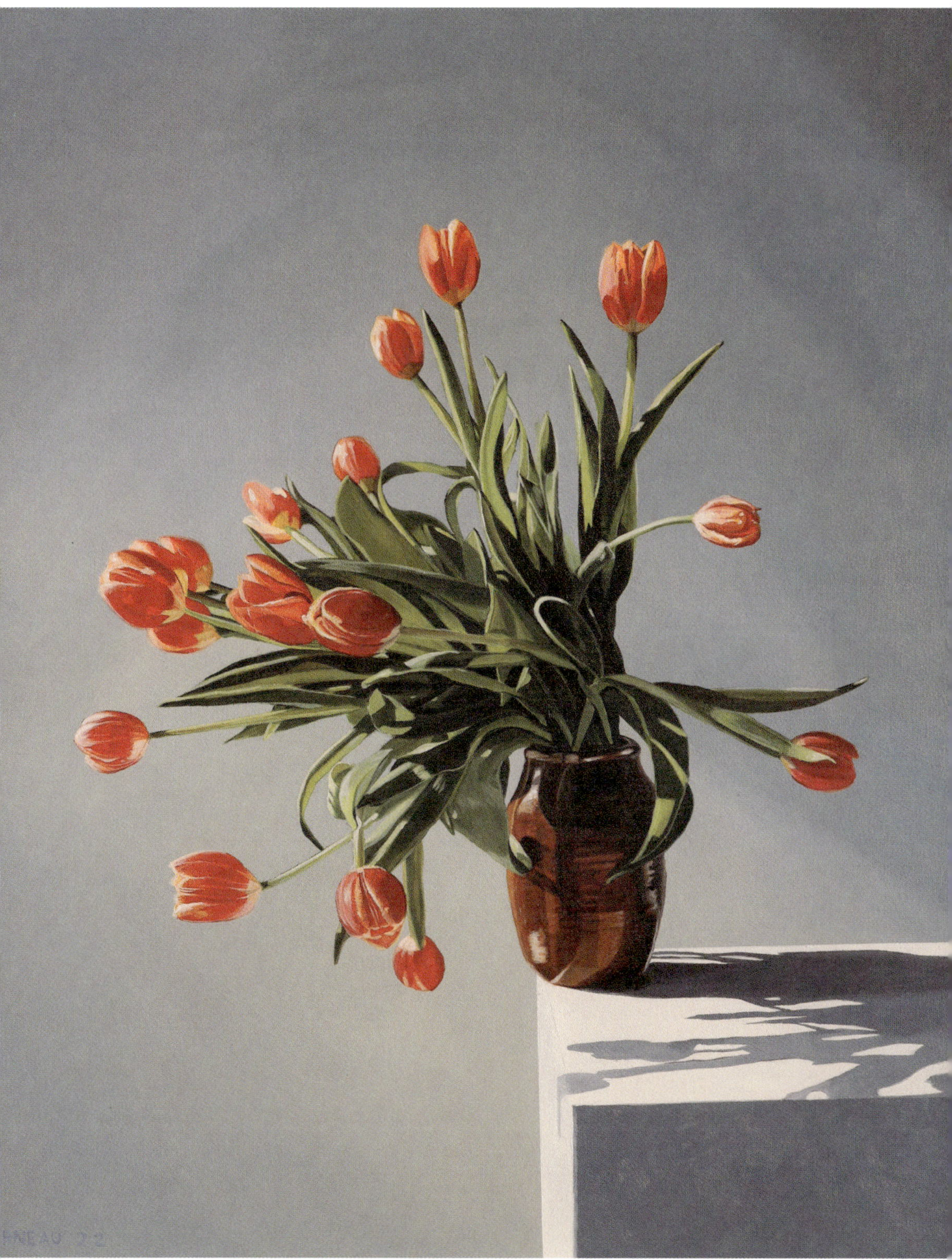

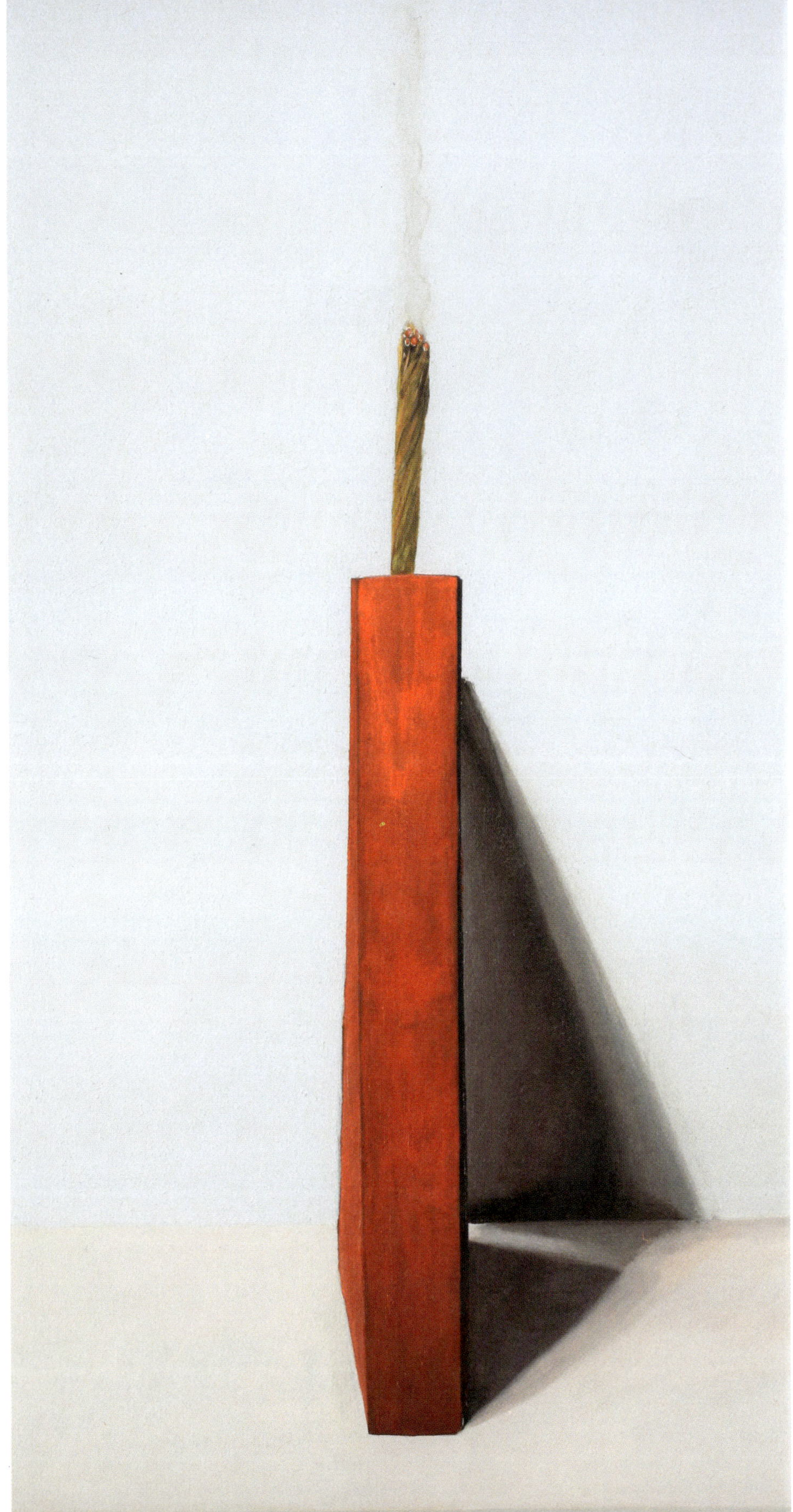

FUSE AND
FORMAL AND INFORMAL EDUCATION
BY JESSE WENTE

t might be dynamite. At least that's my first thought, but then you realize it's a book standing alone. It's alone, which is unusual for an upright book, and it casts a stark geometric shadow. It's an image verging on the fantastic. It speaks to the unusualness of the book that it's only after you reconcile its presence, and the fact that it's not dynamite, that you can take stock that the wick is a smouldering braid of sweetgrass sprouting from the book's top.

Sweetgrass is a medicine for many First Nations, as it is for mine. Used in healing and ceremony, it's harvested, carefully, every year from closely guarded spots. It's often braided, as depicted in the painting, and burned for ceremony. I always have sweetgrass in the house, braids of it hanging in windows, more often freshly harvested, sometimes a little green as it dries. There's always sweetgrass behind my desk where I work, and where I often smudge. It's sacred, and the smell of it, both burning and growing, is a comfort.

The book and the sweetgrass sit against a stark white backdrop, with a cream-coloured tabletop beneath the book. The red book and the sweetgrass, surrounded by whiteness while standing tall. The fact that the sweetgrass is burning suggests ceremony, and that it is being held by the book tells us it's the book that was in ceremony.

I have been this book.

Many of us have.

FACING: "Fuse," 2019, 61 × 30.5 cm, acrylic on panel. Collection of Jesse Wente.

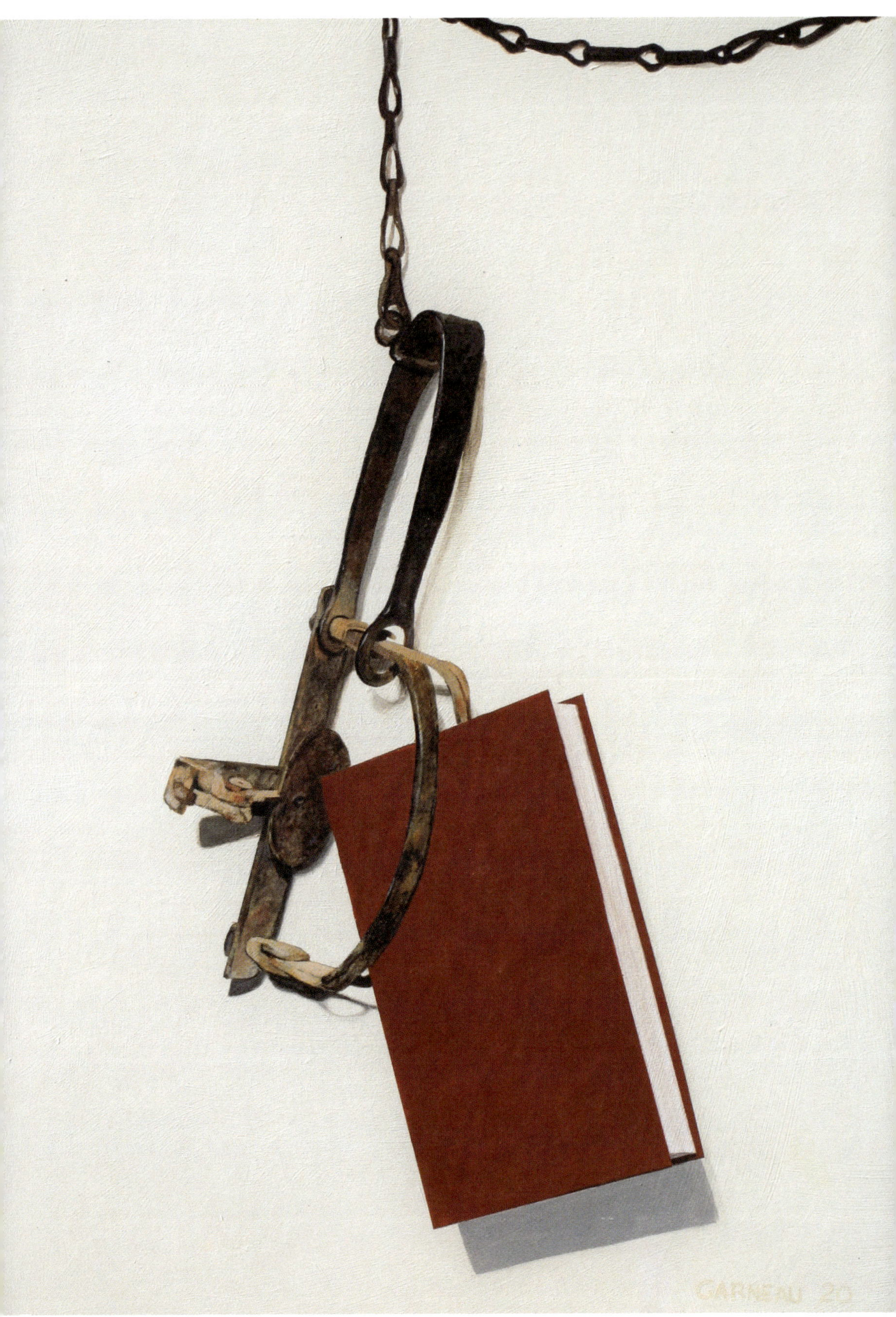
GARNEAU 20

I suspect Garneau has.

I imagine the book is seeking the same comfort from the sweetgrass as I do. As so many of us do.

The challenges of navigating colonial spaces, spaces constructed from whiteness, are plentiful and frustratingly predictable. The isolation from your community and often from collegiality can be agonizing, as can the isolation of our world views, of our understanding. And yet the obligation seems to be to stand tall as the book does, and to hold ceremony in these spaces. That this may be felt as explosive to the same spaces is what conjures the dynamite.

Some years ago I organized a ceremony for the opening of a new cultural space, which included a smudge of the entire space by an Elder. As we neared the date, concerns were raised around the smudging and the fire alarms.

When I told this to the Elder, he turned to me and smiled. "It's sacred smoke" he said. "The only thing that can detect it is inside of us." So we smudged, and nothing happened. I have carried this nugget of wisdom ever since and have smudged when needed. It has been a comfort. That something we find so much safety in could be seen as potentially damaging speaks to the fear that has led to our ways being labelled as dangerous.

This is not a book you would find in other paintings. I am often struck by this simple fact when admiring David's work. He has perfected a form, the still life, and yet uses that form and method to depict elements normally absent. It's a reshaping of meaning that is often evident in modern First Nations, Métis, and Inuit artwork, as the artists turn the mirror to the colonial world they are immersed in. That the items depicted are both recognizable and yet also out of place captures a tension of colonial presence on our lands and how it has distorted our ways of simply being. How it can contort ceremony into threat. Garneau so often depicts vessels of knowing, like books, and places them in this context and then in the context of the gallery, which brings our ways into spaces where they had often been barred before.

Perhaps this is why I so wanted this book and sweetgrass in my home. So perhaps it could be surrounded not by the artworks it contrasts, but by siblings. I also wanted this painting in my home because when I look at it, it feels like a mirror, like a reflection of both myself and my work;

FACING: "Formal and Informal Education," 2020, 60.5 × 45.5 cm, acrylic on panel. Collection of Jesse Wente.

looking upon it gives me a sense of kinship; to it, to David, to the others who have also been this book, and those who will be this book. The knowledge in its pages has already been lit, and the explosion is to come next. The red book seen in *Fuse* is back in *Formal and Informal Education*, but this time instead of being explosive, it's trapped. Snared and displayed, the book dangles from an unseen hook, still in the throes of its capture.

When I first saw this image, it was somehow instantly familiar to me. The red book, a recurring presence in Garneau's work, suggests the formal education of the title, while the trap is the informal education, only taught when triggered. The gallery setting of the objects depicted seems more overt in this work, with the chain of the trap connected above the frame of the painting, suggesting we are seeing a purposeful display. This mirroring of gallery spaces with untypical images within the work means their own display is a further mirroring, distorting traditional Western notions of curation, of what belongs in galleries and what does not. This is again mirrored in the title, which suggests that both forms of education, formal and informal, are present in these spaces, which, of course, they are.

But this image analysis is not why I fell in love with this painting.

My great-grandfather Alex Meawasige was a fur trapper, who traded with the Hudson's Bay Company. His traplines extended beyond our community of Genaabaajing along the north shore of what is now called Lake Huron. His generation was the last of our family, at least up until now, to live on the land, something Alex and his wife, Maggie, were well aware of. Which is why they sent their children to the schools run by the priests and the nuns. They knew their family would not live the life they had led, so they wanted them to get a formal education in order to be successful in this new world.

Sadly, their children received more of a formal education in the violence of colonialism than they did in literacy or numeracy, but their descendants, including myself, would go on to receive the most formal of formal educations. So many of the descendants of Alex and Maggie now use that education, the formal one, in order to revitalize the memory of the other. The painting graphically depicts this duality, the formal and informal, the new and the traditional.

The painting also suggests the violence that inevitably faces us when we seek the formal. That it can snare us, trap us, keep us from moving. This is not uncommon: even as our communities have embraced the formalities of Western learning, it has come at the cost of the revitalization of our traditional ways of knowing and being. The academy, and even the gallery, can be a trap for our people, for our ways, for our spirits.

Yet there is also profound love and hope in this painting. For where the trap and the book meet is a point of union, where the formal and informal touch, where ancestors and future relations can convene in mutual education.

What I see in this painting is my family, my community, and my people. I see our past, present, and future. I see the many ways of knowing and of being that we are capable of. This painting is us, and I think David depicted us beautifully.

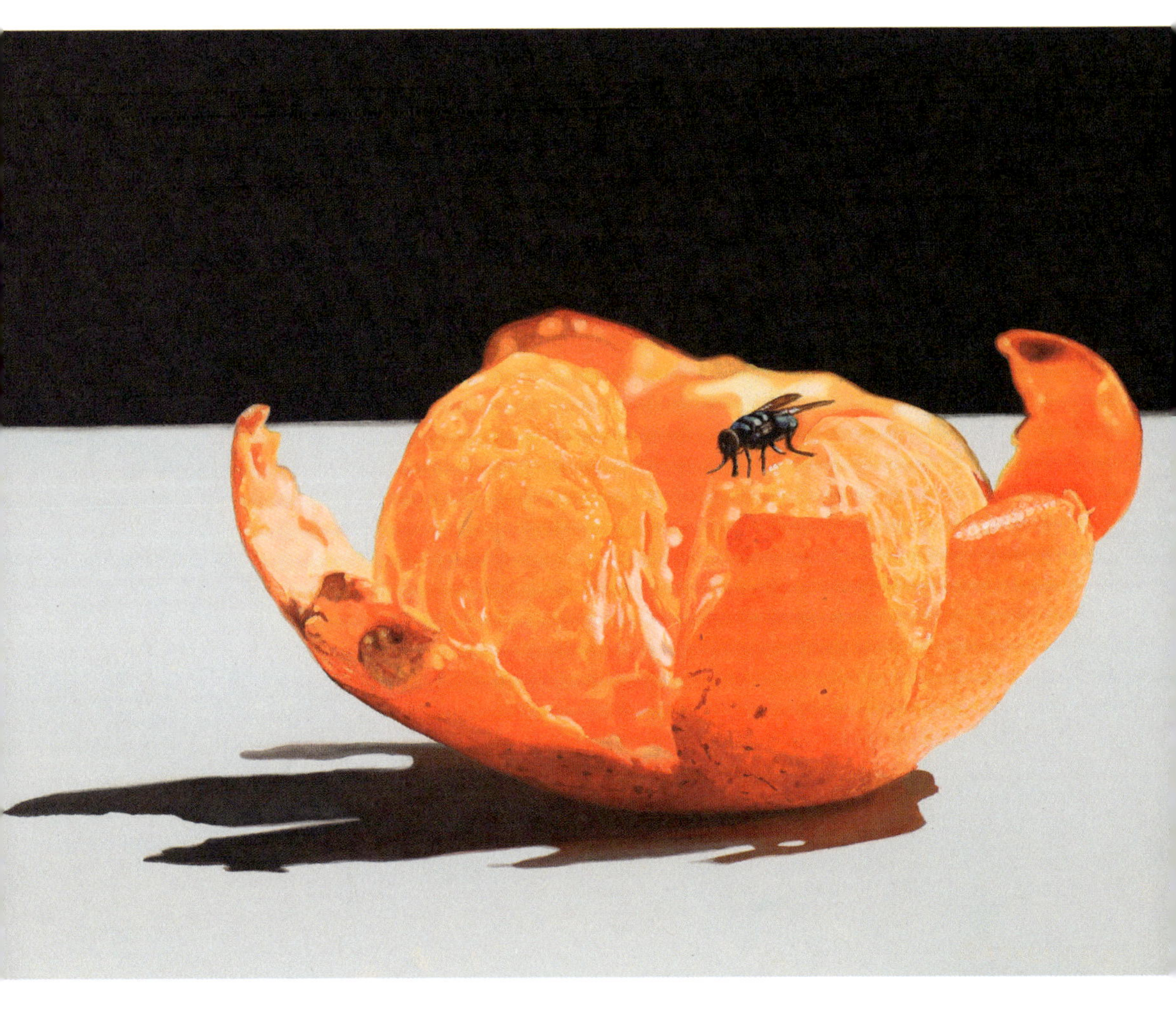

THE PROBLEM WITH PLEASURE
BY BILLY-RAY BELCOURT

Most days I've wanted
to be my desires and not merely
the unrelenting density
from which they rush forth.
The problem with pleasure is that
two people can meet in a room
in order to exist less. It's not that
I disliked myself; it's that no one
told me it was possible to feel
that much of the world all at once.
I felt everything; I was constantly
coming apart, like an orange, half-
peeled on the table, a life split in
two ways: toward the past, which
I couldn't free myself from, and
toward the future, which is to say,
toward both ecstasy and pain.
At some point I decided
there was no use in parsing
the difference. At some point
I realized I had, without
noticing, become the difference.

FACING: "A Problem with Pleasure," 2022, 46 × 61 cm, acrylic on panel.

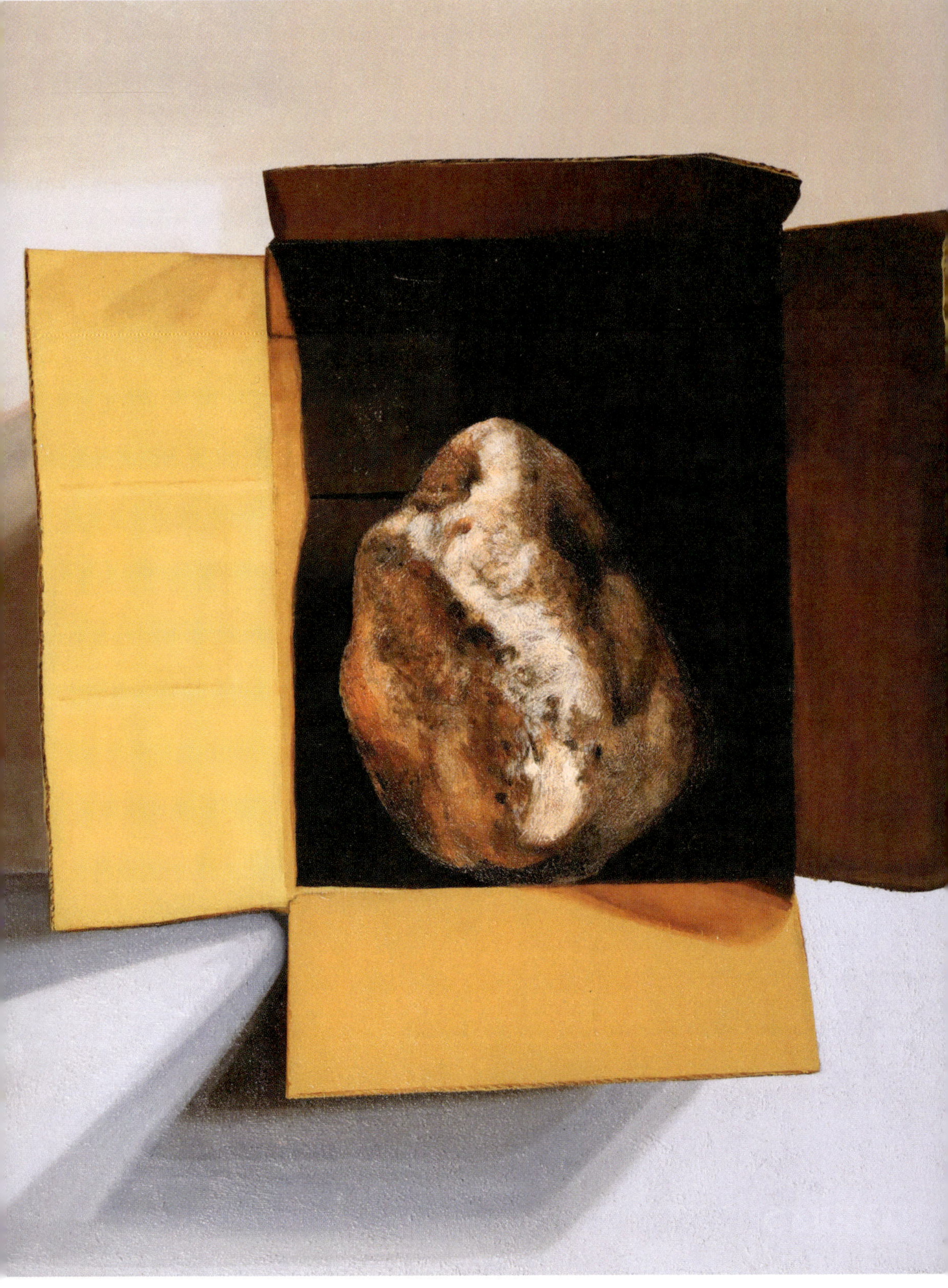

MÉTIS REALISM: ON THE MATERIALITY OF SMOKE AND RELATIONALITY OF ROCKS
BY DAVID HOWES

David Garneau's artistic work typically confounds the viewer. Contemplating it can trigger double, triple, and even quadruple takes. This is due to its uncanny juxtapositions. A parallel could be drawn to René Magritte's paintings, which are known for their tricks of perspective—for example, the Belgian artist's painting of 120 or so dark-suited businessmen in bowler hats hovering in mid-air, or the painting of a painting of a landscape superimposed on that very landscape with no discernible borders. So, too, can certain parallels be drawn between the enigmatic titles of Garneau's paintings and those of Magritte. Magritte is most famous for *The Treachery of Images* (1929). The depiction of a pipe in this painting in conjunction with the sentence "Ceci n'est pas une pipe" scrawled along the base problematizes representation itself. This wordplay fascinated Foucault on account of the way it bedevils the relationship between the signifier and the signified.[42] The realism of the painting is sur-realized by the inscription.

But the comparison stops here, for David Garneau's work does not just playfully deconstruct the Western mindset or gaze. It interjects other epistemologies—most notably, Métis ways of sensing and knowing—and thereby ratchets up the conundrum. Garneau's work opens

42   Michel Foucault, *This Is Not a Pipe* (Berkeley: University of California Press, 1983).

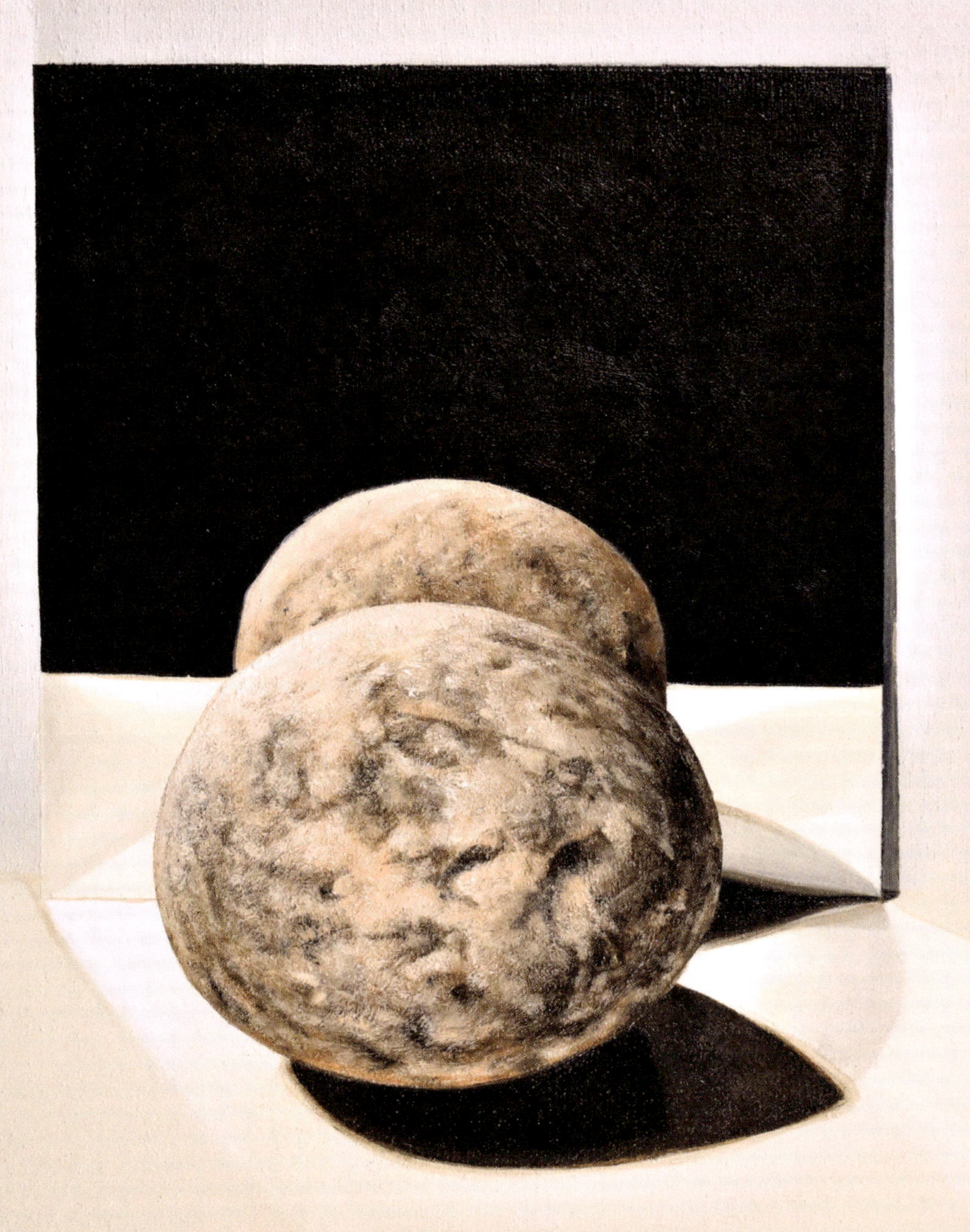

a crack in the prevailing regime of representation, and "that's how the light gets in" (in the immortal words of the late Leonard Cohen in the song "Anthem"). Call it Métis Realism, for there is nothing surreal, nothing illusory, about Garneau's style: it makes uncommon sense when we think about it interculturally, as I propose to show in what follows.

ON ROCKS AS RELATIONS

In the case of the paintings in David Garneau's *Dark Chapters* series, the regime of representation he troubles is principally that of Canadian settler society.[43] Consider the pair of paintings entitled *Grandfather Contemplating Western Ocularcentrism* and *Grandfather, Archived*. The former depicts a rock seated in front of a mirror; the latter portrays a rock in a cardboard storage box. The settler-viewer is immediately plunged into a quandary. Take 1: Rocks are inanimate, therefore devoid of sentience, and certainly don't have eyes. So how can a rock see itself in a mirror? Take 2: It doesn't. Rather, the painting is holding up a mirror to Western ocularcentrism. It exposes the overbearing emphasis on vision, which is presumed to be "the most informative" of the senses, in the traditional Western hierarchy of the senses, and hints at other ways of sensing and knowing, which are not beholden to sight, such as co-presence. Take 3: The rock is called Grandfather, a kinship term. Does the artist mean to suggest that rocks are our relatives?

Now consider *Grandfather, Archived*. Take 1: A rock is a mineral specimen, which therefore belongs in a museum of natural history, or the storeroom of such a museum, hence the storage box. That seems orderly. Take 2: But the rock is not any old specimen; it is a grandfather, as the title suggests, and therefore a living being. You don't archive (i.e., entomb) living people. There is something amiss with this

---

43   Garneau's paintings do more than just disturb the Canadian imaginary, however. For example, they trouble the whole tradition of still life painting (nature morte in French) by scrambling the distinction between the living and the dead, the animate and the inanimate. Significantly, the original title for the series discussed here was *Dark Chapters and Métis Still Life*, or, in other words, life without end: for example, rocks that are animate, not dead game animals or flowers on the verge of wilting, as in conventional Flemish still life painting. Garneau's still life paintings are not reflections on the transience or vanity of existence. They give expression to an alternate ontology, an Indigenous way of being.

FACING: "Grandfather Contemplating Western Ocularcentrism," 2021, 50.5 × 40.5 cm, acrylic on panel. Private collection.

representation then. It appears to scramble the distinction between persons and things, persona and res—the most hallowed distinction in the history of the Western mindset.[44] By doing so, it opens the way for a radical critique of the museum—whether it be a museum of natural history or a cultural history museum, like the Canadian Museum of History (CMH) in Gatineau, Quebec—as mausoleum.

The CMH has an extensive collection of Indigenous artifacts: totem poles and other carvings such as Iroquois False Face masks, drums, clothing, et cetera. Recent decades have witnessed a momentous change in curatorial attitudes towards—and treatment of—such artifacts. Consider the Sacred Materials project at the CMH. In the case of the Iroquois masks, once yearly a pair of Elders from the Haudenosaunee Confederacy are sponsored to come to the CMH and minister to the masks. They chant them, smudge them, and feed them cornmeal. In this way, the senses of the masks are pleased, propitiated. That is what it (now) means to conserve Indigenous artifacts in a culturally conscientious fashion. They are not to be treated as objects.[45]

The Sacred Materials project at the CMH could alternately be called the "sensitive materials" project: the masks are sensitive because they are sentient beings, and the manner of their handling and display is also sensitive, which is to say political. For example, there is the whole issue of repatriation, or whether Indigenous artefacts even belong in (or to) museums, a very sensitive issue indeed.[46]

Rocks are a different matter. They do not receive special treatment because there is nothing sacred or sentient about them, according to the prevailing mindset.[47] Yet we know from the ethnographic record

---

44   Marcel Mauss, "A Category of the Human Mind: The Notion of Person; the Notion of Self," *Sociology and Psychology: Essays* (London: Routledge and Kegan Paul, 1979).

45   David Howes, "Sensorial Investigations: A History of the Senses," *Anthropology, Psychology, and Law* (University Park: Pennsylvania State University Press, 2023), 72–6.

46   Maureen Matthews, *Naamiwan's Drum: The Story of a Contested Repatriation of Anishinaabe Artefacts* (Toronto: University of Toronto Press, 2016).

47   This cast of mind can and should be challenged. On what rocks know—being the "cosmological and ontological repositories" they are—see Shannon Mattern, "Glimmer: Refracting Rock," *LA+ Interdisciplinary Journal of Landscape Architecture*, no. 12 (Fall 2020), 106–115. "We illuminate and irradiate [rocks] in order to extract and collect and classify them; and they, in turn, reflect light back on us" (Mattern, "Glimmer," 111). In Mattern's call for the decolonization of geology and natural history generally, she notes that optical technologies such as UV, backlighting, and especially, the method of "blacklighting" (as proposed by critical race scholar Denise Ferreira da Silva) can help "recalibrate our eyes to bring

that some rocks (not all) are classified as animate in Cree and other Algonquian languages, and therefore possess personhood. Their animacy is a function of the relationships in which they stand to other (e.g., human) persons.[48] This Indigenous apperception of elements of the material environment as kin is profoundly relational and, at the same time, a powerful rebuke to the extractivist logic of the epistemologies of the global North, as discussed by Boaventura de Sousa Santos in *The End of the Cognitive Empire: The Coming of Age of Epistemologies of the South* (2018). As the Canadian philosopher George Grant observes in connection with the "abyssal line" (to use Santos's phrase) that divides the world in two (North/South, colonizer/colonized, scientific knowledge/folk knowledge, etc.), "That conquering relation to place"—by which he means the "Conquest of America," Western expansionism —"has left its marks within us,"—us settlers. Grant continues: "When we go into the Rockies, we may have the sense that gods are there. But if so, they cannot manifest themselves to us as ours. They are the gods of another race, and we cannot know them because of what we are, and what we did. There can be nothing immemorial for us except the environment as object."[49]

ON THE MATERIALITY OF SMOKE

Consider the painting *Scientific Method Applied to the Sacred*. It depicts a smoking bundle of sage on a seashell in a glass bell jar of the sort the scientists of the Enlightenment used to conduct their experiments on phlogiston and other gases in, and in which Victorians kept their knickknacks (dried flowers, shells, human hair, etc.). I like to think of this painting as a veiled allusion to the performance art piece David and I put on at the *Ethnographic Terminalia* exhibition held in conjunction with the 2019 annual meeting of the American Anthropological Association (AAA) in Vancouver, BC. Our "play" lasted all of eleven minutes. Despite its brevity, it was pregnant with all manner of epistemological and cosmo-

---

shine itself into relief—to transform glimmer into a figure on a white supremacist and colonial ground" (Mattern, "Glimmer," 111).

48　Maureen Matthews and Roger Roulette, "'Are All Stones Alive?' Anthropological and Anishinaabe Approaches to Personhood," in *Rethinking Relations and Animism: Personhood and Materiality*, eds. Miguel Astor-Aguilera and Graham Harvey (London: Routledge, 2018), 173–92.

49　George Grant, "In Defense of North America," *Communio: International Catholic Review* 38, no. 2 (Summer 2011): 345.

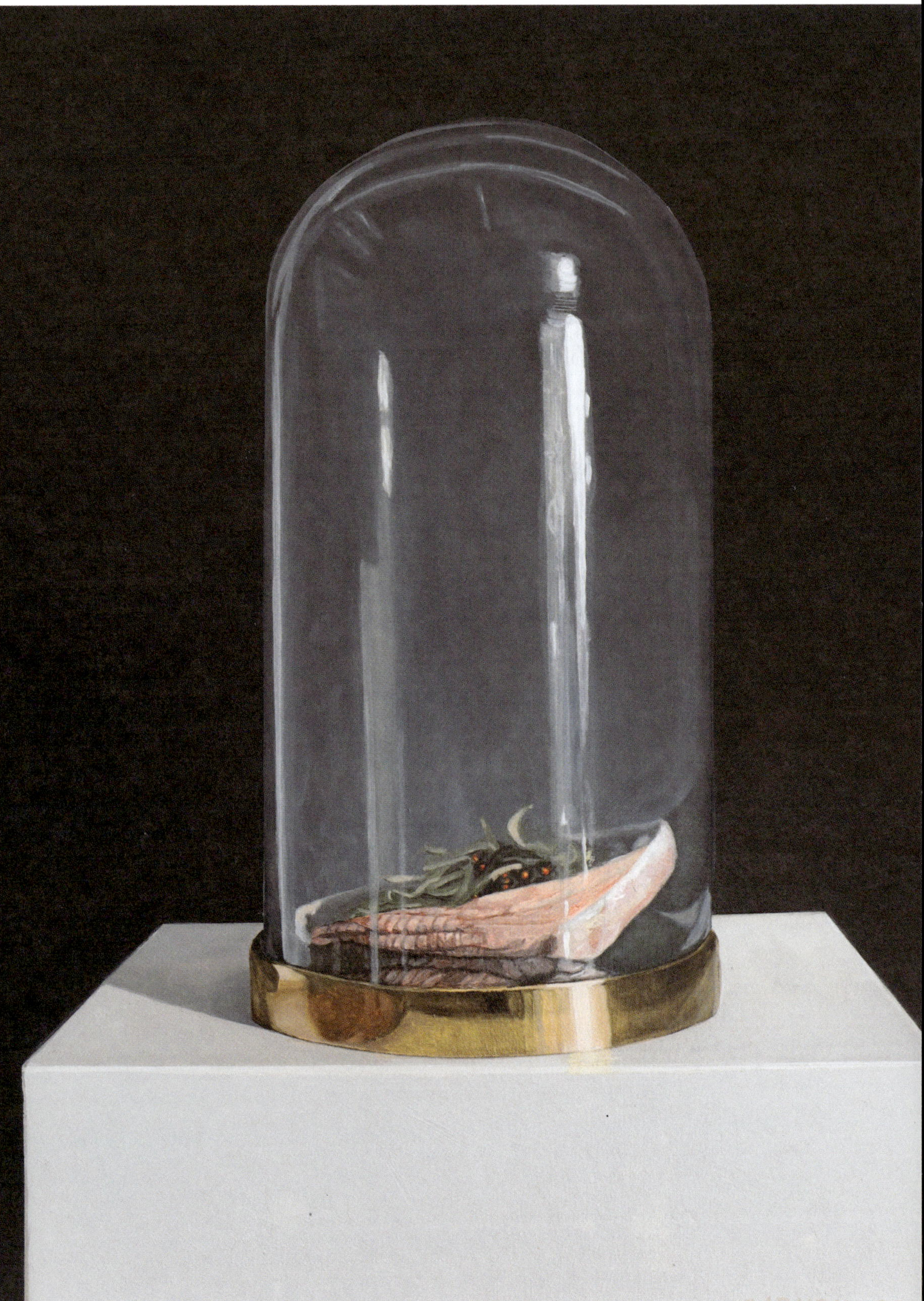

logical implications, providing you knew something about its backstory. Let me fill you in.

At the time of the AAA meeting in Vancouver, David and I were both collaborators on the *Sensory Entanglements* research project directed by intermedia artist and (then) professor of design art at Concordia University Christopher Salter. This project had as its goal the "decolonization of the sensorium" through the production of a series of installation art pieces that crossed cultural borders.[50] One such piece was called *Yahkâskwan Mîkiwahp / Light Tipi* by fellow collaborator Cheryl L'Hirondelle and her artistic partner, the Cree Elder Joseph Naytowhow. What intrigued me about this piece was its use of smoke as a canvas. Unlike a normal canvas, smoke is ephemeral, which shifted the onus onto the temporal or processual nature of the work rather than its "being" an art object. It was also a prime example of "relational art"[51] in that the artistic element consisted mainly in staging novel social relations among the viewer-participants.

Briefly, *Yahkâskwan Mîkiwahp* involved forty or so interested Ontarian citizens who took up an invitation to congregate in a park in downtown Toronto, with the CN Tower looming in the distance, on a cold December night in 2016. Select participants were each handed either a flashlight or a bundle of smouldering sage. (The sage had been ritually gathered by L'Hirondelle and Naytowhow beforehand, back in Saskatchewan, where they were based.) The billowing smoke of the sage both created an aromatic atmosphere and functioned like a projection screen. The participants, distributed in a wide circle, were then invited to hold up their torches to make the image of a tipi out of the light beams. Of note, the image of the tipi was three-dimensional, not two-dimensional (like on an ordinary screen), and stood a good three storeys tall (way grander than an IMAX projection).[52] All the while,

---

50   Christopher Salter, "Disturbance, Translation, Enculturation: Necessary Research in New Media, Technology, and the Senses," *Visual Anthropology Review* 34, no. 1 (Spring 2018): 87–97, doi.org/10.1111/var.12156; David Howes, *The Sensory Studies Manifesto: Tracking the Sensorial Revolution in the Arts and Human Sciences* (Toronto: University of Toronto Press, 2022), 181–204.

51   Nicolas Bourriaud, *Relational Aesthetics*, rev. ed. (1998; repr., Cambridge: MIT Press, 2023).

52   From a certain angle, the tipi of light (a smoke signal) also dwarfed the CN Tower (a telecommunications hub): the medium bristled with messages and was the message. It

L'Hirondelle beat her drum, sang songs in Cree, and told stories with an Indigenous ecological message.

Yahkâskwan Mîkiwahp was unlike any artwork you might see in an art museum or gallery: it was out of doors, it was fleeting, it was an aromatic (rather than a purely visual) spectacle, and it had a proprioceptive dimension due to the way the participants had to position their bodies in order to uphold an Indigenous architectural structure—the phantom tipi—against the settler city skyline. The coercion or cooptation, if one could call it that, of the settler-citizens who made up the audience was ever so subtle—that is, enter-training.

The 2016 performance of *Yahkâskwan Mîkiwahp* took place not long after the release of the *Final Report of the Truth and Reconciliation Commission of Canada* in 2015.[53] I interpret it as a response to the recommendations of the commission regarding the necessity of rebuilding (or re-setting) the relationship between the settler society state and Indigenous Peoples within Canada—here mediated by the remarkable boundary-crossing propensities of the sage smoke.

Contemplating the multisensory aesthetic and cross-cultural dynamics of *Yahkâskwan Mîkiwahp* inspired me to further investigate the role of smoke in mediating intercultural relations. For example, in the "Smoke and Mirrors" chapter of *Sensorial Investigations*,[54] I explored the treaty-making process during the colonial period. The treaty negotiators acting for the Crown believed that getting an Indigenous leader to mark an X on the treaty document sufficed to render the treaty binding. The Indigenous parties, by contrast, insisted on the ceremony of smoking a pipe together. Thus, for the latter, smoke had the same force or binding power as writing. No smoke, no pact. Evidently, the Crown negotiators who participated in the smoking rituals did not think the same way, or there would not have been so many broken treaty promises.[55]

---

ineluctably Indigenized and therefore politicized perception.

53   Truth and Reconciliation Commission of Canada, *Honouring the Truth, Reconciling for the Future* (Truth and Reconciliation Commission of Canada, 2015).

54   Howes, *Sensorial Investigations*, 208–223.

55   David Garneau, "Imaginary Spaces of Conciliation and Reconciliation: Art, Curation, and Healing," in *Arts of Engagement: Taking Aesthetic Action in and beyond the Truth and Reconciliation Commission of Canada*, eds. Dylan Robinson and Keavy Martin (Waterloo: Wilfrid Laurier University Press, 2016) 31–32. The British treaty negotiators set great store in the rationality of writing and its effectiveness as a means of alienation (i.e., the

The publisher of *Dark Chapters* arranged for the contributors (myself included) to meet over Zoom in August 2023 to discuss our contributions together with David. We wanted to be on the same page. During the conversation, David remarked regarding my "sensorial investigations" that he "couldn't smell the smoke on [me]." The words were spoken in jest, but that did not diminish their sting—or their truth. "The fact is I only ever had the chance to witness *Yahkâskwan Mîkiwahp* on YouTube,[56] and I had only ever participated in one smudging ritual: Joseph Naytowhow came to Concordia to present a lecture entitled "Indigenizing the Academy" and led a group of us in a smudge the following day. In effect, I had developed an intellectual understanding of smoke as "a medium of communication" and/or "artistic expression," but I hadn't let it envelope me or penetrate my pores.

WHEN SMOKE GETS IN YOUR EARS

After this rather circuitous backstory, let us turn our sights back to the play. In early November 2019, David and I discussed the performance we would put on at the *Ethnographic Terminalia* exhibition by phone. I came armed with a device (culled from one of my son's physics experiments) that resembled a TV remote control with wires sticking out of it, which I intended to use as a scanner. We did not have a chance to rehearse our skit.

The performance began with me seated on the edge of the stage, while David lit a bundle of sage grass and, after a few moments, bottled and sealed its smoke in a large glass jar. He then handed the jar to me, and I proceeded to inspect it with the scanner, humming and hawing as I went. It was impossible to smell the smoke, of course. I thought this was an ingenious send-up of "the innocent anthropologist" who looks but does not smell, and therefore does not really see.[57] Pointing out the

"extinguishment" of aboriginal title that followed on the apposition of an *X*, (supposedly signalling consent), on the treaty document by an Indigenous sachem). The Indigenous chiefs came to hold a different view of the power of the written word: "pen-and-ink witchcraft" is how Odawa Chief Egushawa branded it. See Howes, *Sensorial Investigations*, 215.

56 You can watch *Yahkâskwan Mîkiwahp / Light Tipi* at youtube.com/watch?v=dZmcb-EA1Q9Y.

57 The potential epistemological value of the olfactory sense is not well recognized in modern Western culture. For example, in *Visual Thinking* (the title speaks volumes), the psychologist Rudolf Arnheim opined, "one can indulge in smells and tastes, but one can hardly think in them" (Berkeley: University of California Press, 1969). Compare Hsuan L. Hsu, *The Smell of Risk: Environmental Disparities and Olfactory Aesthetics* (New York: New York University Press, 2020).

limits of the ethnographic gaze—was all I really had to say. But as it turned out, this was only act one.

Act two (for which I was not prepared) involved David tying a colourful Métis sash around my head, which blinded me (and also irritated the skin on my face). Then, unbeknownst to me, he opened the jar, inhaled the smoke, and proceeded to blow it quite forcefully in my right ear. This action provoked a profound revelation in me. You see, I have often written about synaesthesia, the "mingling of sensations" or "unity of the senses,"[58] but this idea of crossing the senses remained an intellectual abstraction for me. When David blew the smoke in my ear, however, I smelled it—that is, I swear I smelled it through my ear. Ears are for hearing, not for smelling, but in effect, by his gesture, David short-circuited my hearing and my smelling. When he removed the sash from my eyes, all I could do was stammer "Wow!" I was rendered speechless. Suddenly, synaesthesia was no longer another cultural construction or intellectual abstraction. It was palpable. I had lived it.

The plot of our little play was simple enough: the innocent anthropologist who looks when they should be smelling, who is then blinded and begins to see things in a whole new way when the smoke gets in their ears. In its performance, though, the renvoi, or "criss-crossing multiplicity of the senses,"[59] was literally mind-blowing and imbued with all sorts of implications.

Fathoming the implications of this experience, like fathoming the implications of *Yahkâskwan Mîkiwahp*, is not easy, for the circumstances of its production were wholly unlike those of the "ideal speech situation,"[60] which is normally supposed to undergird public consensus-building in liberal democratic societies. These experiences went beyond words. But by this very fact, they created the conditions for

---

58   David Howes, "Cultural Synaesthesia: Neurological vs. Anthropological Approaches to the Study of Intersensoriality," *Intellectica* 55 (2011): 156–87; David Howes and Constance Classen, "Synaesthesia Unravelled: The Union of the Senses from a Cultural Perspective," *Ways of Sensing: Understanding the Senses in Society* (Abingdon, Oxon: Routledge, 2013).

59   Boaventura de Sousa Santos, "The Deep Experience of the Senses," *The End of the Cognitive Empire: The Coming of Age of the Epistemologies of the South* (Durham: Duke University Press, 2018).

60   Jürgen Habermas, *Moral Consciousness and Communicative Action* (Cambridge: The MIT Press, 1991).

forging "a new legal common sense"[61] that bridges cultural borders just as it modulates the divisions among the senses and holds out the promise of "conciliating"[62] diametrically opposed world views.

Since November 2019, as I have reflected further on the epiphany I experienced at *Ethnographic Terminalia* thanks to the way David ministered to my senses, I have come to think of it as an annunciation ("the Word materialized as smell," one might say). In that moment, my habitual way of thinking came to be inspired by David's Métis wisdom concerning the interconnectedness of all things and all peoples (for which smell is such a fine medium), and the effect has been everlasting.

CONCLUSION

Garneau's painting *Scientific Method Applied to the Sacred* problematizes the way the smell of sage smoke is contained and objectified by the glass bell jar, eradicating its border-crossing potential or relationality. Garneau's paintings of Grandfather rocks also trouble the scientific imaginary, which divides the world into subject and object, person and thing, the animate and the inanimate. His point is that rocks have the potential to be recognized as sentient beings or persons—that is, as kin.[63] The world he depicts in his Métis still lifes (in contradistinction to the still life tradition in the history of Western art) courses with life, courses with animacy. His paintings envision "Being" as all sentient—a multisensory ontology, which overspills the logic of the settler and scientific gaze (or, epistemology of the global North). Crossing borders, whether sensorial, social, or ontological, goes to the heart of what it means to be Métis—how to get real.[64]

---

61   Boaventura de Sousa Santos, *Toward a New Legal Common Sense: Law, Globalization, and Emancipation*, 3rd ed. (Cambridge: Cambridge University Press, 2020); Caroline A. Jones, David Mather, Rebecca Uchill, eds., *Experience: Culture, Cognition, and the Common Sense* (Cambridge: MIT Press, 2016), 8.

62   Garneau, "Imaginary Spaces of Conciliation and Reconciliation," 30–34.

63   Zoe Todd, "Fossil Fuels and Fossil Kin: An Environmental Kin Study of Weaponised Fossil Kin and Alberta's So-Called 'Energy Resources Heritage,'" *Antipode* (November 2022), doi.org/10.1111/anti.12897.

64   The research on which this chapter is based was supported (partially) by the Canadian Government through multiple Social Sciences and Humanities Research Council Insight Grants and by the Australian Government through the Australian Research Council's Discovery Projects funding scheme (DP170102969).

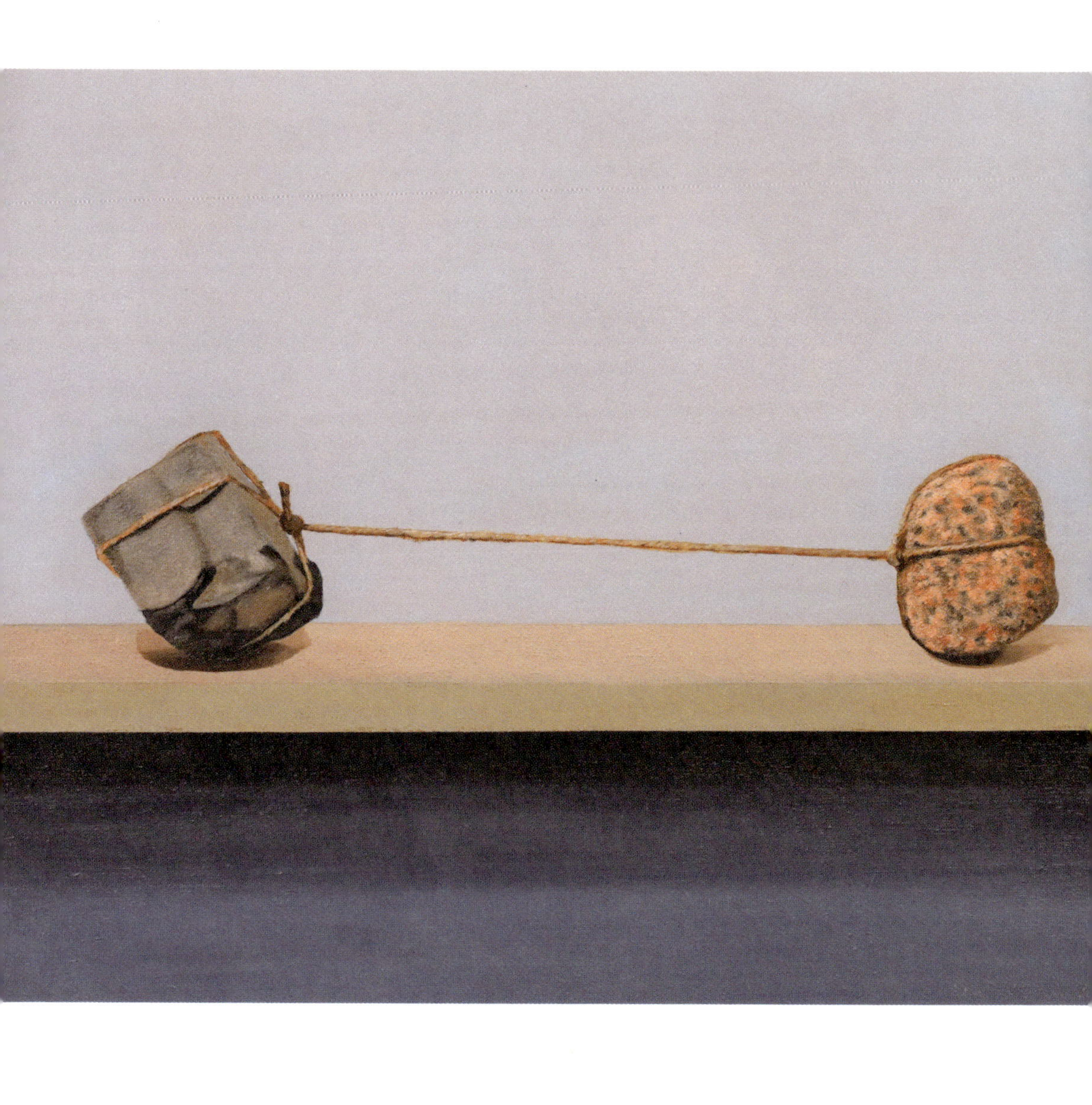

ALLIES (AFTER HSIEH AND MONTANO)

BY LARISSA LAI

nitially a term of connection across difference, allyship has gotten a bad rap. The concept was born from the best of intentions, a way to declare connection and solidarity with another who has been harmed by colonialism and other oppressive systems. But perhaps its bad reputation is deserved. Those who claim allyship usually do so from a position of power; allyship is what one declares when one inherits structural privilege yet doesn't want to be seen as the villain. The ally is the one in the know. They are hip enough to know that you can't say "We are all the same" anymore, wise to the disingenuity of "I don't see race." But it's precisely that shot from the hip that's the problem. The ally is cool, the ally is with it, the ally doesn't see how the claim to connection in fact places a burden on the one claimed in alliance.

To the claimed, the ally is freight added to the weight of oppression, one more rock in a sack of rocks to carry while attempting to lead an ordinary life, a life of fullness and meaning, perhaps even a political life, beside others who carry no rocks at all. Who needs an ally if the ally weighs you down and silences you with their declarations of goodwill and friendship? When you are just trying to get on with your work. How can you push back against a stance that is simultaneously kind and possessive? The ally can be a millstone around the neck. The ally understands power relations, but only partially, only when it suits them. Sometimes, too, the ally uses you as a shield against accusations of privilege, as a way to evade accountability. The ally understands that the state has exercised legislation against you. The ally understands name-calling. They might understand structural racism too: the ways in which society, institutions, and the dupe on the street overlook you or treats you as different and unworthy. The ally might even march with you, chant with you, shout slogans on your behalf. But all the while, every fibre of their being cries out, Look at me! See how good I am! (Because I stoop to stand beside the unwanted one.) Your unwant-edness stands out in stark relief to their shining goodness. Their good-ness shouts louder than your pain. Another rock.

But maybe one day you, with your sack of grey slate fragments, encounter another carrying a sack of orange speckled granite. Although your slate and their granite are not the same rocks, you can see a paral-lel between your burden and theirs. What language do you use to say, *I would like to stand beside you; I'd like to talk about these rocks?*

The relative weight of the rocks, the relative exhaustion of the car-rier is not the same. The qualities of the rocks, the qualities of the carri-ers are not the same. And yet that conversation, that possibility. Allies?

The arithmetic of power and pain needs to be read against more complex unfoldings in the field of experience.

The performance artists Linda Montano and Tehching Hsieh gave us early insight into allyship's bad rap (though they never used the term, which belongs more to our moment than theirs) with their *Art/ Life One Year Performance*,[65] conducted between July 4, 1983, and July 4, 1984—starting and ending on American Independence Day. For a year, they were tied together with an eight-foot rope, passed loosely around their waists and secured at each end.[66] They signed a statement, essen-tially a contract, stating the constraints of the performance, namely that they would be tied together at the waist for a year, never alone, in the same room most of the time. They agreed that they would never touch.[67]

---

65   Francky Knapp, "For a Year, They Lived Tied Together with 8 Feet of Social Distance," *Messy Nessy*, June 17, 2020, messynessychic.com/2020/06/16/for-a-year-they-lived-tied-together-with-8-feet-of-social-distance.

66   Thomas McEvilley, "Tehching Hsieh, Linda Montano," *Artforum* 23, no. 3 (November 1984): 98–99, artforum.com/events/tehching-hsieh-linda-montano-224861.

67   Linda Montano and Tehching Hsieh, "*Art/Life One Year Performance 1983–1984*, Statement," tehchinghsieh.net/artlife-oneyearperformance1983-1984?lightbox=dataItem-jg99f2kb.

They slept a few feet apart, in separate beds. When one showered, the other waited outside the door, but otherwise they were always in the same room, and both remained celibate for the duration.[68] Both had prior experience of durational performance. They were interested, as the title of the piece suggests, in blurring the boundary between art and life, experienced over time.

Montano, in an interview with Alex and Allyson Grey, said that she thinks of art and life as one and the same. Thomas McEvilley's astute review notes, however, that the two artists had very different philosophies in terms of what the performance meant. For Montano, to call something art meant "to give it a special quality of alert but nonaggressive appreciation not unlike the frame of mind developed . . . in a vipassana meditation retreat." For Hsieh, on the other hand, the process was more abstract and impersonal, an attempt to override questions of individual attitude. McEvilley writes, "While she thought of meditation retreats, he thought in terms of his three [compulsory] years in the Taiwanese army."[69] The difference became the source of much contention over the course of the year—the root of the struggle between them, which devolved, according to Montano, into yanks and tugs on the rope and communication in the form of grunts. Hsieh said, "We became each other's cage," and later, "The piece is about being like an animal, naked."[70]

McEvilley reads the agon that developed between them as devastatingly painful. Yet both Hsieh and Montano, in the last days of the performance, recognized their strife as inevitable, tied together as they were, at such close quarters. Hsieh said, "We had a lot of fights and I don't feel that is negative. Anybody who was tied in this way, even if they were a nice couple, I'm sure they would fight too. . . . We cannot hide our negative sides. . . . It's more than just honesty—we show our weakness."[71] Montano said, "Besides training the mind, the piece raises so many emotions to the surface that the soap opera quality eventually gets boring. I feel as if I've dredged up ancient rages and frustrations

68   McEvilley, "Tehching Hsieh, Linda Montano."

69   McEvilley, "Tehching Hsieh, Linda Montano."

70   Kristine Stiles and Peter Selz, "Linda Montano and Tehching Hsieh: *One Year Art/Life Performance*: Interview with Alex and Allyson Grey (1984)," *Theories and Documents of Contemporary Art* (Berkeley: University of California Press, 1996), 780, 782.

71   Stiles and Selz, "Linda Montano and Tehching Hsieh," 782.

this year, and although I'm glad that I went through with them, I now feel that holding any emotional state for too long is actually an obsolete strategy. On the other hand, because I believe that everything we do is art—fighting, eating, sleeping—then even the negatives are raised to the dignity of art. As a result I now feel much more comfortable with the negative. It's all part of the same picture."[72]

Speaking of pictures, David Garneau's *Allies (after Hsieh and Montano)* depicts two rocks, a chunk of grey slate and a chunk of orange-tinged granite, tied together with string, like Hsieh and Montano. Because it directly references the rope piece, the painting asks us, at least in one mode of viewing, to anthropomorphize the rocks, to read one as Hsieh and the other as Montano. The addition of a contemporary, racializing valence over the *Art/Life* struggle asks us to read their binding in contemporary terms. In our moment, the term *ally* is usually used to figure a friendly relationship between a white person and an Indigenous person, or a white person and an Asian person. We can, but don't usually, talk about Indigenous people and Asian people as allies. However, this piece struck me as an implicit invitation to do so. In the wake of Rita Wong and Dorothy Christian's important work together on water, *downstream*, and Lisa Lowe's important book *The Intimacies of Four Continents*, as well as my own connection with David Garneau through the *Primary Colours* project at the Banff Centre several years ago, I want to think about what *Allies (After Hsieh and Montano)* might offer, in spite of the uneasiness of the term, for Asian-Indigenous connection.

For indeed, the rap of allyship is like the rope of Montano and Hsieh's *Art/Life* performance, but only if we understand allyship's contradictions. The grey slate cube is bound to the very different orange granite pear in a similar knot, tailored to its shape. They sit on a level board, and the string that binds them is almost, though not quite, level. Their differences in shape and colour remain, though they are of curiously similar size.

The playing field on which Asian and Indigenous people meet, however, is not level. (And in fact, the metaphor of the playing field is both limiting and overdetermining.) While both are affected by historically entrenched state oppression, including racist laws (the Indian Act, including the amendments of 1884 that brought residential schools into being; the Chinese Exclusion Act; the Chinese head

---

72   Stiles and Selz, "Linda Montano and Tehching Hsieh," 780.

tax; the Orders-in-Council that disenfranchised Japanese Canadians during World War II; the continuous journey rule), Indigenous people are affected by land theft while Asians participate in land theft, albeit sometimes as a matter of survival (as, for instance, when indentured Chinese workers assisted in the building of the Canadian Pacific Railway in order to send money back to their impoverished families in China, themselves in distress because of Western imperial incursions into China, bad government at home, and their own human foibles, obligations, and other enmeshments. Arguably the Chinese head tax paid for the railway; our oppression and our complicity in this understanding become one and the same). When Asians participate, however, it is because of displacement in other places disturbed by the colonial process. This doesn't make us innocent—we never were. But by making a few historical recognitions, we find that our oppressions are not so much parallel as entangled. Because the colonial state has historically pitted us against one another, allyship is difficult—harder, I'd suggest, than white-Indigenous allyship or white-Asian allyship because of the strategy of divide and conquer and because there are so few articulated lines through which to connect. The string that binds us together in the colonial project is the most obvious, and the strongest, yet also the most fraught because it pits us against one another. We yank. If you get something, I don't, and vice versa. It's not a good dynamic.

The rope or string as metaphor is limited in that it doesn't make room for more than one string. What if instead of being bound by a single cord, we were bound by a skein? For indeed, relations beyond the state are possible and have been documented. For instance, the documentary *All Our Father's Relations* tells the story of the Grant siblings' trip from their home in Musqueam to visit Sei Moon, the village of their Chinese father,[73] and Lee Maracle's "Polka Partners, Uptown Indians and White Folks" tells the story of a local Chinese Canadian café as a beloved site for Indigenous gatherings.[74] Though the state produces racial positionings, we don't need to accept the forms of relationship it imposes. If we are connected by a complex skein, then if one thread is yanked, another goes slack; the shape of the skein shifts,

73 *All Our Father's Relations*, directed by Alejandro Yoshizawa, featuring Howard E. Grant, Larry Grant, Helen Callbreath, and Gordon J. Grant (Right Relations, 2016).

74 Lee Maracle, "Polka Partners, Uptown Indians, and White Folks," *Sojourners and Sundogs* (Vancouver: Press Gang Publishers, 1999), 286–304.

though the difficulties of relationality remain. A spider scuttles onto the web to show us the limitations of the binary at work in Hsieh and Montano's *Art/Life* piece.

I know from conversations with Lee Maracle (Sto:lo) and Doreen Spence (Cree) and from other contexts, too,[75] that stones are Grandfathers who hold story. John G. Hampton, through their interesting project on the Foothills Erratics Train, makes a distinction between rocks as beings tossed up by Nature, without humans having anything to do with it, and stones, imbued with meaning and being through human relationship with them.[76] As David Garneau takes stones up in his paintings, he enriches them, adding more story to the story they already carry. Insofar as they represent, they talk back to Montano and Hsieh. They talk back to all the struggles around allyship that have come to the surface in recent years. But why painting? And why a painting that references a durational performance? It is clear that Garneau is trained in contemporary global painting practices and representational practices as well. In painting Grandfather stones, he references Indigenous storytelling as a mode outside Western painting practices. Lee Maracle teaches us: "Stone is our oldest grandfather. We refer to the stones that keep our songs and stories as grandfather."[77] But, she says, "our grandmothers move us from that stone in the direction of relationship with others. They are the keepers of the stories that teach us about relations; they are the flesh of our bones that are stones."[78]

By giving us the two stones—one grey and cubic, the other pink and round—Garneau engages questions of how gender and race are understood in Métis contexts. However, in his adoption of a range of representational modes, he breaks binaries by showing us that art and life are not poles that can be merged (as Hsieh and Montano attempt to do), but rather that they are complex entities that are entangled, not just in practice but philosophically. There is a different kind of art/life entanglement here, not in the sense that Hsieh and Montano

75   Larissa Lai, "Bone to Bone, Spirit to Spirit—Sovereign Matriarchy, Asian/Indigenous Relations, and the Work of Directed Re-Membering," *Ideology in Postcolonial Texts and Contexts*, eds. Katja Sarkowsky and Mark U. Stein (Leiden: Brill Rodopi, 2021), 223–58.

76   John G. Hampton, "Rocks, Stones, and Grandfathers," *Rocks, Stones, and Dust* exhibition catalogue, 2015.

77   Lee Maracle, *Memory Serves: Oratories* (Edmonton: NeWest Press, 2015), 3.

78   Maracle, *Memory Serves*, 3–4.

seem to mean when they work so deliberately to blur the distinctions between individual human lives lived and call it art. Here, it is the reverberative entanglement that occurs when Garneau uses an older form—painting—to refer to a newer form—performance art—that emerged in the first place from painting's drive to become more life-like. By using Western painting techniques to show us the life already present in both rocks and stones, Garneau disorients our notions of progress and innovation. He goes back to go forward and seems to revel in the polydirectionality of temporal movement. By engaging painting, he acknowledges his own implication, his own contemporaneity along a Western trajectory, but he is also taking up his Métis positionality to trace a different line—a Métis pathway—that brings him to this moment in a different way. In a sense, he is creating another skein, one that doesn't disavow the thread of Western progress—he's humble; he sees how hard it is to cut that thread. Instead, he weaves it in while affirming other trajectories for other beings and other ways of know-ing—Métis, Plains Cree, perhaps even Chinese earth ways. The string between stones is one thread in a web or weaving. As such, it gestures to textile art, the art of entanglement, often coded as feminine. The softness of fibre is put in conversation with the hardness of stone, and painting is put in conversation with storytelling. Though there is just one line of string binding the two stones in the painting, this work is far from monologic; it is entangled in the most productive of ways, draw-ing many of us unevenly together—as allies? Though the painting is neat, the story it tells is beautifully messy in the most moving of ways.

With thanks to David Garneau for inviting me to contribute in the first place, and for the email exchange that clarified and opened up the conversation. Appreciation also to Arin Fay, Karen Clark, and Nic Wilson for their generous support and patience.

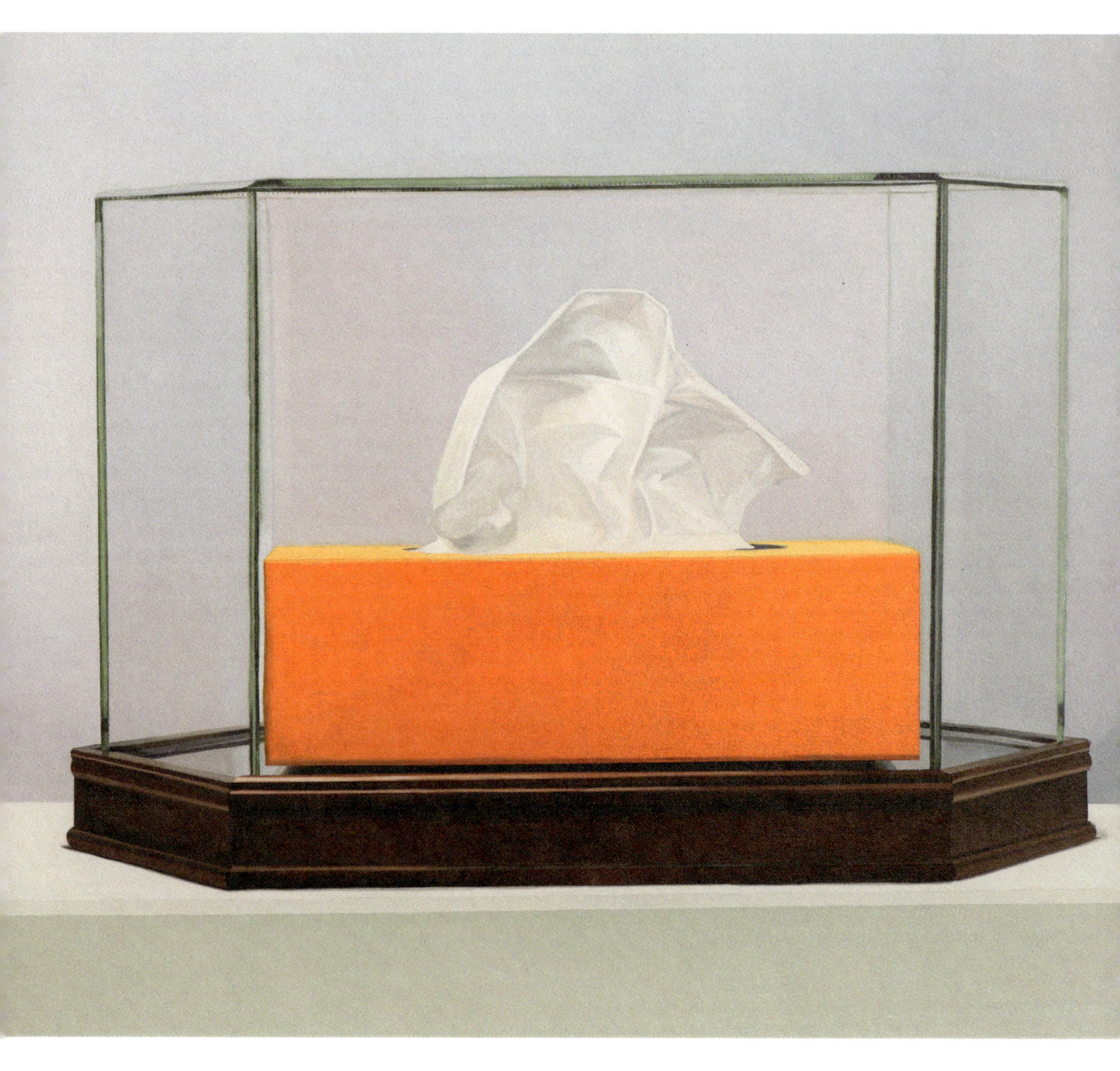

ALLY TEAR RELIQUARY
BY ARIN FAY

David Garneau's still life paintings both expand upon and usurp the long-standing genre of still life representation, creating a new vernacular for this much maligned mode of painting. I grew up watching endless slides of still life paintings in darkened classrooms and was told that cracked vases represented the loss of virginity and mouldering fruit, mortality. For an art nerd raised on European still life, among other homogenized histories, Garneau's paintings feel both reminiscent and confronting. The works expand upon and challenge the vanitas and memento mori styles, introducing a modern Métis iteration of still life painting that could be called l'honneur (honour) and/or ayka chi kishikwuhk (enlighten). The works pose open-hearted quandaries about the opposition and/or similarity of symbolic objects, with humour, beauty, and a distinctly Indigenous perspective.

Borrowing from the ethical intimations of the aforementioned styles, a painting such as *Ally Tear Reliquary* meaningfully elevates a box of tissues to the status of relic, illustrating the arbitrary and often absurd nature of overt veneration, pomp, and ceremony, presented in opposition to oral history, lived experience, or memory. Just one of many inversions that these works pose. Such an object of reverence and contemplation is traditionally something from an ethnocentric past, something understood as saintly or significant, and often stolen; all are loaded concepts that are tied to colonization, genocide, and an

FACING: "Ally Tear Reliquary (TRC Archive. 2014, 1.01a)," 2023, 76.5 × 92 cm, acrylic on canvas.

interpretation of history broadly—the usurpation or reconstruction of value(s). The transition between the still life subject and object is jarring in this work, since what we are seeing is a modern artifact and one customarily deemed unworthy of praise or attention. The title sets the stage, but the objects themselves carry the connotations. The colonial cabinet of curiosity is here upended, and the concept of ally is under investigation, the hothouse flower of reconciliation.

The critical tone of this artwork does sting somewhat, for hand-wringing white people like me who want to be a part of the cultural conversation in a country that some call Canada and some see as an unauthorized rebranding of place and peoples. On first pass, the painting comments on the preciousness of white privilege from an Indigenous perspective, a not-so-subtle jibe; like all witticisms, it carries a kernel of truth. The work acknowledges the wellspring of settler sentiment and captures, in one strange arrangement, the uneasy reality of allyship. The source for *Ally Tear Reliquary* was Garneau's involvement in many of the Truth and Reconciliation Commission (TRC) gatherings across the country, events that involved tears on all sides of the circle—impossible analogy intended. The specially made tissues for these events were gathered and burned in ritual, a cathartic end for throw-away things, but here in Garneau's painting memorialized as a museum artifact, one that both honours the sentiments expressed and lambasts the too-little-too-late sympathy of some spectators. Both can be true.

Is it exhausting and sometimes irritating for Indigenous people to absorb and respect ally tears? Of course it is, hence the ironic and over-wrought reliquary. Are settler allies part of the equation? Of course we are, unless some extreme decolonial exodus happens and we all return to our countries of origin, as a wise friend once suggested. Instead, uneasy relationships have become inextricably commodified and rote, branded like the Kleenex box and transformed into mass-marketed orange shirts and Canada 150 campaigns that might mean well but are subsumed by the jingoistic ocean of public opinion. Yet the effort to find meaning and "truth" could also be something that all viewers of this work have in common—an effort that exemplifies compassion—which is arguably a much better response than, say, racism (overt or covert), hate, indifference, or the legion of other micro- and macro-aggressions that exist. Tears can represent so many emotions: love, guilt, rage, sorrow, empathy. . . . They can be the purest form of honesty

and sincere emotion, or function as a shield, crutch, or distraction—
much like the delivery of land acknowledgements that run the gamut
from profound to stilted to hollow to parodic (*Baroness von Sketch*'s "If
we're on someone else's land, should we . . . leave?" or Cliff Cardinal's
awesome adaption of Shakespeare's *As You Like It* in which he expresses
his profound impatience for performative pathos). *Ally Tear Reliquary*
speaks to an uncomfortable tension and reality that needs to be considered and acknowledged.

The *Dark Chapters* series contributes a new chapter to the exclusion-
ary and ethnocentrically selective canon of Western art history, which
represents a significant corollary for a world grappling with ways to
reframe fundamental cultural and societal conversations. The series
challenges the preconception of a linear and selective historical time-
line with the presentation of geological time and other ways of knowing, concepts present in the ponderous appearance of stones and other
land-connected objects alongside more constructed or manufactured
creations. *Ally Tear Reliquary* is one of the more lighthearted pieces in
this series, yet it still pulls punches. It presents the idea of an ally as
other, a meaningful reversal and a concrete caricature—and a reminder
that it is not about a settler status quo, or an annihilating melting pot,
but a retelling of stories that reject the doctrine of discovery. The side-
kick status of the Indigenous other has been overturned and the butt
of the joke swapped in a small symbolic sample of what it feels like
to be simplified, belittled, or written out within a dominant narrative.
There is also an offering inherent in the perspectives proposed, akin
to the round peg, square hole polarity of Garneau's previous work *Not
to Confuse Politeness with Agreement* in which even conciliatory stances
involve adversity and critical conversation.

Dark Chapters is a disarmingly straightforward and accessible series
in some respects, yet symbolically and aesthetically sophisticated,
inviting the myriad interpretations that emblems employ. The genre
of still life is enriched by the representative yet salacious mashups presented, a friction which extends to the gallery in which the works are
installed. The white gallery space has historically been an inhospitable
environment for Indigenous and BIPOC art and artists into which they
would be invited in, quantified, and catalogued in an often patroniz-
ing and paternalistic relationship. Such spaces continue to be places of
privilege, which for curators, such as myself, can only be mediated by
honesty, relationship-building, and trust, intentions that are naturally

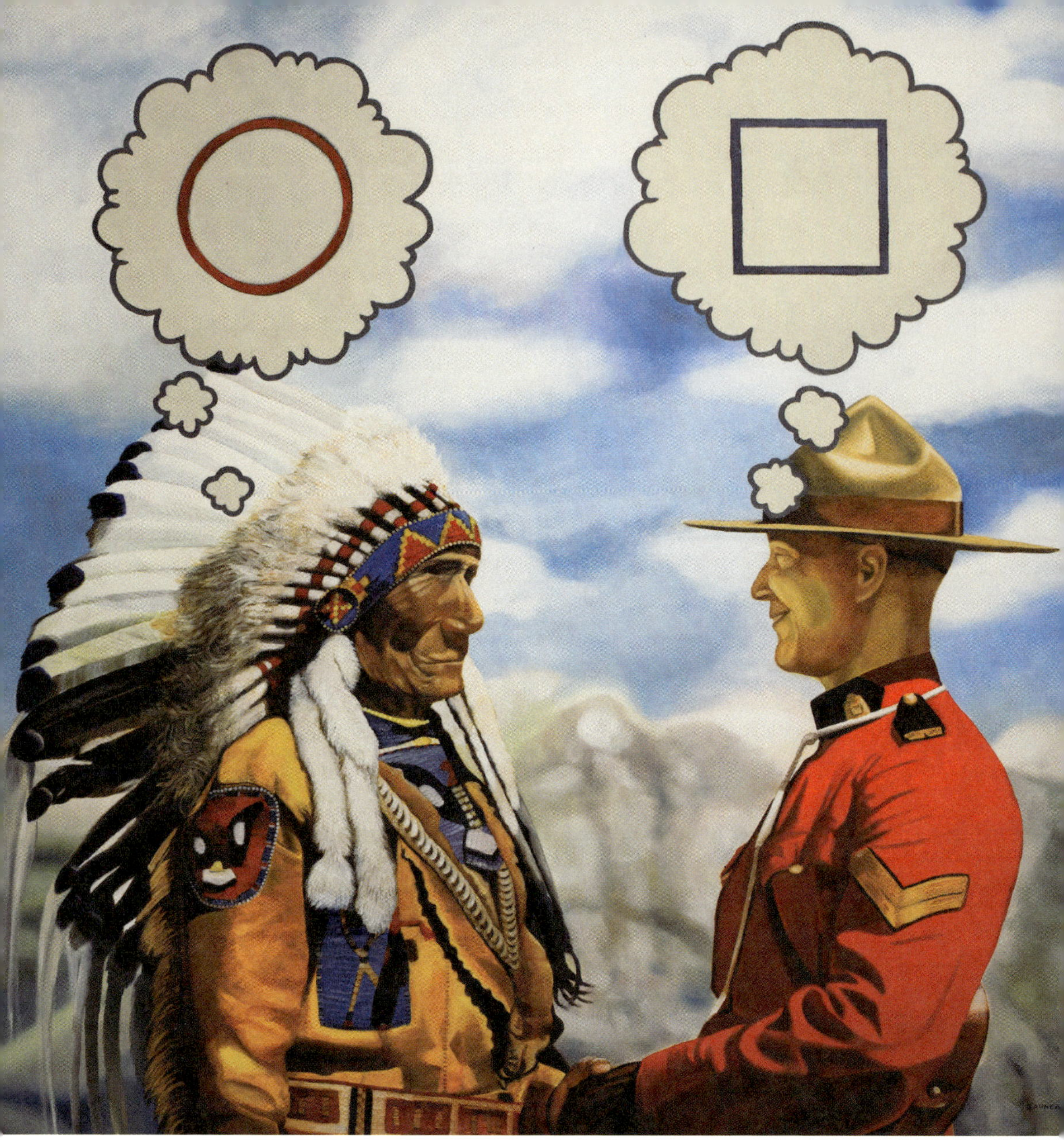

"Not to Confuse Politeness with Agreement," 2013, 122 × 122 cm, oil on canvas. Collection of the Montreal Museum of Fine Arts.

unpredictable and prone to ego and human frailty. *Ally Tear Reliquary* offers another way of seeing the settler ally position within a visual retelling of history that is not our recognized norm, a negotiation that allows settler viewers to sit with the insecurity of being encased within a narrative that does not always reflect one's intentions or worth. Garneau's still lifes and his use of wit, vernacular, and visual tropes illustrate the power of art to elicit feelings that would otherwise not be observed or appreciated.

I navigate this work through the lens of my own lived experience: the love and empathy of a mother, which is where my tears come from; the second-class status of being born a woman, where rage and empathy reside; and the creative impulse of an artist and a curator, which propels my constant search for ways of seeing and knowing. I understand fundamentally what privilege looks like, because I embody it, even as I try, like others, to understand what the evolving role of an ally can, should, and does look like in an ever-shifting landscape. There is no gold star distributed to white people, who run the gamut from altruistic to narcissistic, at the end of decolonization; it is a journey that never ends. *Ally Tear Reliquary* has put this idea on a literal and gilded platform, an important page within the *Dark Chapters* series, an indictment and a joke between friends.

"Indigenous Research Methodology (I)," 2019, 40 × 50 cm, acrylic on masonite. Collection of Arin Fay.

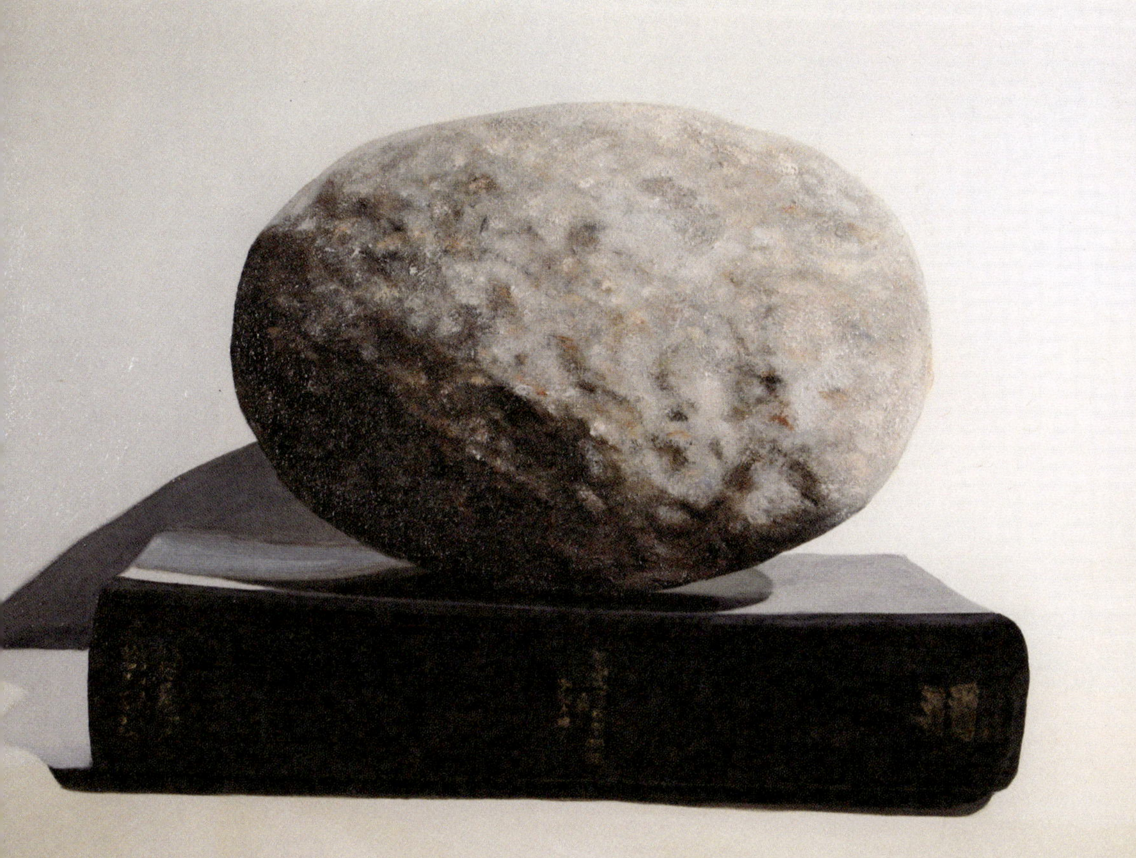

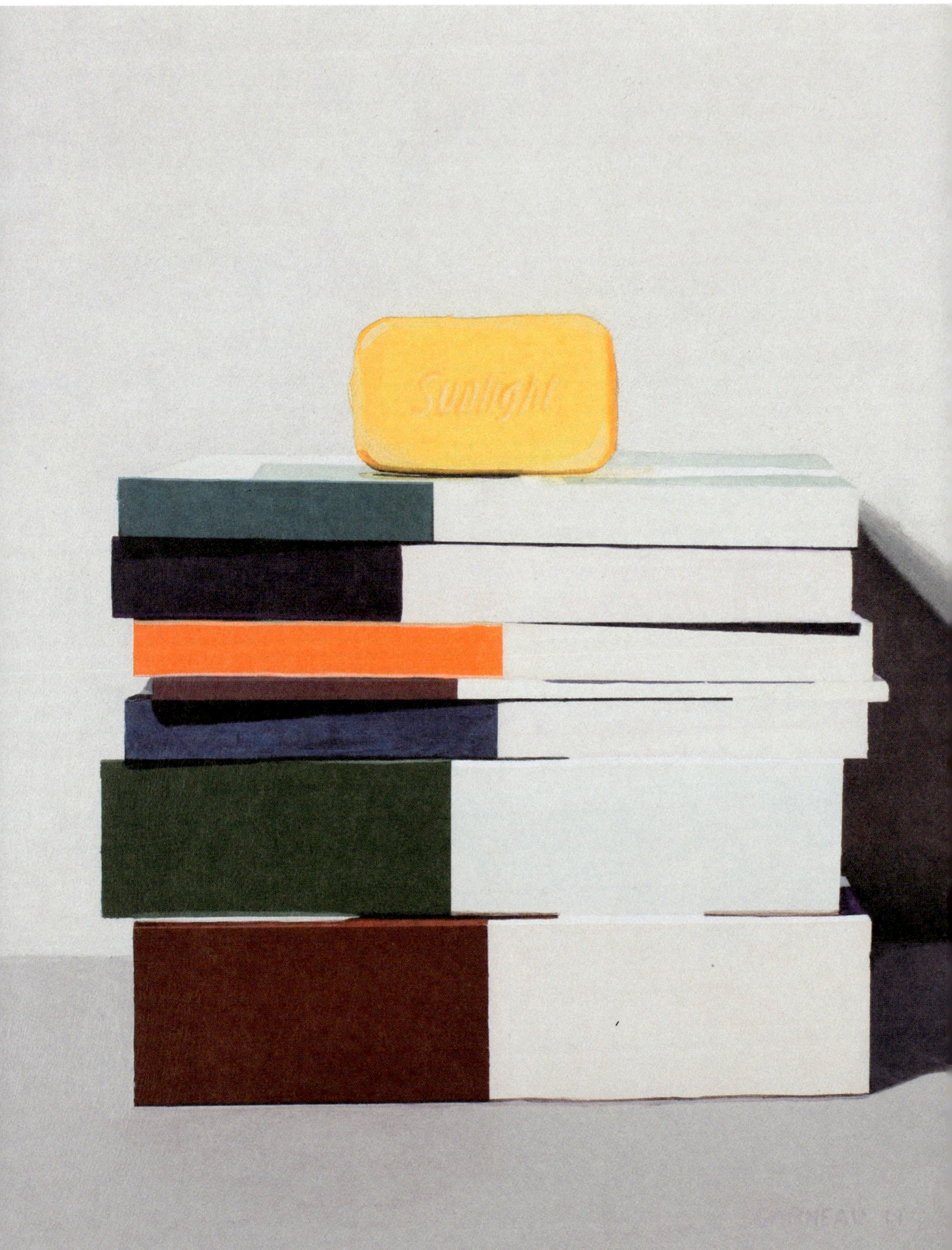

Sunlight

UNDERSTANDING *ATTEMPTED ENLIGHTENING:* BETWEEN LANGUAGE AS POWER . . . AND LIGHT AS LIFE
BY DICK AVERNS

I. IN THE BEGINNING WAS ~~THE WORD~~ CREATIVITY

A stack of wordless books surmounted by a bar of yellow soap, offset by an abruptly truncated shadow, defies immediate legibility. With no glossary or original tomes, we have only David Garneau's painterly forms and titles of artworks as ciphers. To begin understanding the painting *Attempted Enlightening* contextualized within the artist's larger series *Dark Chapters*—at once still lifes and history paintings—consider that Garneau is encouraging us to contemplate both these encrypted books and our dead reckoning. In doing so, we can decipher many a conflicted episode and appreciate the value of creativity in recalibrating conflicted histories.

In parsing confliction, I'll begin with one of the older texts in Garneau's extensive series, the Bible, identifiable by the crucifix and binding (see p. 105). The fact that many Indigenous Peoples have been disenfranchised by this god, for instance through Christian-governed residential schools, is not my only point. In a powerful testament to the mettle of the Word, the book of John opens with this proclamation: "In the beginning was the Word, and the Word was with God, and the Word was God."[79] Put another way, it is widely accepted that language is power, to which I add that words (and images) are constantly

79   John 1:1 (King James Version).

currencies. Why else would colonizers and imperialists destroy the languages of others, if not to suppress peoples and their cultures? For example, in the sixteenth century, Spanish priests destroyed Mayan codices en-masse; the Nazis burned books;[80] and more pertinently here, the British Crown banned the speaking of Indigenous languages in a defining dark chapter of Canada's 1876 Indian Act.

Garneau is aware of such dynamics and willing to address related subjugated histories. He effaces and erases words from his bookish tablets while simultaneously acknowledging the open-and-shut case that books, or the knowledge and arguments therein, are also power. Thus, he supplants words and the Word with creativity, for which his muscular studio output is a testament to one of the four interwoven underpinnings of Indigenous well-being: physical wellness.[81]

But where do we go from here, if our communities and humanity are to find wellness beyond conflict? How to shed light on the double bindings of missing words and lost worlds? As with many an artwork or text, mining titles and footnotes make good entry points.

Attempted Enlightening indicates significant effort (i.e., the *attempted* of the title) towards positivity, perhaps towards Buddhist calm, free from desire and conflict. More philosophically, I suggest a nod towards the Enlightenment, or the Age of Reason. To locate the light in enlightenment, Garneau offers us appropriated sunlight, writ large and stamped on a hybrid, pseudo-soapstone readymade sculpture[82] and keystone heir apparent, a bar of yellow Sunlight soap sitting atop seven books. More light is discovered when further unpacking the artwork's title: an enlightenment unfettered from religious dogma.

Looking more closely at Garneau's Bible brushing by observing another of Garneau's paintings we see crucifixes in *Syncretism* beneath

---

80   Caleb A. Zavala, "The Maya Codex of Mexico (MCM)." *Historical Mexico* (Huntsville, TX, Sam Houston University), https://www.historicalmx.org/items/show/67. And, United States Holocaust Memorial Museum, "Book Burnings." *Holocaust Encyclopedia* (Washington, DC: United States Holocaust Memorial Museum), encyclopedia.ushmm.org/content/en/article/book-burning.

81   Charlotte Loppie Reading and Fred Wien, *Health Inequalities and Social Determinants of Aboriginal People's Health* (Prince George, BC: National Collaborating Centre for Aboriginal Health, 2009), 3.

82   A readymade is an industrially manufactured object that is appropriated from everyday life into the form of an artwork, to conceptually introduce new subject matter and content at the behest of an artist, while still referencing its origins.

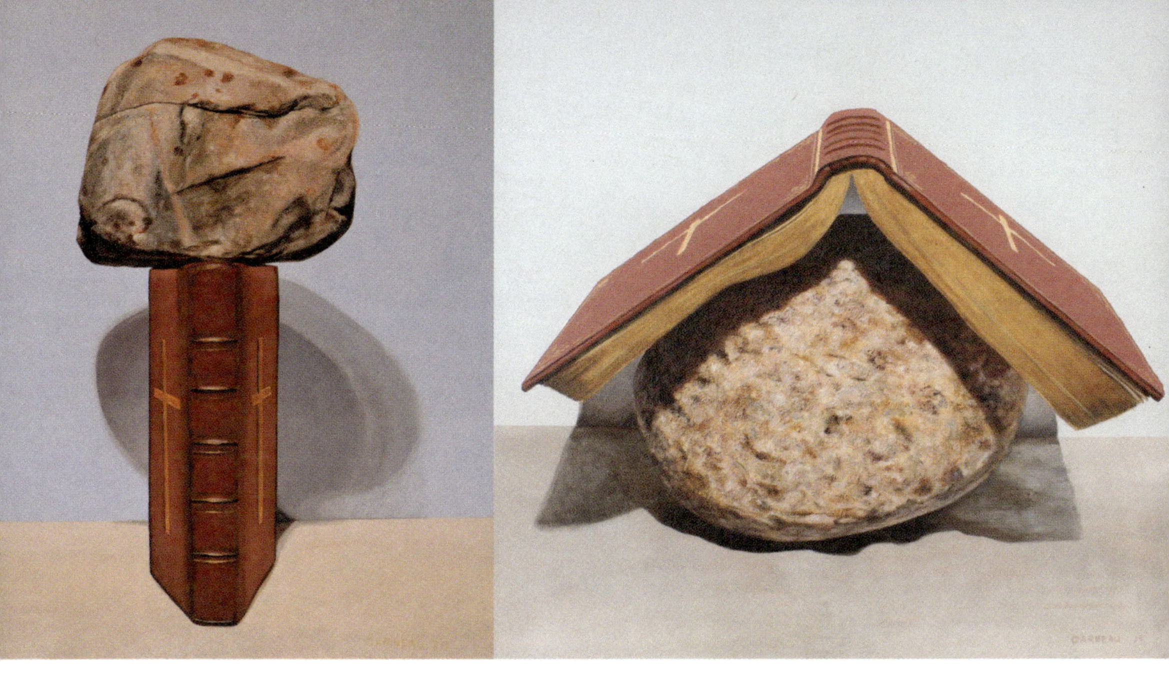

L: "Syncretism," 2020, 61 × 51 cm, acrylic on panel. **R:** "Upon this Rock," 2021, 58.5 × 58.5 cm, acrylic on canvas.

a Grandfather keystone. The Bible appears again in *Upon this Rock*, cloaking and shadowing another Grandfather rock. I see such balancing acts functioning on at least two levels.

Firstly, syncretism is defined by *Merriam-Webster* as "the combination of different forms of belief or practice." Secondly, the Truth and Reconciliation Commission's ninety-four Calls to Action are invoked, specifically number 60, wherein the Church needs "to respect Indigenous spirituality in its own right."[83] With this comes a connection to a second Indigenous whole-person cornerstone: spirituality.

As a corollary to Garneau's decision to paint hundreds of books, disguising their identities and omitting virtually all words, while clearly revealing the Bible, I locate a telling footnote in the aforementioned quotation from John in Genesis 1:1: "In the beginning God created the heavens and the earth," followed on the first day by God saying, "Let there be light."

With many Indigenous people having long given thanks to the Creator, respecting nature-inspired spiritual figureheads for the earth's bounty and our being—free from a Christian God synonymous with power through the Word—it becomes clearer why, referring to this

---

83   Truth and Reconciliation Commission of Canada, *Truth and Reconciliation Commission of Canada: Calls to Action* (Truth and Reconciliation Commission of Canada, 2015).

section's subheading, we are alighting on creativity.[84] Indigenous Peoples thrived for centuries pre-contact with an oral culture, and the revivification of creation, or the Creator rather than God, does not remove light from the equation. The sun is still here, and with it comes light as life.

II. SUNLIGHT—WHAT OF IT?

The conjoining of sun and light into sunlight and Sunlight allows an expansive look at both worldly and cosmic cultures, as well as notions of cleansing derived from the soap in *Attempted Enlightening*. All the while, let's not forget the props beneath: nameless books codified by form, mass, and colour—a stratified plinth or conceptual foundation of considerable heft.

Bearing in mind Garneau is also an author, often penning critical writing on art and culture, it becomes necessary to probe encryption within the stack of books that hold this light of sun aloft. To foreground this conundrum, let's consider two factors: 1) What are the predominant forms or objects in *Dark Chapters*? and 2) Which other paintings depict words?

The recurring objects in the series are books, rocks, bones, bindings, readymades, life forms, tools, and assemblages comprising the above. Many of the artworks echo, or rely upon, colonizer conventions of still life painting[85] but advance today's narratives and art history by repositioning the power dynamics and critical value of such conventions.

Some books are held in the jaws of a spring trap or noosed, and Grandfather rocks are in dialogue with the wordless tomes, significant when considering that found objects (encompassing naturally occurring forms) are actively problematizing the power of the word. Materials most closely derived from nature are in contestation with the order, or often disorder, of formalized words and books. In sum, I see a critical privileging of Indigenous tenets over the readymades and a clear invoking of a third Indigenous key to wholeness: mental or intellectual strength.

---

84   I recognize that creativity is, of course, a word and that we're relying on words to discuss creativity, but let's not let semantics get in the way when there are bigger conflicts to address and resolve.

85   Still life painting is a Western genre that variously depicts celebrations of life's trappings or serves as a warning of human fallaciousness or mortality.

Paintings declaring their textual "aboutness"[86] by conveying words in the picture plane total only ten canvasses out of 108. Put another way, there are a total of 288 publications (books, magazines, and the novel Sunlight soap) appearing in the 108 paintings but only ten of them overtly express their source through words or logos:[87]

1. Crucifixes and the Bible in *Syncretism* and *Upon this Rock*
2. Three books, *Halfbreed* and *The Inconvenient Indian*, in *Displacement. Indigenous on Indigenous Scholarship*, and *Lives of the Saints* in *Syncretism II*
3. Publishers' logos: Routledge in *Apple Press*, Pantheon in *Two Degrees*, and HarperCollins in *Empathetic Conformation* and *Indigenous Research Methodology (I)*
4. *Canadian Art* magazine in *Indigenous Art Shaping Canadian Art*
5. Sunlight in *Attempted Enlightening*

For an artist of Garneau's rigour and merit, we must consider this sprinkling of words and logos as linguistic breadcrumbs: ciphers indicating why only these few publications and paintings are bestowed with the power of words. Conversely, not deploying written words re-emphasizes and privileges oral history and storytelling as millennia-old means of conveying and preserving culture among Indigenous Peoples, including Métis ancestors.

Summing up the above, we have a Bible, two books written to lay bare and highlight the marginalization of Indigenous life and scholarship, publishers' logos, and a bar of soap. From here, I see clearer creative and conflicted relationships at play between Church and state, Indigenous belief systems, the value of learning, and power derived from agents of cleansing.

Pursuing this last point, let us probe the choice of Sunlight soap, as opposed to, say, Dove or Imperial Leather (both of which are also strong

---

86　Terry Barrett, "Principles of Interpretation," *Criticizing Art: Understanding the Contemporary* (Mountain View, CA: Mayfield Publishing, 1994), 71.

87　It may not be possible to concretely discern the artist's intent, but at the very least we can agree that David Garneau is not a text-based artist, unlike others who use printed matter in their art and retain the words, such as Hannah Höch, John Heartfield, or Carl Beam. For readers wishing to consider other artists who have used wordless book forms to address cultural genocide, a strong parallel can be found in Rachel Whiteread's Holocaust memorial in Vienna.

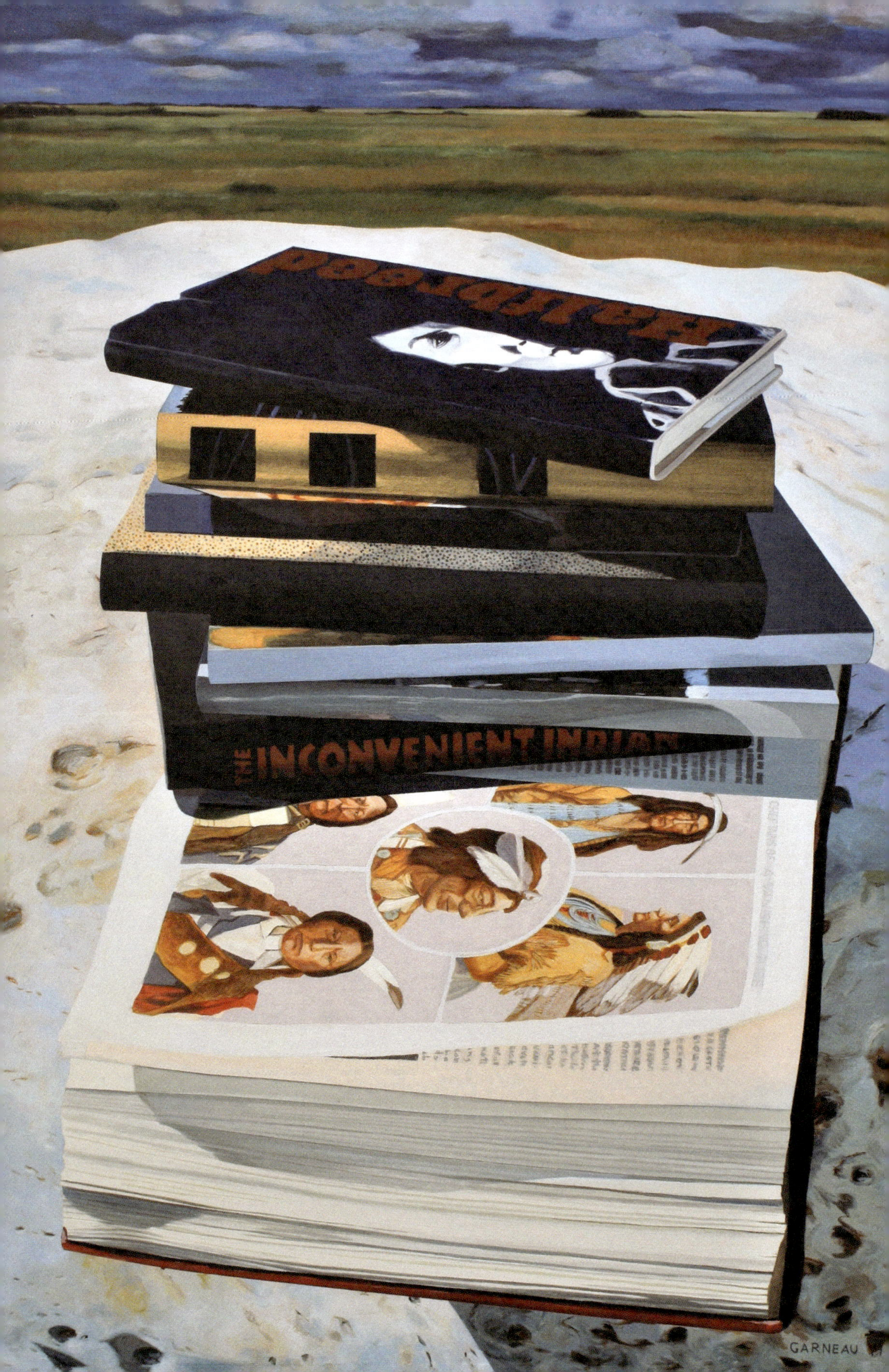

Hollywood
THE INCONVENIENT INDIAN
GARNEAU

conceptual contenders), in the context of a set of words that are at once founding and confounding: Canada's Indian Act. Not forgetting the imperative of sunlight supporting all life, Sunlight sells itself as "pure," with "real lemon," and as "multipurpose." The Indian Act sought to wash away Indigenous rights and was far from pure, with clauses that barred students from exercising their mother tongue, denied rights to women, expropriated land, and until 1960 denied "Indians" the right to vote unless they surrendered their treaty rights and status.[88]

Some people assert that the impact upon Indigenous Peoples from the colonial project in Canada—which my antecedents were part of, and I acknowledge I'm implicated and committed to meaningfully redress— is tantamount to ethnic cleansing.[89] If this is too strong, consider the TRC's report acknowledging "cultural genocide" in Canada.[90] All point to the negative power of "cleaning house" rather than light as life.

But there is more being invoked with Garneau's choice of Sunlight, an interpretation that gains currency when noting that early twentieth-century U.S. Justice Louis Brandeis wrote that "Sunlight is said to be the best of disinfectants."[91] Underlying Brandeis's statement is a proposition to ensure democratic fairness, free from self-serving power-broking, by adopting transparency, as in letting processes see the light of day. We now have a code for combatting the abuse of power: sunlight as a positive agent for cleaning house, and *Attempted Enlightening* presenting a natural, creative, and colourful path to righting injustices.

88   Bob Joseph, *21 Things You May Not Know about the Indian Act: Helping Canadians Make Reconciliation with Indigenous Peoples a Reality* (Saanichton, BC: Indigenous Corporate Training, 2018).

89   James Daschuk, "When Canada Used Hunger to Clear the West," *Globe and Mail*, July 19, 2013, theglobeandmail.com/opinion/when-canada-used-hunger-to-clear-the-west/article13316877; James Daschuk, *Clearing the Plains: Disease, Politics of Starvation, and the Loss of Aboriginal Life* (Regina: University of Regina Press, 2013), 123.

90   See the conclusion to the first paragraph on page 1 of *Honouring the Truth, Reconciling for the Future: Summary of the Final Report of the Truth and Reconciliation Commission of Canada* (Truth and Reconciliation Commission of Canada, 2015).

91   Louis Brandeis, "What Publicity Can Do," *Harper's Weekly*, December 20, 1913; Louis Brandeis, *Other People's Money and How the Bankers Use It* (New York: Frederick A. Stokes, 1914), 92.

FACING: "Displacement. Indigenous on Indigenous Scholarship," 2019, 122 × 79 cm, acrylic on canvas. Collection of the Dunlop Art Gallery.

Having now wordsmithed the Bible, bookends, and sunlight, what of deciphering the anonymous books in this painting? The majority of stylized books in *Dark Chapters* are suggestive of the authority of writing, some publications recognizable, most deliberately not, and others perhaps fictive. What I can't ignore is the uncanny resemblance of the stacked tomes in *Attempted Enlightening* to three encryptions.

First, the books are similar in colour and form to the TRC's seven volumes, for which each volume's colour matches the book cover hues in Garneau's painting. The Routledge series of critical dictionaries also has similar colours. Second, the white of each duotone book could be the result of sun bleaching, a cleansing of content, or even a whiting-out of vernacular Indigeneity by settler word-driven power. Third, the books carry the colours of the rainbow, albeit reordered and earth-toned, suggestive of diversity. The rainbow has been a symbol of championing marginalized communities since artist Gilbert Baker adopted it for a pride parade in 1978.

A profound example is the strong resemblance of the green book in *Attempted Enlightening* to the TRC's *Canada's Residential Schools: The History, Part 2, 1939–2000* or to *The Routledge Critical Dictionary of Postmodern Thought*.

III. SUNSHINE ON MY SHOULDERS

Writing this chapter during the Israel–Hamas war makes it hard to concentrate on artful words. Not because Garneau's work is less deserving, but because there is an amplification of rawness, pain, and torment through human oppression, factors highly pertinent to *Dark Chapters*. With this comes the fourth tenet of Indigenous being: an emotional connection, both to painful histories and memories and to optimism.

David Garneau is acutely aware of his ancestors' disenfranchisement, as, too, am I conscious of my connection to colonialism. As the Crown saw fit to approve Canadian Confederation, so my grandparents' generation gave the nod for the abandonment of the British Mandate for Palestine, itself a colonial vestige from World War I and the Balfour Declaration.[92] My father's conscription to the Middle East in 1948, where he worked intelligence in the infantry, is a parallel dark

---

92   I am not wishing to simplify the carving up of the Middle East by colonial powers. I have witnessed the reality as a war artist, including hearing the Etzel freedom fighter Yokse Nachmias tell me of a British saying, "The Arab oil is thicker than the Jewish blood."

chapter, particularly seen in his letters home that use slurs to describe locals. Much of this shaped my decision to be deployed as an official war artist to the same territories—Egypt, Sinai, Palestine, the West Bank, and Israel—to calibrate how nation states constitute conflict-related cultural canons.

Crucially, *Attempted Enlightening* spans the above and more, wary of suggesting a grand narrative yet positing the value of sunlight as an antidote to conflicted words and worlds. Further, to temper the Enlightenment as a vaunted Eurocentric philosophy, I note that *The Dawn of Everything* by anthropologist David Graeber and archaeologist David Wengrow dispels such notions by pointing to North American Indigenous thinking and wisdom being exported to Europe, where it influenced the very architects of the Enlightenment.[93] Having shed light on many a shoulder with a healthy dose of disinfectant, what else can sunlight offer in the realm of our everyday?

I asked my peers this question, and the answers were illuminating. Light from the sun sends us happiness, warmth to aid healing and growth, and fosters self-nourishment. Meanwhile Sunlight washes away the dirt, sanitizes, and purifies, and lemon is a natural disinfectant.[94]

Beyond Garneau's compelling and eloquent Sunlight illumination of human travesty, he embraces sunlight to generate healthy understanding. His endeavours are evidence of bringing divergent communities together, making good on the TRC's Calls to Action, such as number 93: "Indigenous and non-Indigenous artists . . . undertake collaborative projects and produce works that contribute to the reconciliation process."

Moving beyond the black and white world of printed pages, we have art, colour, and theory. Inky shadows symbolic of black marring and earlier losses of Métis culture; green symbolizing growth and prosperity of the Métis Nation today and in the future.[95]

---

93   David Graeber and David Wengrow, *The Dawn of Everything: A New History of Humanity* (New York: Farrar, Straus and Giroux, 2021), 19.

94   Much of the shaping of this paragraph came through discussions with, and contributions from, my hairdresser, Michelle Baker.

95   "Métis Sash," Eastern Woodlands Métis Nation, easternwoodlandmetisnation.ca/metis-sash. Colour theory is a complex realm, although black is often associated with darkness and despair, while green is widely associated with nature, health, and rebirth. These

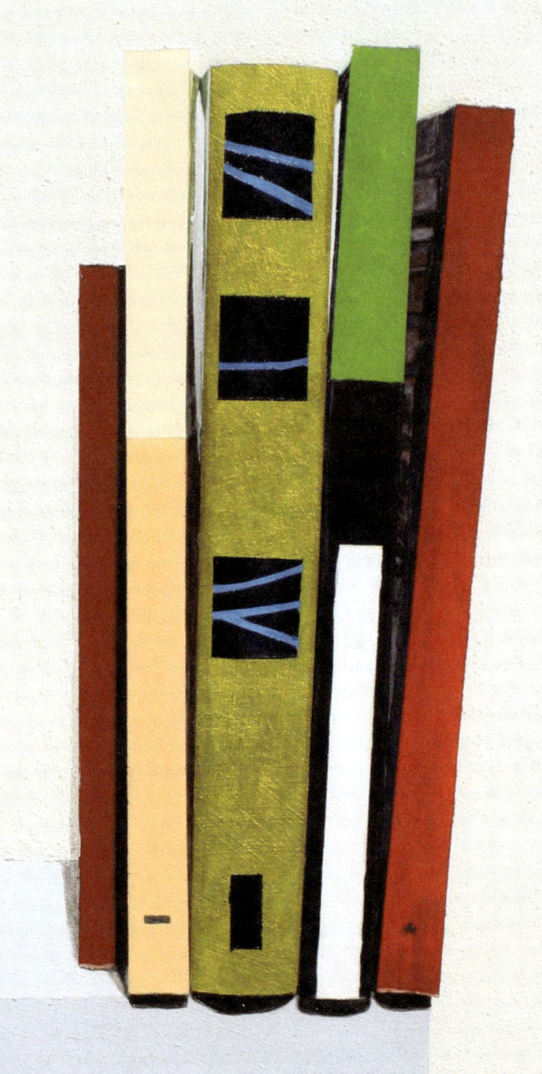

The identity of the books in *Attempted Enlightening* are undoubtedly loaded and burdensome. What do you think?[96] My best offerings are to focus on the intertextuality that is central to *Dark Chapters* and to let the TRC findings, hue, cry, and all, positively colour our souls and actions. Take stock from Garneau that trying to recalibrate the value of art and humanity within an interwoven Indigenous-settler dynamic is a struggle—yet surely a valued aim with a compelling essence.

Ultimately, the sun's rays are now creatively reworded to optimize our locus between language as power and light as life, preparing us to move forward productively as stewards of Turtle Island. We must not shy away from probing dark pasts and reconciling shady practices, as we challenge our vision to see beyond what we normally apprehend and comprehend. Beware the words that cast the darkest shadows . . . but never shy away from eclipsing them.

BIBLIOGRAPHY

Barrett, Terry. *About Art Criticism.* Mountain View: Mayfield Publishing, 1994.

Brandeis, Louis D. "What Publicity Can Do." *Harper's Weekly, A Journal of Civilization,* December 20, 1913.

Daschuk, James. *Clearing the Plains: Disease, Politics of Starvation, and the Loss of Aboriginal Life.* Regina: University of Regina Press, 2013.

First Nations Education Steering Committee. "First People's Principles of Learning," accessed October 25, 2023. https://www.fnesc.CA/first-peoples-principles-of-learning/.

Graeber, David, and David Wengrow. *The Dawn of Everything: A New History of Humanity.* New York: Farrar, Straus and Giroux, 2021.

Joseph, Bob. *21 Things You May Not Know about the Indian Act: Helping Canadians Make Reconciliation with Indigenous Peoples a Reality.* Saanichton, BC: Indigenous Corporate Training, 2018.

interpretations hold water for Métis symbolism, but it should be noted that colour symbology across Métis regions may vary.

96   At a writers' meeting, David Garneau spoke about his role in assisting the writing process: "Don't come to me and ask, 'What does this mean?' Make your own read." At some point, we all have to do this.

FACING: "Indigenous Academics," 2020, 50.5 × 40.5 cm, acrylic on panel.

"Métis Sash." Eastern Woodland Métis Nation. Accessed June 8, 2024. https://easternwoodlandmetisnation.ca/metis-sash

Reading, Charlotte Loppie, and Fred Wien. "Health Inequalities and Social Determinants of Aboriginal People's Health." National Collaborating Centre for Aboriginal Health, Prince George, 2009.

Sim, Stuart. *The Routledge Dictionary of Postmodern Thought*. London: Routledge, 1999.

The Holy Bible, trans. from the original languages (being the version set forth 1611, revised A.D. 1881–1885 and A.D. 1901, compared with the most ancient authorities and revised A.D. 1946–1952, second edition of the New Testament, New York, Glasgow & Toronto: William Collins Sons & Co., Ltd., 1971).

Truth and Reconciliation Commission of Canada. *Honouring the Truth, Reconciling for the Future: Summary of the Final Report of the Truth and Reconciliation Commission of Canada.* Manitoba: Truth and Reconciliation Commission of Canada, 2015.

Truth and Reconciliation Commission of Canada. *Truth and Reconciliation Commission of Canada: Calls to Action.* Manitoba: Truth and Reconciliation Commission of Canada, 2015.

United States Holocaust Memorial Museum. "Book Burnings." *Holocaust Encyclopedia*. Washington, DC: United States Holocaust Memorial Museum. Accessed October 25, 2023. https://encyclopedia.ushmm.org/content/en/article/book-burning

Zavala, Caleb A. "The Maya Codex of Mexico (MCM)." *Historical Mexico*. Huntsville, TX: Sam Houston University. Accessed August 12, 2024. https://www.historicalmx.org/items/show/67

FACING: "Waiting Out the Guests," 2021, 61 × 46 cm, acrylic on panel.

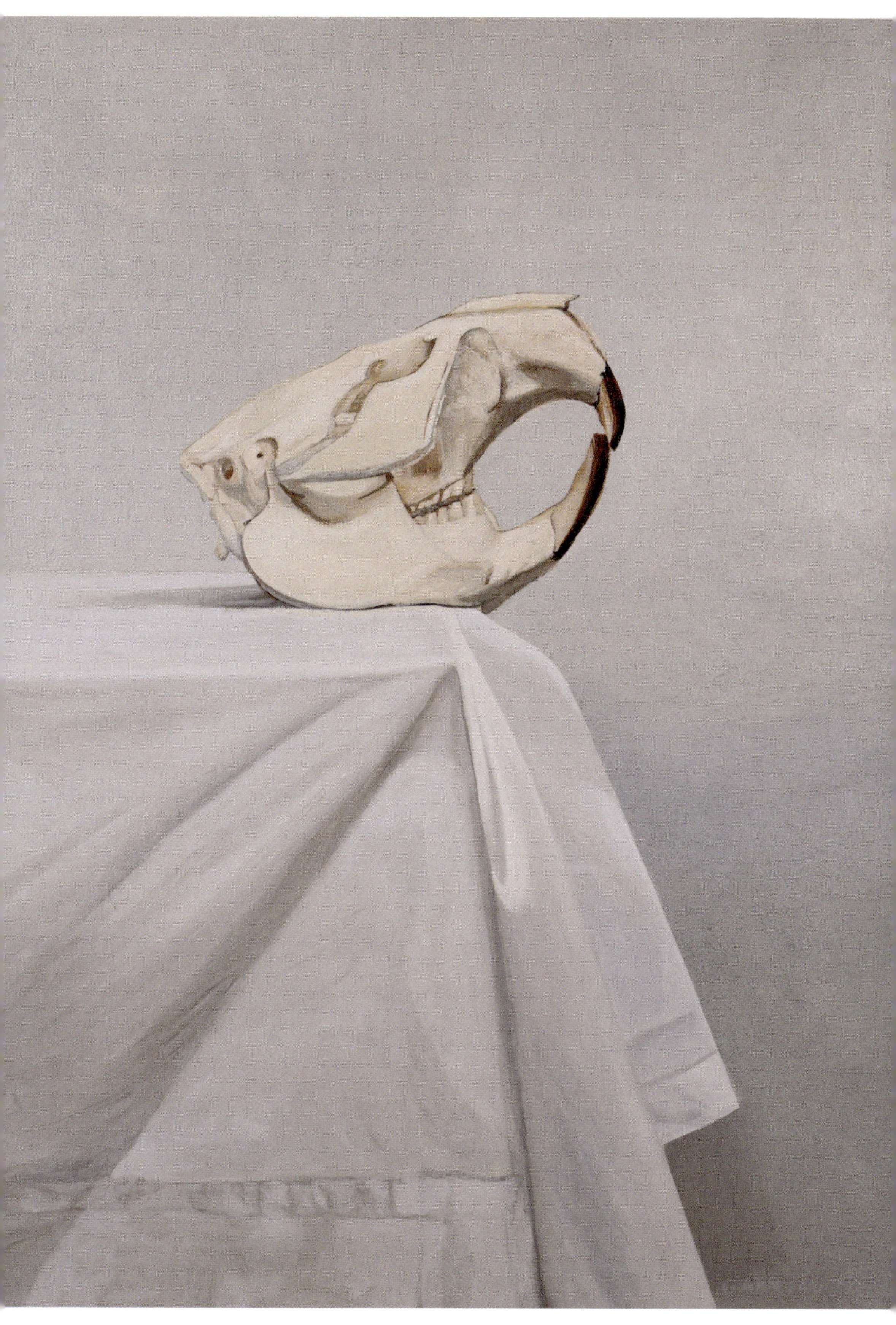

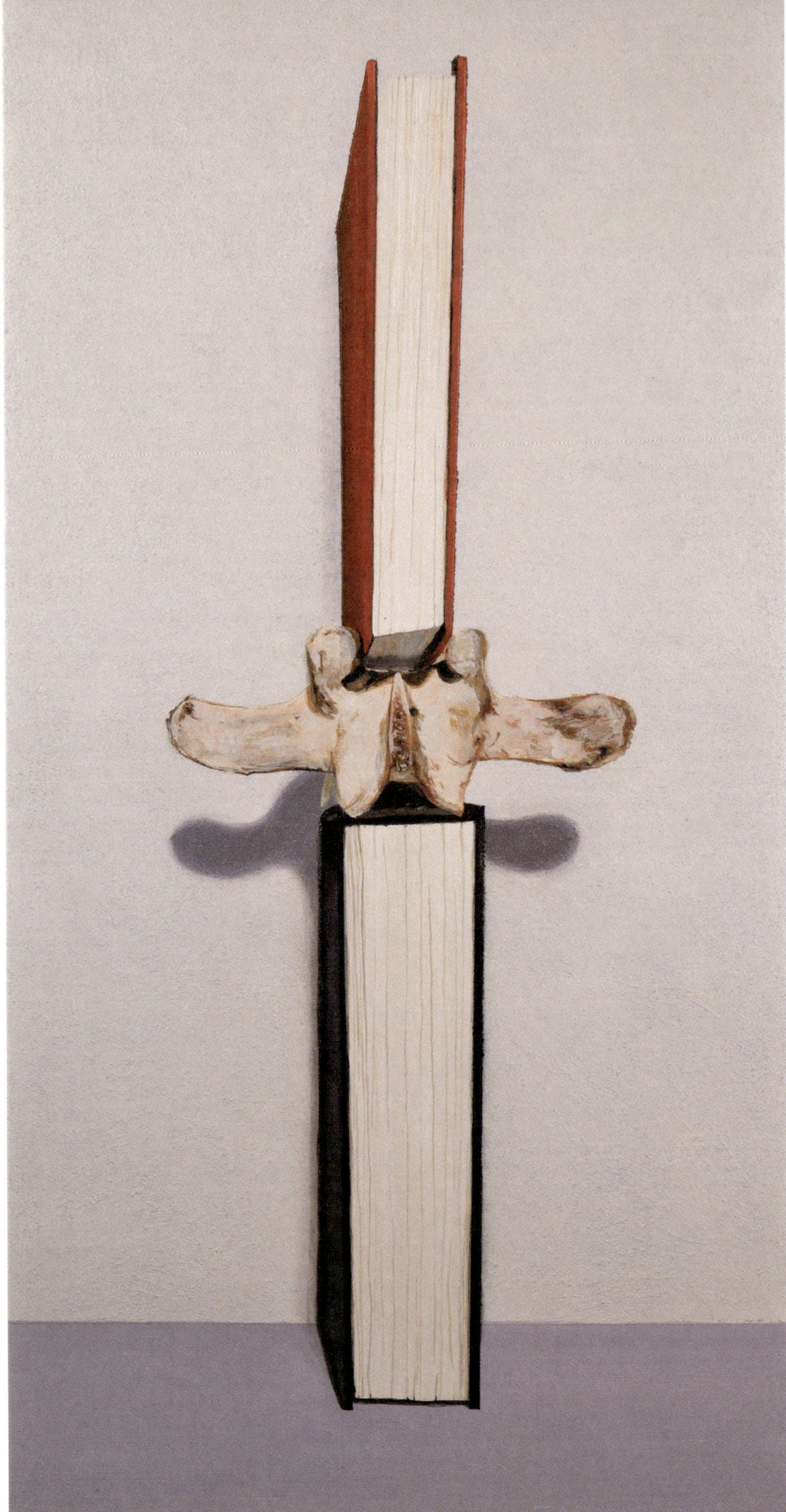

SPINE
BY FRED WAH

1.
Two books and a bone
's what the artist has shown

heads smashed in
story chained to a stone

Rock of ages scissor paper
one after the other
the chapters go, still

life hastens slowly
we've read this before

the plotline of truth
is a pain in the spine.

2.
Up to now the artist
in composing his chapters

FACING: "Spine," 2021, 61 × 30.5, acrylic on panel.

> has scanned over
>   the paved, ditched, and gravelled
>   roads and right - of - ways
> that sweep the prairies
> resist containment
> and fill the eyes
> with elusive floaters of struggle
> and dissent.

". . . a wound could be a wheatfield"[97]

> Its Pleistocene horizon
> blurred by the asymmetry
> of miscegenation
> has led the artist to stare and hunt
> for the roadkill, the cloudland
> of cowboys and Indians,
> wood and stone,
> sun-bleached bison bones,
> and now that machine of colonization—
>   the book.

"Gliding down the highway, my eyes sweep left and right for signs of death. Eschewing disgusting indefinite wrecks but also the fresh and pathetic, I scan for disfigures in the landscape, unbeings that inspire an affective oscillation between engagement and estrangement; an animal about to pass from being to mere thing. Glimpsing a discordant shape splayed in the grassy verge, I wheel, loop back for another pass. Seeing the ruined bird, I pull over, switch on the hazard lights, grab a camera and walk into the ditch, to my prey."[98]

> The truth is still
> art is a good read
> of this most troubling chapter

---

97   Christine Stewart "*From April, Before May* (2020)," *Some*, no. 3 (2021): 77.

98   David Garneau, "Road Kill and the Space of the Ditch: An Artist's Meditation," *Overlooking Saskatchewan: Minding the Gap*, eds. Randal Rogers and Christine Ramsay (Regina: University of Regina Press, 2014), 113.

in "this" nation's history, "our"
truth turned to stone.

[Hey you! Who me? I wasn't a Chink until she called me one. Guilty.
Hard to flip those pronouns into normal so that I'm the "who" who
speaks "our" truth.

"Hard to believe / Enough of this to make / The horizontal land appear
/ A place or highway / Here or in the starry sky / And trust my eyes to
speak."[99]]

"Whose" nation, "whose" truth
                         stoned,
too much "rubbaboo
        the murky soup
                 somewhere
        a mix up . . .

    [the artist's] politics
        the eyes of absolute necessity"[100]

3.
The reader over the artist's shoulder

mutters a reading of the Spine

the silence of the middle voice
talking to himself:

"This bone-upright crucifix
seems but an image of the red Assiniboine
which, like the last spike, mirrors
to me my own real backbone
bound like a wolf
on a bison's backside

---

99   Fred Wah, *Scree: The Collected Earlier Poems, 1962–1991* (Vancouver: Talonbooks, 2015), 135.

100   Wah, *Scree*, 139.

to God's infinite Book."

It becomes an old rugged cross
that he hopes to stick to John A.'s story
and it does,
a sticky memory, a scream

that troubles sea to shining sea
a "prickly trickle" in the throat of image nation,
a thoracic curve in the spines of intention

"I believe," he continued
crossing the border of belief,
"this has to be
in the table of contents, the result
of a REAL signature."

[Genetically drifting along this Spine I want that bone to be a hyphen.
A bookmark outside the book to mark another place to return to, a
bone to pick up where we left off. A hard reminder?]

This life of the eye is anything but still.

The citizen imagination relocates itself
between the covers of a decolonial non-fiction,
the mental stenosis of the nation's motto
("From Sea to Sea"), seen
in the lived reality
of a more situational discourse,
rendered into the sticky marrow
of osteo-Métisity, a kind of muddy ditch
of frustrated ambivalence.

"In fact," the reader reflects,
"out here between the seas
it should be 'from ditch to ditch,'
red water black earth,

a hyphen of bone, a slipped disk
between two closed books."

[The coercion between these prepositions (propositions) "from" and "to" disengages the messy syntax of colonization. How to voice that silent dash of bone bound "between" the stories covered over in a coat of arms. Spine echoes a shared location, standing in the doorway, shouting "blindfold, hinge, thorn, spike, rope, slash . . . head tax, railway car to an internment camp, non - status outskirts of town nomad other side of tracks no track. Mi - nus mark, not equal sign. . . . How float this sign . . ."[101] between, the real proposition shadowing these stories.]

> Over the shoulder
> he imagines the title on the spine of the red book
> is VÉRITÉ.
>   And underneath the bone
> along the spine of the black book
> he pictures the word DOUX.
>
> Or maybe ESPÉRER.
>
> In the pages of the red book
> he sees his hand write a poetry of hunger
> for the Métis nation while the black book
> collects an index of surplus memory
> detailing the bones of genocide.
>
> And in that bleached chunk of vertebrae
> he reads an amulet of LAW:
>   "do not hunt on Sunday."

---

101 Fred Wah, "Half-Bred Poetics," *Faking It: Critical Writing 1984–1999* (Edmonton: NeWest Press, 2000), 94–95.

4.
"here's signs and wonders truly!"[102]

Gabriel Dumont, looking over the artist's other shoulder,
soliloquizes:

> "what's bound by this bison bone
> are the collected petitions of our needs
> and our rights.
>> Don't make us pay to cut firewood
>> Give us the same as you give Indians
>> Land and hunting rights
>>> and not to lose our lands
>> Honour our scrip
>> Let us join Treaty Four
>> Give us tools and seed to settle the land
>> Re-open the buffalo hunt
>> Grant us reserve land
>> Give us our Nation."

Not.

All the signatures didn't matter.
Left with nothing
but still on his horse.

5.
Still
after life
we expect to be rescued.

We spoke upright,
ignored the curvature
and split the plan
between the crushed apple

102 Herman Melville, "Chapter 99: The Doubloon," *Moby Dick* (London: Richard Bentley, 1851).

of John A.'s eye and the stone soup
of necessity.

That chunk of bone is still a shadow,
an inconvenient splinter yet
the crux of this sad story.

Let's spin awhile in the gutters of these books
between the threads

in the ligaments of intention
where we find the bullets of belief.

Do the pages list the signatures
Do the endnotes cite the prayers of reconciliation.

"a certain wild longing, if not hopefulness."[103]

Do all those pages speak the gospel truth
Is this how doublespeak is bound

Are the pages blank, the words not there
Not an open book but a broken promise

Are those bison spurs the wings of precarity
Or open arms that bespeak solidarity?

103   Melville, "Chapter 99: The Doubloon."

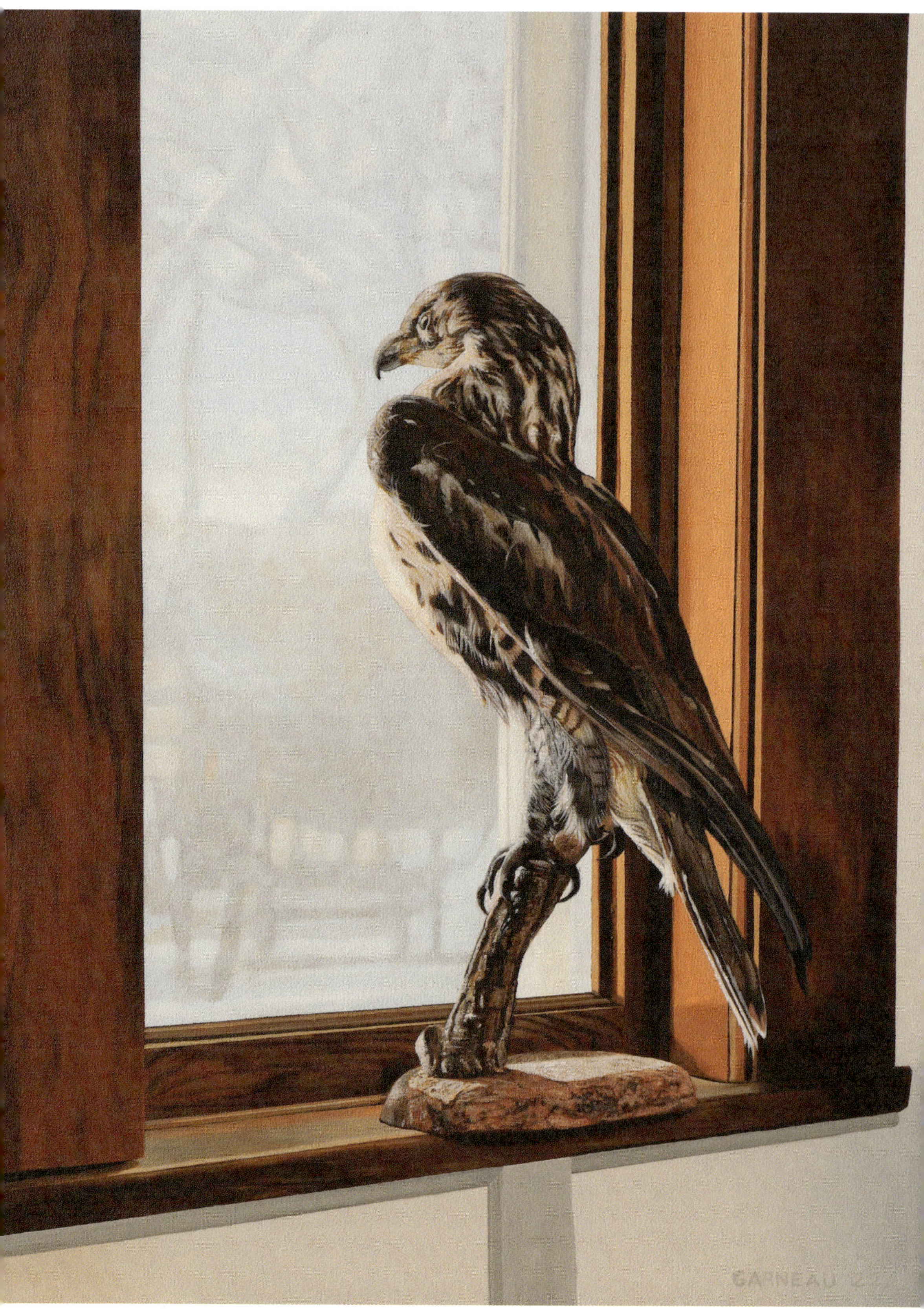
GARNEAU

THE RESTING HEARTBEAT
OF A WOUNDED BIRD
BY SUSAN MUSGRAVE

You kissed me in the laundry room,
your socks on spin cycle, your jeans
tumbling dry. I hadn't been kissed since the day
my love died; I had been faithful to a ghost, not
wanting to be disloyal—till death do us part never
seemed long enough for me, didn't hold water.
Look, I am sinking now into the hands of your words.

I watch the strike of a hawk break the body
of its prey, a hapless shorebird guddling amongst reeds.
To be a bird you don't need faith, only the ability
to fly. It sounds as simple as a kiss, but it is
never simple, the union of tongues and lips;
it became my whole undoing in the time it took
for your socks to wick away their excessive moisture.

But your kiss would not withstand the criticism
of the October storms: land, sea, and sky agreed
on one thing: faith, or lack of faith, a white cirrus of wings.
In the dunes above the beach, tiny flowers of lady's bedstraw
and tormentil, the tortuosities of the coastline where
your kiss slipped through the cracks of my unbeing.

FACING: "Faith," 2022, 92 × 71, acrylic on canvas.

There is no anything-ever-after, only an infinity
of headlights licking wet asphalt on an unending road.
Behind is darkness and darkness lies ahead; a hurt
hawk loops around my house in the long ascendancy of rain,
drops through my open window and comes to rest
in the bewildering light. It would be ironic to lose an eye
to a half-blind bird who can't find his way out of any passing
moment: the wind, the insinuating rain, a following sea.
You tried to warn me about the dangers of loving
too faithfully but I was more enchanted by the hawk
settling on my windowsill, his still eyes intent
upon mine, entranced by his diminishing reflection.
Isn't the faith you have in your own being
all the faith you need?

Sandpipers jacked up on the northwest wind,
jinking in and out of the tide, while I
go about the world in a moony love-flap,
saying kiss me like I'll die tomorrow; no matter
what you possess, or how lucky you think you are,
there is nothing in this life you can hold on to
so fiercely that it can't be snatched from you.
Even when I sit and watch the river it reminds me
how everything is on its way to somewhere else.

Faith is our hopeful belief in an afterlife for which
there is no evidence, though some say this world
and the world we will go to after death are not so far
apart. Why does everything memorable make me lament
the past? I remember leaving a bouquet of Baby's
Breath on Oscar Wilde's plot in Père Lachaise, kissing
a stranger in the dirt on Jim Morrison's desecrated grave
(*He Was True to His Demons* inscribed on his headstone),
and later being followed through narrow streets
by a firebreather who promised he could make the rain
stop falling if I let myself be made whole again
by a man as faithless and broken as he was; I believed him.

Do you know what loving too faithfully taught me?
The dead don't care. They are gone. You bury them
where they can no longer reach you, and you go on.

The hawk hasn't moved from his perch since the day
we kissed in the laundry room where the dark kept growing
dimmer: how does the brain, which lives without hope of light,
prepare us for a world of shadows and brilliance? What about
the heart, that lonely muscle, beating to death in the holy
darkness of your body?

The hawk stirs only when I sing to him and stroke
his bloodied claws. He casts a cold eye on my life
as if trying to decide whether trusting me would be worth
the effort, and I think let me love this wild thing anyway,
let the grief of this world be contained within
the resting heartbeat of a wounded bird.

You have to want me more than you fear me.
Let me rest my faith in you. Let me
touch you with a gloved hand.

GALLERY

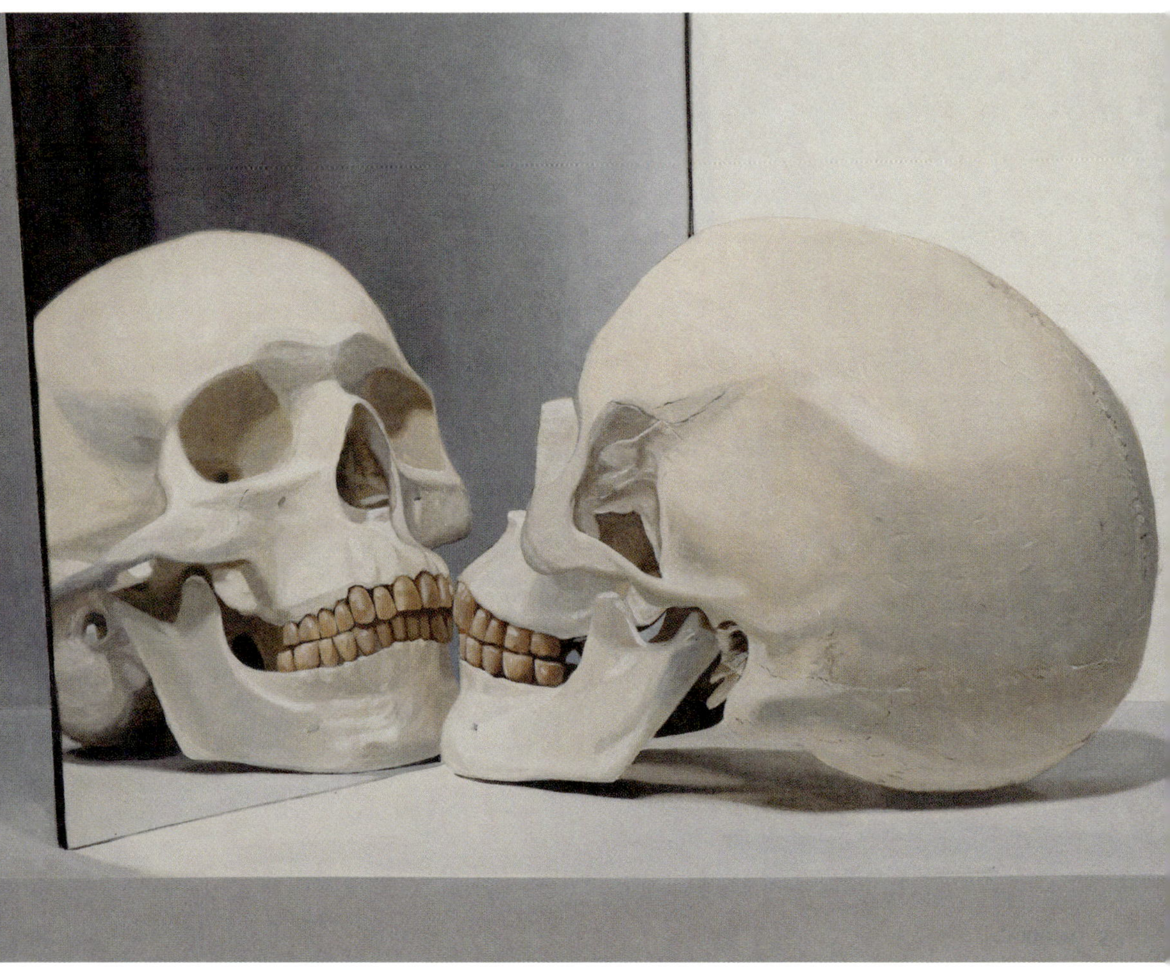

"Confirmation Bias," 2023, 46 × 61 cm, acrylic on panel.

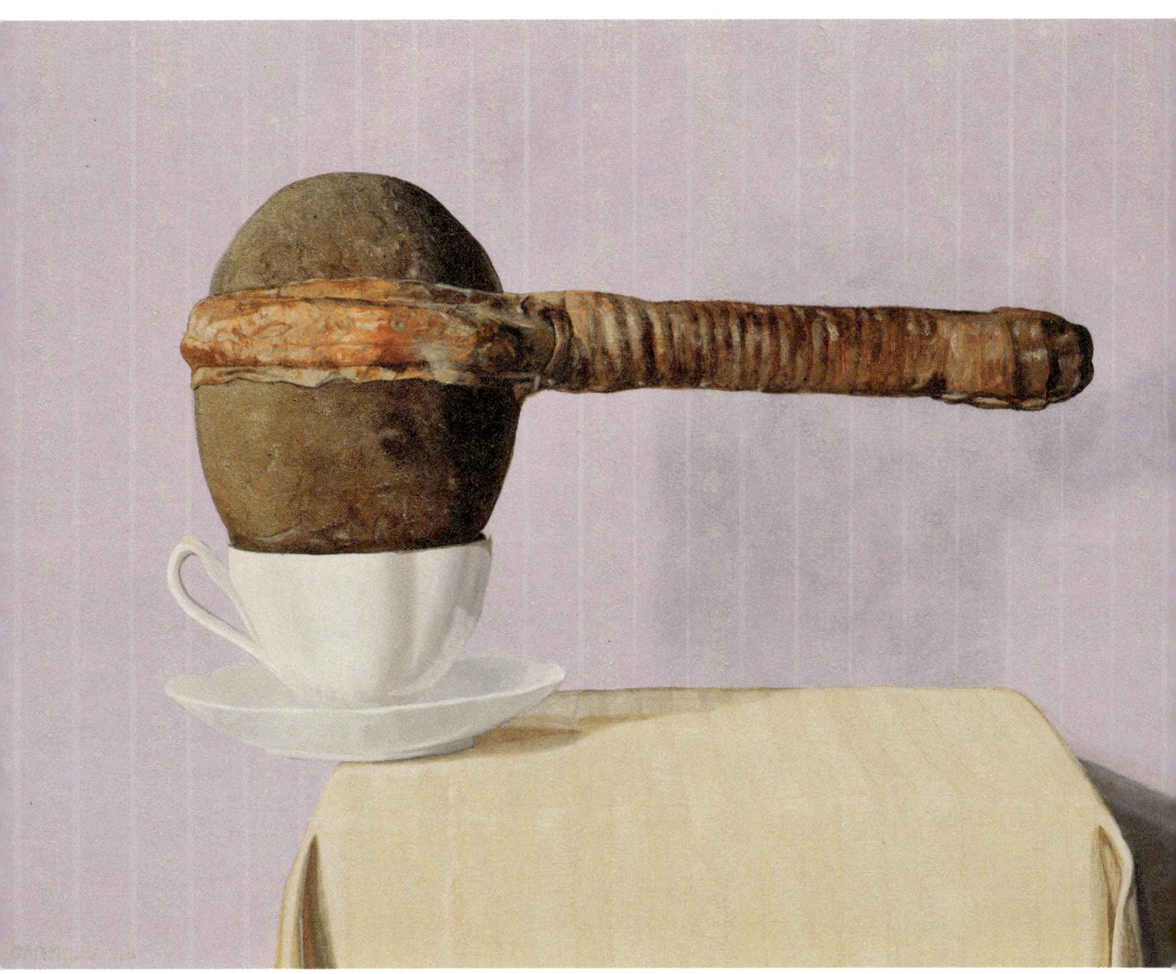

"Post-Colonial Tension," 2023, 45.5 × 61 cm, acrylic on panel.

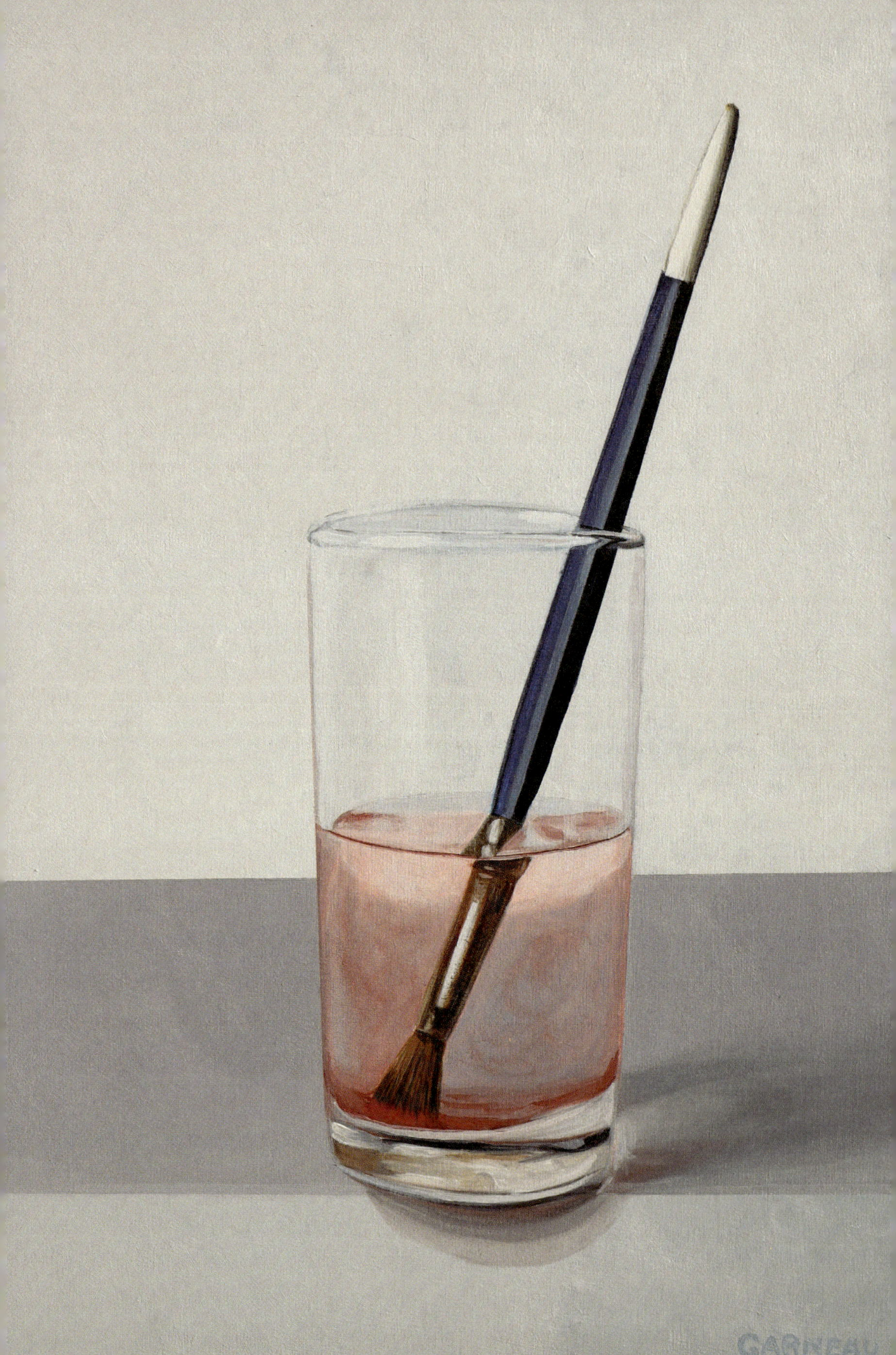
GARNEAU

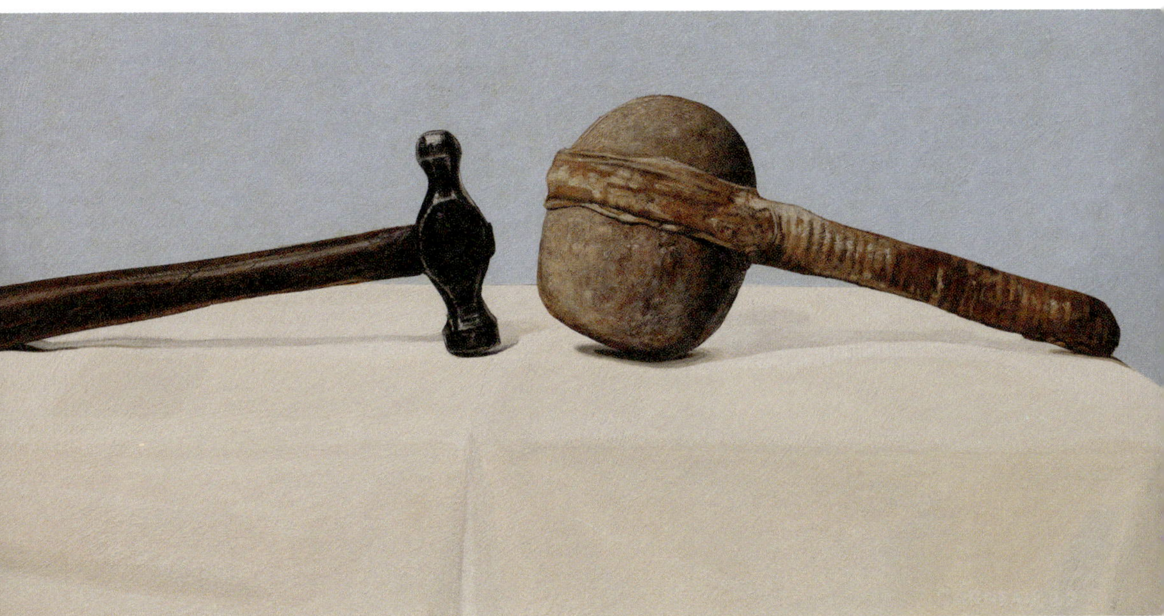

"Potential Collaborators," 2022, 30.5 × 61 cm, acrylic on panel. Collection of Michael Garneau.

FACING: "Art and Violence I," 2022, 45.5 × 35.5 cm, acrylic on panel.

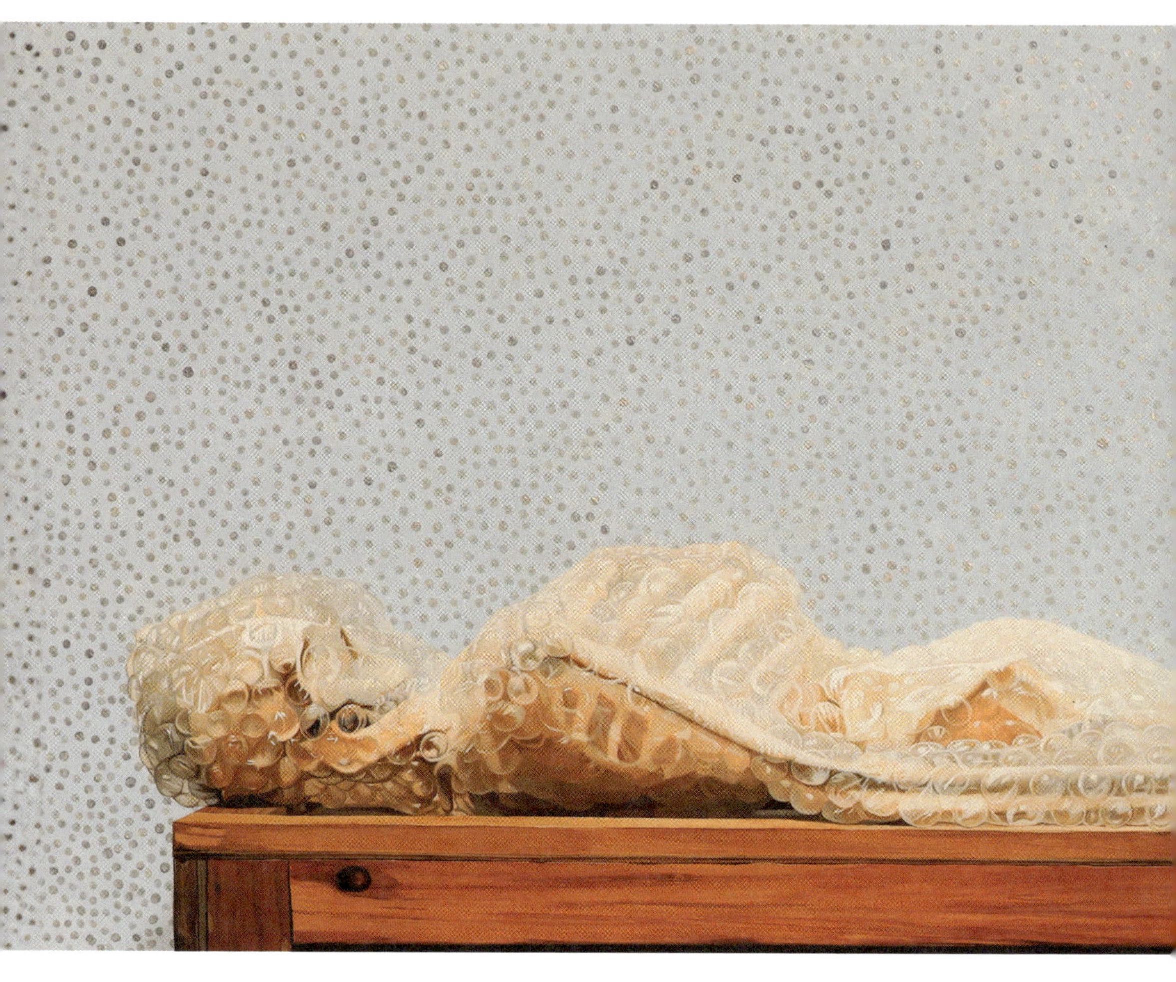

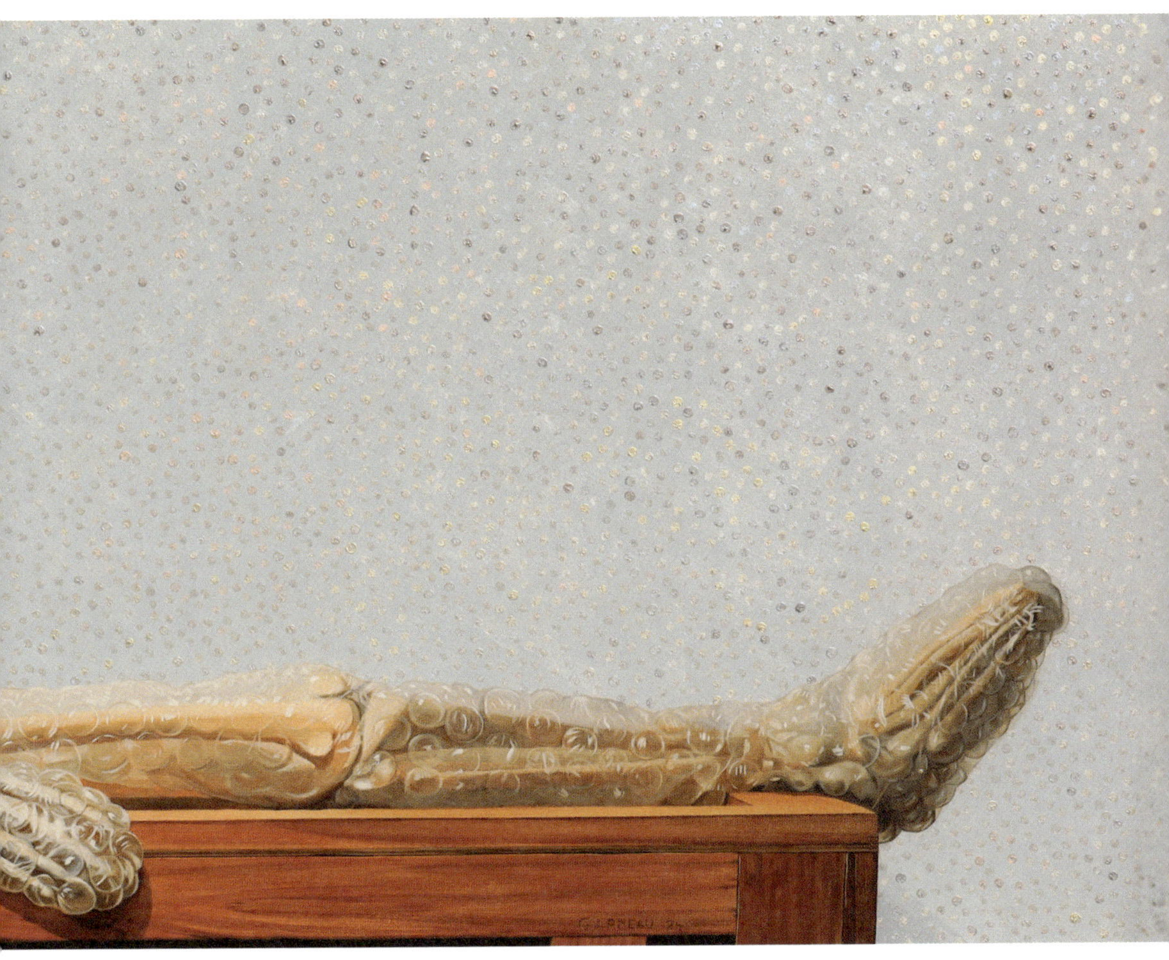

"The Museum and its Discontents (after Holbein and Luna)," 2024, 76.5 × 198.5 cm, acrylic on canvas.

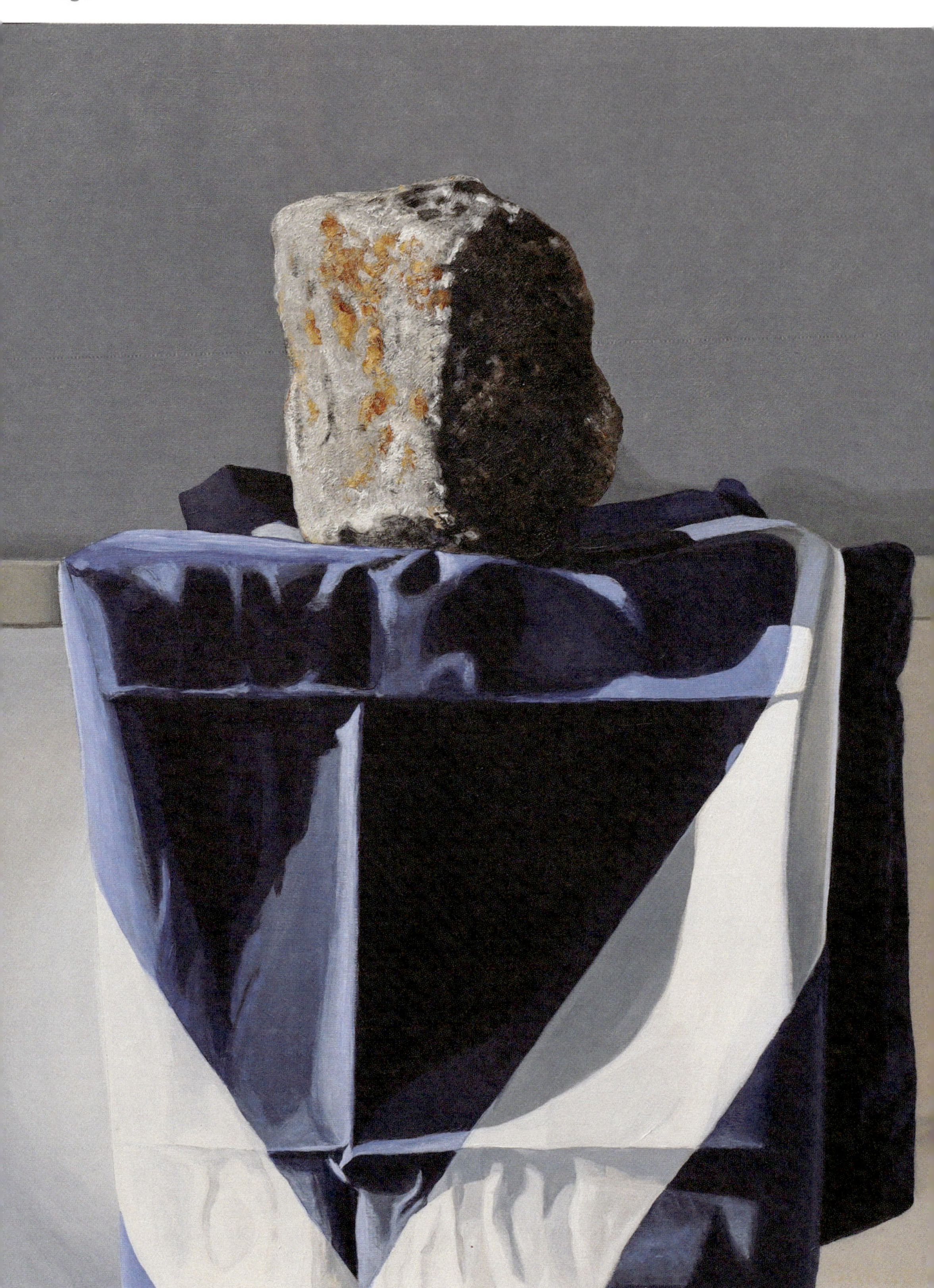

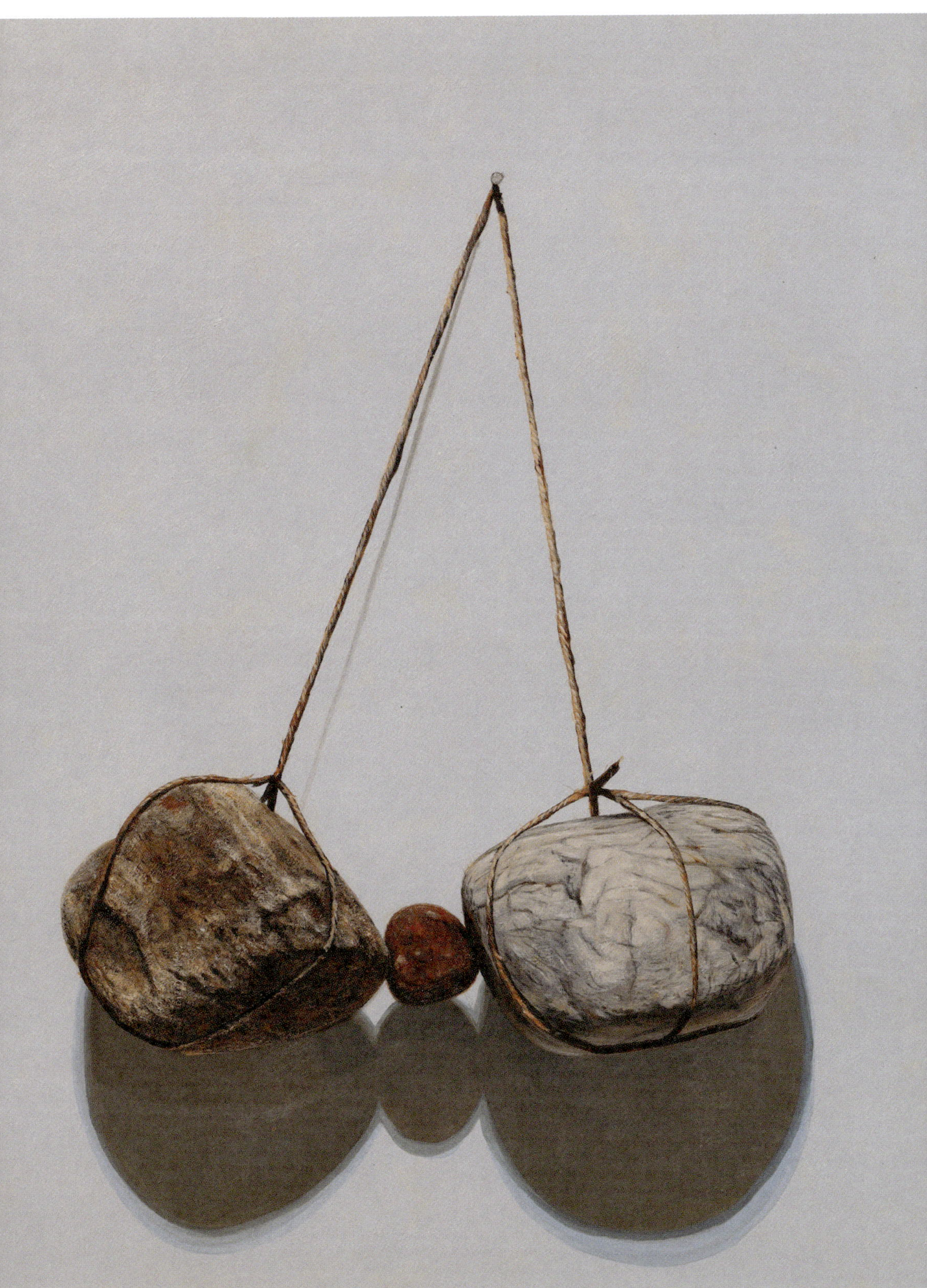

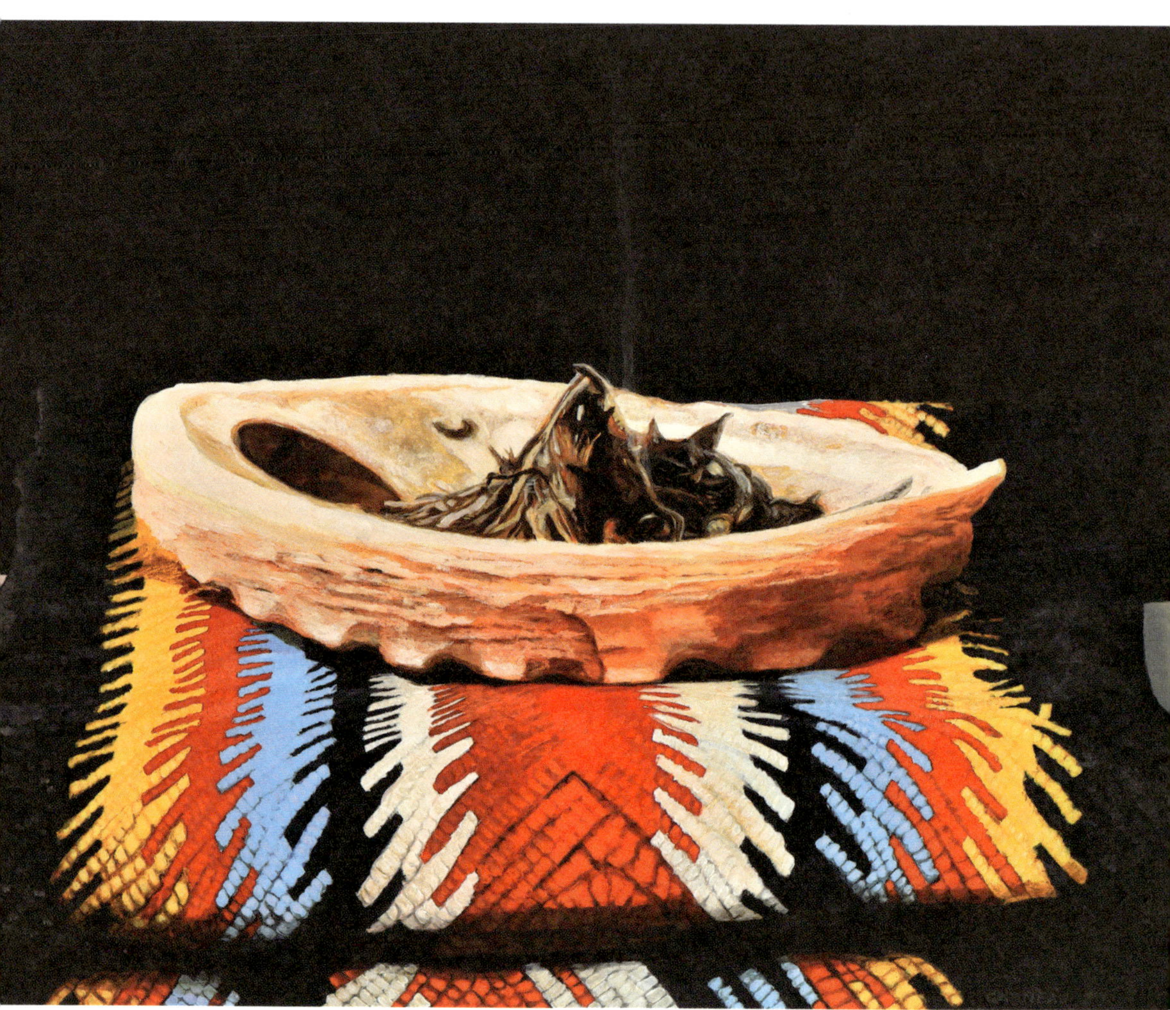

"Maternal Influence," 2023, 51 × 61 cm, acrylic on panel.

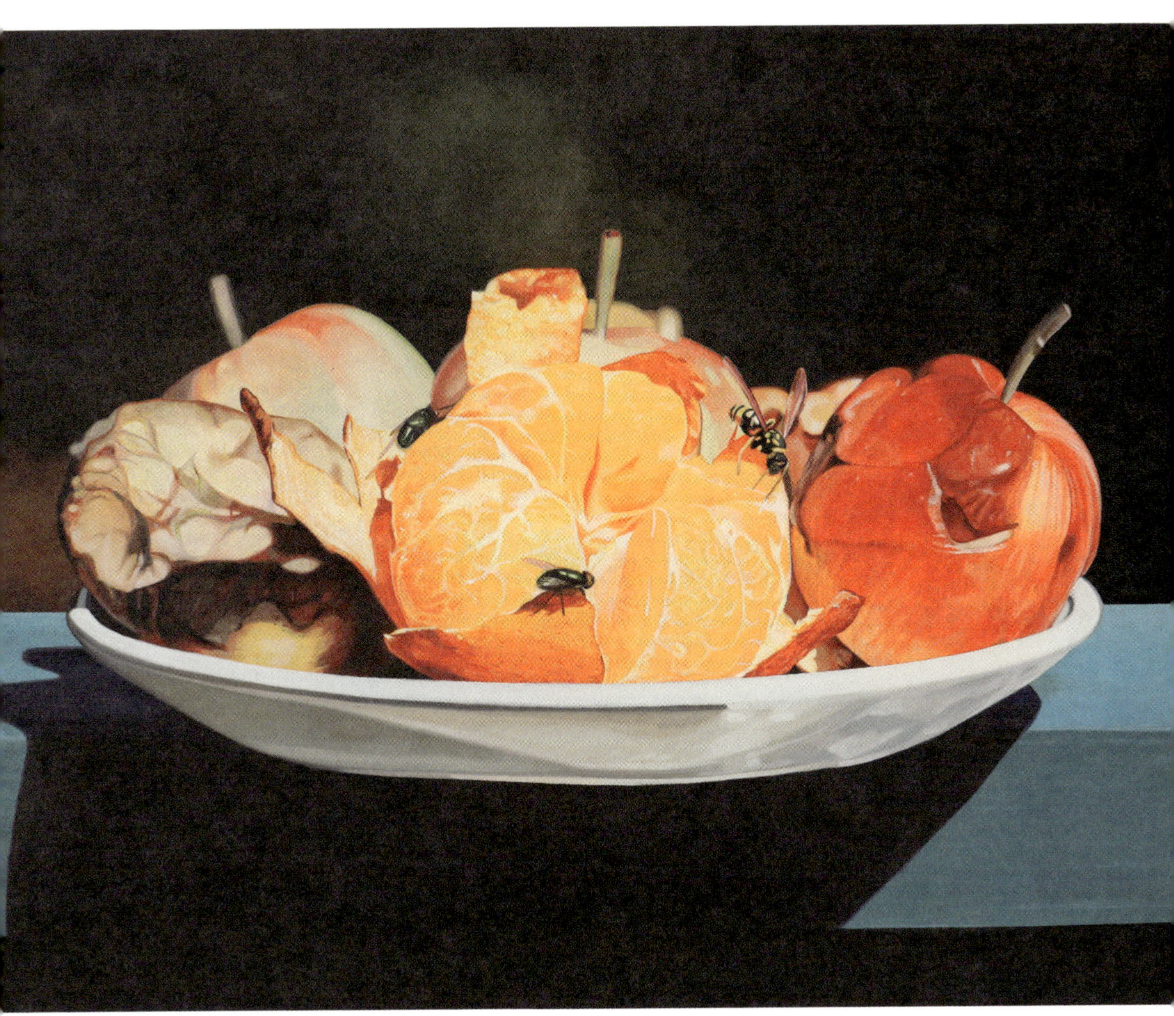

"The Way of All Flesh," 2022, 71 × 92, acrylic on canvas.

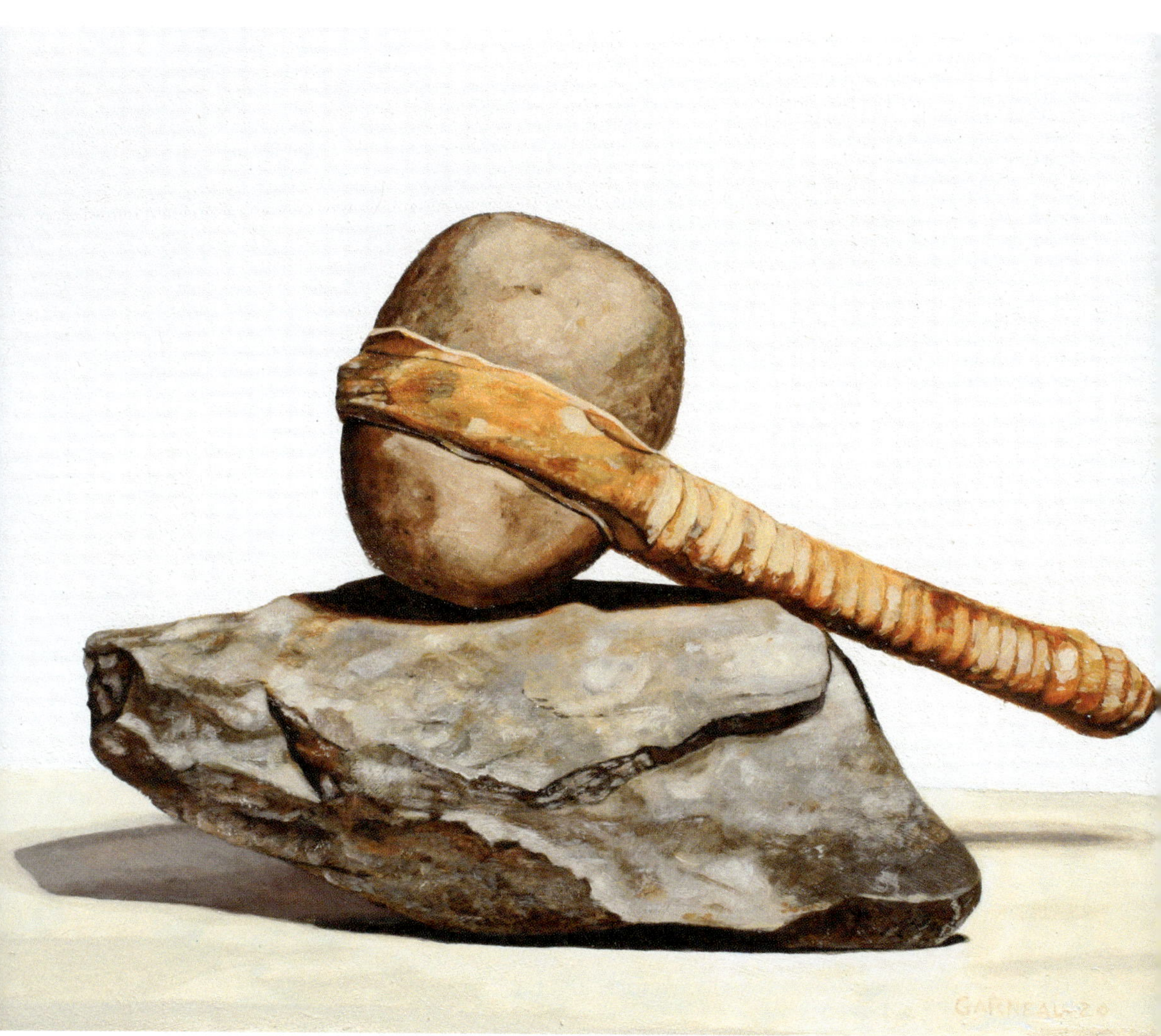

"Dialectical Materialism I," 2020, 40.5 × 50.5 cm, acrylic on panel.

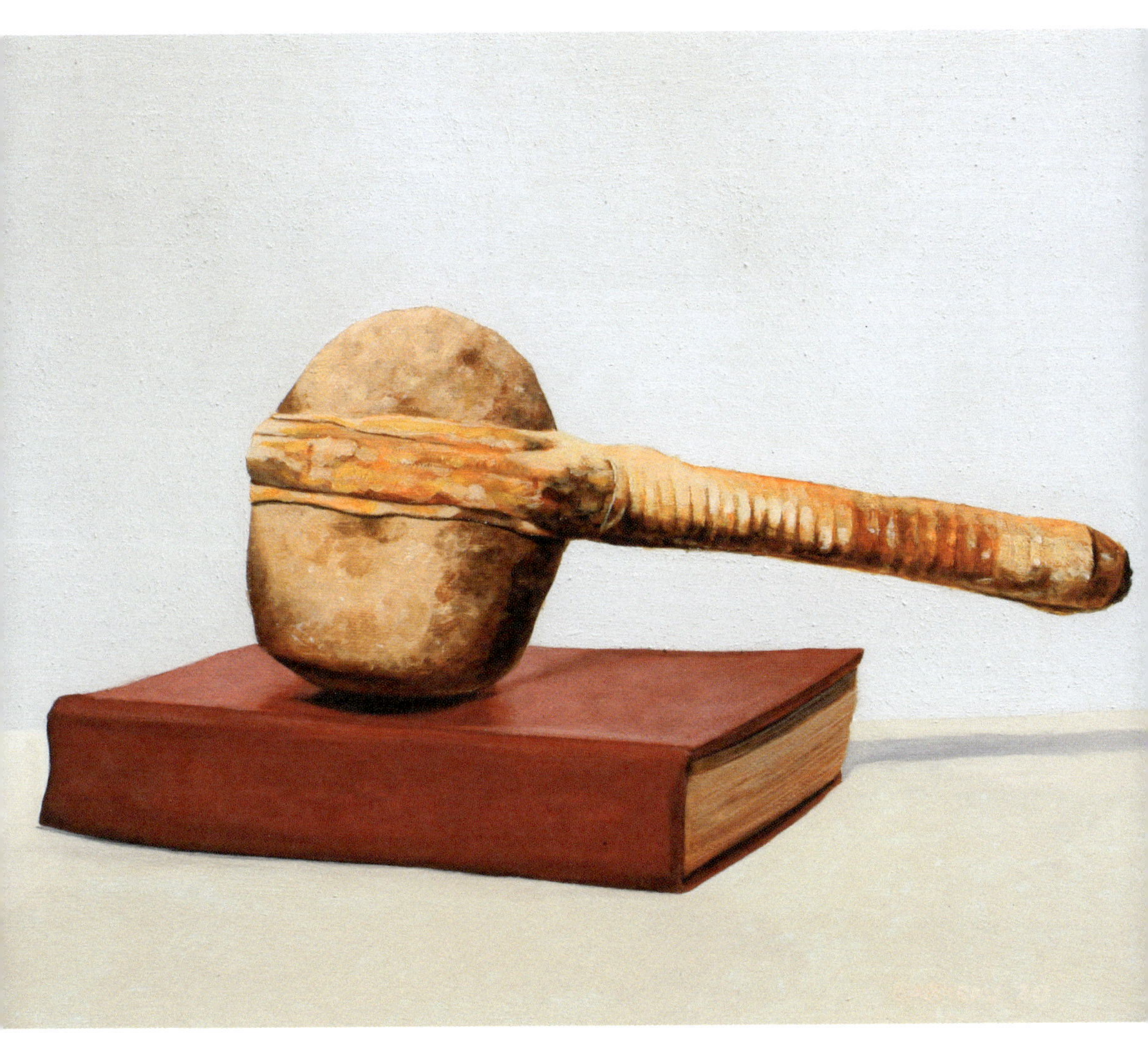

"Dialectical Materialism II," 2020, 40.5 × 50.5 cm, acrylic on panel.

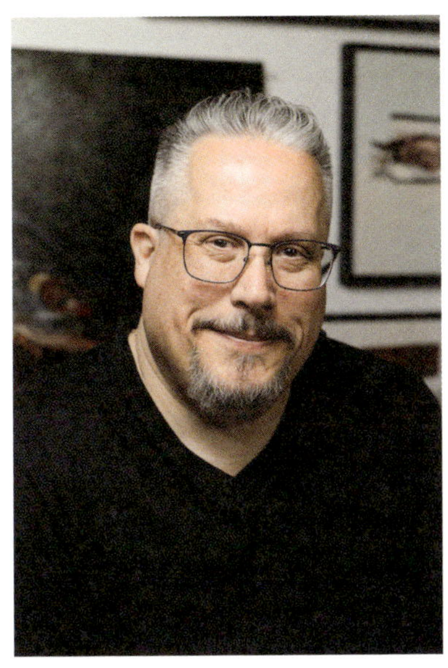

ABOUT THE ARTIST

DAVID GARNEAU is a Métis painter, writer, curator, and educator who creates metaphorical still life paintings. Based on Treaty 4 lands, Saskatchewan, David Garneau is one of Canada's foremost Métis artists, painters, and public intellectuals, and has been leading the charge in complex conversations around the nuances of Métis identity and the politics of Indigeneity, Indigenization, and non-colonial aesthetics in the colonized lands of Canada.

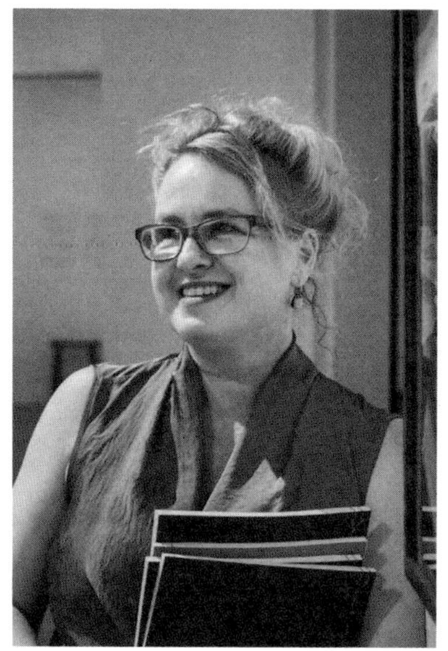

ABOUT THE CURATOR

ARIN FAY is a curator living near Kaslo, British Columbia. Her areas of special interest include publications, curatorial writing, and advocating for art and artists. Fay has been an active member of the arts and culture community in the Kootenay region for thirty years as an artist, volunteer, board member, and curator. She is currently Curator at the Nelson Museum, Archives & Gallery (NMAG).

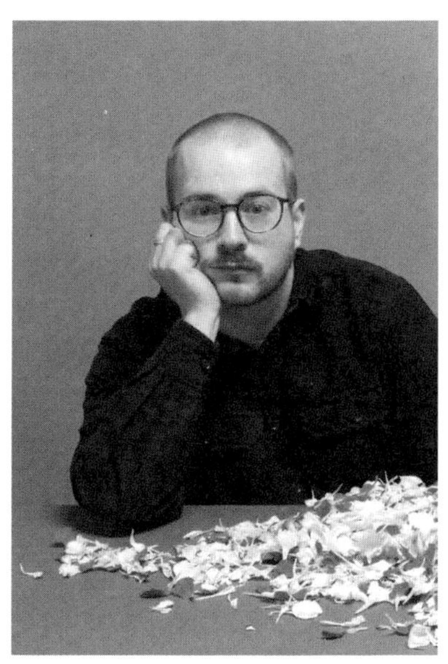

ABOUT THE EDITOR

NIC WILSON (they/he) is an artist and writer who was born in the Wolastoqiyik territory known as Fredericton, NB in 1988. Their work often engages time, queer lineage, decay, and the distance between art practice and literature. Their writing has appeared in *BlackFlash Magazine*, *Peripheral Review*, *NORK*, *C Magazine*, and *Border Crossings*. Their book of essays *Colossal Equine Statue* was published by ARP Books in 2024.

ABOUT THE CONTRIBUTORS

BILLY-RAY BELCOURT is a writer and academic from the Driftpile Cree Nation. He is an Associate Professor in the School of Creative Writing at the University of British Columbia. He is the author of five books: *This Wound is a World, NDN Coping Mechanisms: Notes from the Field, A History of My Brief Body, A Minor Chorus*, and *Coexistence.*

CECILY NICHOLSON is the author of four books and past recipient of the Dorothy Livesay Poetry Prize (2015) and the Governor General's Literary Award for poetry (2018). She is the first honouree of the Phyllis Webb Memorial Reading award from the Poetry in Canada Society (2023) and a 2024/2025 Holloway Lecturer in Poetry and Poetics at UC Berkeley.

DAVID HOWES is a Canadian anthropologist and legal scholar. He is a professor in the Department of Sociology and Anthropology and Co-Director of the Centre for Sensory Studies at Concordia University, and an adjunct professor in the Faculty of Law at McGill University. He has authored, co-authored, or edited 15 books, ranging from *The Varieties of Sensory Experience* (1991) to *Sensorium* (2024).

DICK AVERNS is an interdisciplinary artist, curator, and educator, currently residing in Mohkinstsis, as an uninvited settler. The first non-fiction writer selected as an official Canadian war artist, deployed to the Middle East, his work has been published by *Momus*, the CBC, *Galleries West, Canadian Art*, and in numerous catalogues and journals. He has taught at the University of Calgary, the Alberta University of the Arts, and UBC, and received the Calgary Mayor's Leadership Award for Healing Through the Arts (2020).

FRED WAH is a poet, novelist, scholar, and an Officer of the Order of Canada. Born in Swift Current, Saskatchewan, he's also the author of more than 17 chapbooks and full-length collections of poetry, the winner of the Governor General's Literary Award for Poetry, a former parliamentary poet laureate, and a founding editor of the poetry journal *TISH*.

JEFF DERKSEN is a poet, critic, and scholar. His poetry books include *The Vestiges, Transnational Muscle Cars*, and *Down Time* (Winner of the Dorothy Livesay Poetry Prize). His critical books include *After Euphoria, Annhilated Time: Poetry and Other Politics*, and the folio *How High is the City, How Deep is Our Love*. A former professor of English at Simon Fraser University, he now serves as their Dean and Associate Provost, Graduate and Postdoctoral Studies. He is a founding member of the Kootenay School of Writing in Vancouver and a former editor of *Writing* magazine. He lives in British Columbia.

JESSE WENTE is an Ojibwe broadcaster, curator, producer, activist, and public speaker. He is Head of TIFF Cinematheque, where he oversees the historical film programme year-round at TIFF Bell Lightbox. An outspoken advocate for Indigenous rights and First Nations, Métis, and Inuit art, he has spoken at the Smithsonian's National Museum of the American Indian, the Canadian Arts Summit, CMPA's Prime Time, and numerous universities and colleges.

Artist and Chickasaw curator JOHN G. HAMPTON currently resides on Treaty 4 territory, Saskatchewan, where they work as Executive Director and CEO at the MacKenzie Art Gallery in Regina. In this role, John became the first Indigenous Director of a major Canadian art gallery. In addition to their role at the MacKenzie Art Gallery, Hampton holds an adjunct professorship at the University of Regina, is co-chair of the Canadian Arts Summit Steering Committee, and is a member of the Canada Gallery Committee for the High Commission of Canada in the United Kingdom.

LARISSA LAI is the author of nine books including, *The Lost Century, The Tiger Flu, Salt Fish Girl*, and *Iron Goddess of Mercy*. She is the recipient of the Jim Duggins Novelist's Prize, the Lambda Literary Award, the Astraea Award, and the Otherwise Honor Book Award. She has held a Canada Research Chair in Creative Writing at the University of Calgary, and a Maria Zambrano Fellowship at the University of Huelva. She is currently the Richard Charles Lee Chair of Chinese Canadian Studies at the University of Toronto.

LILLIAN ALLEN is a poet, educator, and spoken word performer. The seventh Poet Laureate of Toronto, she is a professor of creative writing at OCAD and a two-time JUNO award winner and trailblazer in the field of spoken word and dub poetry. Allen's debut book of poetry, *Rhythm An' Hardtimes*, became a Canadian bestseller, blazing new trails for poetic expression and opening up the form. Lillian Allen's latest collection, *Make the World New: The Poetry of Lillian Allen*, edited by Ronald Cummings, was published in Spring 2021.

PAUL SEESEQUASIS is a nîpisîhkopâwiyiniw (Willow Cree) writer, journalist, cultural advocate, and commentator currently residing in Saskatoon, Saskatchewan. Since 2015, he has curated the *Indigenous Archival Photo Project*, an online and physical exhibition of archival Indigenous photographs that explores history, identity, and the process of visual reclamation. His writing has appeared in the *Globe and Mail*, *The Walrus*, *Brick*, and *Granta* magazines, among others. He has been active in the Indigenous arts, both as an artist and a policy maker, since the 1990s.

PETER MORIN is a Tahltan Nation artist and curator. Throughout his artistic practice, Morin investigates the impact zones that occur when Indigenous practices collide with Western-settler colonialism. In addition to his exhibition history, Morin has curated exhibitions for the Museum of Anthropology, Western Front, Bill Reid Gallery, and Burnaby Art Gallery. In 2016, Morin received the Hnatyshyn Foundation Award for Outstanding Achievements by a Canadian Mid-Career Artist. He currently holds a tenured appointment in the Faculty of Arts at the Ontario College of Art and Design University in Toronto.

RITA BOUVIER is a Métis writer, editor, and retired educator who has received numerous awards for her service and leadership in public education. Her fourth book of poetry, *a beautiful rebellion*, was released in April 2023 by Thistledown Press and honours an ongoing resistance and unconquerable love for family, community, land, and life itself. She lives in Saskatoon, Saskatchewan (Treaty 6), but home is sakitawak— Île-à-la-Crosse, Saskatchewan, Canada situated on the historic trading and meeting grounds of Cree and Dene people (Treaty 10). She serves as a volunteer with the Saskatchewan Ânskohk Writers Circle Inc. and the Indigenous Editors Association.

SUSAN MUSGRAVE has published more than 35 books and received awards in six categories—poetry, novels, non-fiction, food writing, editing, and books for children. She teaches poetry in UBC's School of Creative Writing (online) and lives on Haida Gwaii where she owns and manages Copper Beech House. Her most recent book, *Exculpatory Lilies*, was a finalist for the Griffin Poetry Prize, the Governor General's Award for Poetry, 2023, and the Derek Walcott Poetry Prize. A selection of her poems, *Hunger*, edited by Micheline Maylor, will be published in 2025 by Wilfred Laurier University Press, as part of the Laurier Poetry Series.

TARENE THOMAS is a writer and scholar from Enoch Cree Nation and the Northwest Coast. Her work examines the world through an Indigenous feminist lens, whilst critiquing the institutions she works inside of. Tarene fuses together the personal and political while telling stories of sadness, joy, rebellion, and refusal.

TREVOR HERRIOT is a prairie naturalist, activist, and writer living on the northern edge of the Great Plains in Regina, Saskatchewan. He recently published his debut novel, *The Economy of Sparrows* (Thistledown Press, 2023), and his writing has been shortlisted for the Writer's Trust Non-Fiction Prize, the Governor General's Award for Non-fiction, and the William Saroyan International Prize for Writing, and his work has appeared in the *Globe & Mail* and *Canadian Geographic*, among others.

LIST OF ARTWORKS

INDEX

A

abundance, xiii, 32

academy, 2, 29, 34, 35–37,
39, 41, 44, 55, 73, 85

allyship, 38, 89–90, 92–93, 97–101

American Anthropological
Association, 81

anthropology, 7

Assiniboine River, 119

B

balance, 3, 16, 21, 24, 46, 131, 137

Barthes, Roland, 15

beartrap, 70

bible, 26, 103–05, 107, 110, 120

birds, x, 21, 118, 124, 125–127

bone, ix, 20, 48, 60, 63, 94, 106,
116, 117–123, 134–135

see also skull, 45, 61, 115, 130

books, vi–vii, viii, xvi, ix, 3, 4, 16,
23, 24, 25, 28, 30, 31, 32, 34,
36, 42, 45, 46, 50, 53, 54, 55, 57,
62, 68, 70, 71, 72, 101, 102, 103,
105, 108, 112, 116, 120, 141

Brady, James, 25

Brandeis, Louis, 109

Bryson, Norman, 29, 31

C

Cabinet of Curiosities, 98

Campbell, Maria, 108

Canadian Museum of History, 80

ceremony, 7, 69, 71, 84

chains, 53

Chinese Exclusion Act, 92

Chinese Head Tax, 93

Christian, Dorothy, 92

collaboration, 90–91

colonial violence, 65, 72

commodities, xiii

crucifix/cross, 103–104, 107, 119

D

de Sousa Santos, Boaventura, 81

decay, xiii, 139

decolonization, 19, 35, 38,
40–41, 80, 101, 120

desire, xi, 11, 48, 63, 65, 75, 104

ditch, 118, 120

drum, 40, 80, 84

Dumont, Gabriel, 122

Durée, 19

Dutch Golden Age, xi

E

education, 4, 29, 44, 50–52, 72–73

eggshells, 1

Elders, 4, 71, 80, 83

Eurocentrism, 111